WOODCRAFT
IN DESIGN AND PRACTICE

Frontispiece

DINING-ROOM TREATMENT WITH BUILT-IN SIDEBOARD

WOODCRAFT
IN DESIGN AND PRACTICE

BY RODNEY HOOPER

This edition digitally re-mastered and
published by JM Classic Editions © 2008
Original text © Rodney Hooper 1937

ISBN 978-1-906600-02-0

All rights reserved. No part of this book subject
to copyright may be reproduced in any form or
by any means without prior permission in writing
from the publisher.

CONTENTS

CHAP.		PAGE
I.	FURNITURE DESIGN AND DECORATIVE TREATMENT	1
II.	FURNITURE AS A PART OF THE DECORATIVE SCHEME	6
III.	FURNITURE FOR THE LIVING-ROOM AND DINING-ROOM	10

SECTION		PAGE
1.	Bookcases and Book-Tables	10
2.	Boxes and Caskets	17
3.	Cabinets	20
4.	Chairs	27
5.	Chimney-Pieces	33
6.	Clocks	37
7.	Handles, Handholes, and Knobs	49
8.	Lighting Fittings	51
9.	Radio and Radio-gramophone Cabinets	57
10.	Sideboards	61
11.	Stools	68
12.	Tables	71
13.	Trays	81
14.	Wagons	83
15.	Wall Mirrors	86
16.	Writing Tables	90

CONTENTS

CHAP.		PAGE
IV. FURNITURE FOR THE BEDROOM		97
SECTION 1. Bedsteads		97
„ 2. Chests of Drawers		106
„ 3. Dressing Mirrors		109
„ 4. Dressing Tables		113
„ 5. Wardrobes		119
V. FURNITURE FOR THE GARDEN		125
VI. GARDEN ITEMS IN CAST CONCRETE		135
VII. WOODWORK FOR SCHOOLS		143
INDEX		157

CHAPTER I

FURNITURE DESIGN AND DECORATIVE TREATMENT

DESIGN in furniture involves a synthesis of practical utility, right use of material, and pleasant appearance, as summed up in the slogan "Fitness for purpose." Smaller houses and flats, and the desire to save labour, necessitate furniture that is for living with rather than for show, that makes the best use of the space available and that is easy to clean.

The recognition of usefulness as the first essential of design has led to the designer seeking decorative quality in the shapes of use and in the nature of materials instead of applying it, as an afterthought, to something that would do the job but was not considered quite presentable. Making the most of what is already there by necessity has resulted in a striving towards simplicity rather than complexity of form.

The problem of achieving a real fitness for purpose is simplified by welcoming the limitations of function and material, instead of trying to escape from them or to force them into the mould of a preconceived style. In designing a bookcase, for example, the starting point will obviously be the length, breadth, and height of shelving necessary to accommodate one's books. This could be arranged, to take extremes, in either a tall upright shape or a long low one. The former, if very high, would prevent the upper shelves being easily reached and the top would be difficult to clean. The low formation would give useful space on top but would take up more of the floor; perhaps it could be raised on a stand to make the lower shelves more accessible. If doors are to be fitted, a squarish shape might be preferable so that only two doors would be necessary, and those of a manageable proportion. If the books differ greatly in depth, a "break-front" would enable the deeper books to be accommodated in the centre with the shallower ones at either side. Practical considerations such as these apply not only to bookcases but to all furniture, and provide a working basis for the design which is enlarged by a consideration of the material.

Wood is obtained in straight boards, it resists bending, and the strongest and simplest joints between two pieces of wood are either when they are at right angles, as in the dovetail or mortise-and-tenon, or parallel, as when rubbed-jointed or tongued. The right use of the material, therefore, involves a certain straightness and squareness. Apart from moulding and the rounding of corners, in wood a curved surface involves elaborate preparation and is perhaps more characteristic of plastic materials such as clay or metal. Curves built up of laminations of thin wood glued together under pressure in a matrix are a different matter, as the material is, in effect, reduced to the condition of a plastic. This process, although of recent application, has already had considerable effects on design.

A further example of the influence of material on design is seen in the case of ordinary plywood or laminated board. Plywood is wood with one of its most annoying characteristics removed—the tendency to shrink or swell in accordance with the degree of humidity in the air. In designing for solid wood it is necessary to make allowances for this, and a wide area consists of a rigid tenoned frame with loose panels which are free to move without affecting the overall size. Before the use of plywood most large pieces of furniture were made up of an assemblage of panels, and there was a tendency to regard these as the units of design and to place the decoration, such as moulding or carving, either round the edges or symmetrically in the centre of the rectangular panels. With plywood, which neither shrinks nor swells, perfectly flat surfaces of large size are possible, and the designer does not have to concern himself with applied mouldings and other devices for concealing movement. Also, the unit of design has become enlarged; the piece may be built up in geometrical units veneered to suggest a horizontal or a vertical tendency, cross-banded, or pattern-veneered without the necessity for division into panels. The veneering of plywood has resulted in a greatly extended range of beautiful woods being made available, while design has tended towards simplicity and flush surfaces in order to display them effectively.

Construction and decorative treatment vary considerably with different woods, particularly when these are used in the solid. Oak seems to call for simplicity and massiveness; it will stand hard wear and is effective when unpolished or simply waxed. Visible construction, such as through-tenoning or dovetailing, is not out of place, as it would be in the more sophisticated mahogany. Exuberant shaping should be avoided and a rather austere effect aimed at with slow and flattened curves. The open character of the grain renders oak unsuitable for fine and delicate detail in moulding, turning, or carving. For mahogany an almost opposite treatment is indicated. The close, mild texture permits of sinuous shaping, as in the curves of the cabriole leg, and delicate moulding and carving. The wood will take a high polish which will bring out slight variations of surface, such as fluting, reeding, or slightly raised panels, which would be lost in oak. Walnut lends itself to a direct constructional treatment, as in the case of oak, while the hard and close texture also permits of fineness in detail. The soft woods are more suitable for carcase work than for such things as chairs and tables, the legs of which would have to be made clumsily thick in order to give the requisite strength. Sharp corners, too great projection of mouldings, and anything likely to be easily dented or split should be avoided. Mouldings should be very simple and rounded in character. Few soft woods have enough interest of colour or figure to be left unpainted; pine is perhaps an exception, as it tones to an attractive golden colour when waxed. Oregon pine has an interesting irregular figure which might be made use of in panels.

Decorative quality is obtained by the manipulation of the proportions, line, and colour left behind, as it were, by construction. To the purist anything added to function is unforgivable, but there is a difference between decoration that grows out of construction and that which is planted on as an afterthought. To return to the hypothetical bookcase mentioned earlier in this chapter; the proportions could, perhaps, be insisted upon by accentuating the edges of the carcase with cross-banding, with a simple carved pattern, or with an inlaid line of a contrasting colour. Such treatment would not make the piece any the less useful, could bring out certain characteristics of the material, and would give the maker a further opportunity of impressing his individuality upon his work. On the other hand, to treat the top with an entablature and elaborately carved pediment would disguise the characteristic shape of the bookcase and would mean a doubtful gain in appearance at the cost of additional labour in dusting and cleaning.

Decoration can emphasize proportion and line, as in shaping and moulded or patterned borders, or it can enrich surfaces, as in veneering or carving. The object is to add to the effectiveness of the design as a whole rather than that the decoration should be effective by itself. The primary shape should not be too much interfered with or split up. A wardrobe, for instance, is essentially a box. To shape the top into florid curves would add a certain interest to the upper part, but this would not be convincingly related to the straight sides and bottom. Similarly, doors with excessively heavy panel mouldings would lose the essential effect of flatness. Restrained decorative treatment, such as a slightly arched top and flat and simple mouldings, could be used to relieve the severity of the characteristic shape but would not destroy it.

Mouldings have a practical as well as a decorative use. The chamfering of a table leg, for instance, removes the sharp corner and prevents it damaging, or being damaged by, anything that comes into contact with it. The rounding or working of a bead along such edges has a similar effect. The decorative value of mouldings lies in the bands of light and shade which they produce, which may be used to underline certain features in the design or to give repetitions of a shape. Another application of mouldings is to give a gentle transition from one part of the design to another. Thus a projecting plinth might be moulded on its top edge in order to lead the eye gently upwards; now that long low furniture is popular this might be replaced by a receding plinth which would have a line of shadow cast on it and help to emphasize the horizontal feeling. In the same way the tendency towards simplicity of form has resulted in heavy moulded cornices being replaced by plain tops, slightly stepped back to break the joint and give a definite finish. In contemporary work the tendency is for mouldings to be as simple as possible and flattened in section to prevent them catching dust, and they are largely confined to utilitarian roundings and bevellings. Slight checks and sinkings are often used to give lines of shadow where required.

Carving may be used to accentuate line, as in a gouge-cut border, or to enrich a surface with contrasts of light and shade. Direct carving into the actual wood of the furniture is preferable to anything applied to it afterwards. Low relief work (chip carving) is more suitable than heavy undercutting, as it produces an effect with more economy of means, does not interfere too greatly with the flatness of the surface, and does not catch the dust. In the case of frankly decorative work, such as the carved head of a mirror, a more developed carving is not out of place. Carved running patterns serve a similar purpose to a moulding in underlining and strengthening certain features; an otherwise plain refectory table could have a simple geometrical pattern carved round the edges of the top. There are great possibilities in line patterns incised with a vee-tool, and perhaps coloured or gilded. These could be developed by bevelling down the outer face of the vee-groove so that the pattern became a silhouette rather than an outline.

Veneering makes use of few characteristics of a wood apart from its colour and figure. Work for veneering should be as simple and plain as possible; it may even have a certain "boxiness" which would be lumpy and uninteresting in solid wood. The tendency now is to simplify even further, as seen in such devices as carrying drawer fronts over the carcase ends, in order to give as large an undisturbed surface as possible. The placing of the veneers will vary with different woods; with woods such as figured mahogany and burr walnut, leaves with the same figure may be reversed and "matched" on a centre line to produce a symmetrical pattern. With stripy walnut, oak, macassar ebony, and other timbers with a more or less straight grain, interest may be given by cross-banding and by contrasting the direction of the grain in chequered and other simple geometrical patterns. In veneered patterns employing two or more different woods anything approaching a contrast of black and white should be avoided, or parts of the pattern will "jump" and destroy the effect of flatness of the surface. In both veneered patterns and inlaid patterns on solid wood a stiff and formal effect should be aimed at; an inlaid flower pattern, for instance, will be quite different in feeling from a pattern painted with a flexible brush. Few methods of decoration mix well with veneering except simple mouldings and inlaid lines of ebony or box used for emphasis. The simpler "strings" and "bandings" are effective when used on small pieces such as caskets, but they usually have a pettiness of detail which is out of scale with large work.

Painted and veneered work are akin in that the effect comes rather from interesting flat surfaces than from the play of light and shade. A similar squareness and simplicity is desirable. Sharp angles should be avoided, as they are difficult to finish in paint and show wear first; a feature could be made of bevelled, rounded, or moulded corners. Mouldings should be very simple and rounded in character, or they will become dulled by successive coats of paint. Schemes with painted furniture are full of possibilities and often provide a useful solution when room and furniture refuse to go together. A restful treatment is to have the walls and furniture painted in two tones of the same colour and to introduce a contrasting colour into the carpet or fabrics. For example: walls ivory white, furniture deep cream, curtains and upholstery in blue-grey or lavender. Painted patterns are free of the limitations of veneered and inlaid work and should be done as directly as possible, the brush being used as a flexible drawing-tool rather than employed merely to fill in a pattern which has previously been drawn in pencil. Effective border patterns, made up of straight lines, curves and waves, may be drawn with a sable lining brush.

CHAPTER II

FURNITURE AS A PART OF THE DECORATIVE SCHEME

THE problem of furnishing and decorating a room is often complicated, rather unnecessarily, by considerations of "style." When furniture can be designed for a definite architectural setting a complete unity of style does become possible, but this happens rarely. Otherwise, a period scheme, Jacobean, eighteenth century, or "modern," usually means replacing much of one's furniture and drastically altering the room. Good work of any period will usually mix quite happily, and outside the bonds of a too rigid style there is wider scope for making the room an agreeable place to live in. This may seem to be forestalled by a room which is badly lit, awkwardly proportioned, or with unpleasant architectural detail. Apart from structural alterations, much may be done to redeem such features by the treatment of walls and ceiling and by the choice of fabrics.

Rooms with an air of simplicity and repose are easier to live in than those which stimulate and arouse, so restfulness should not be restricted to bedrooms. For the entrance hall and the bathroom, in which one does not spend hours at a time, more exciting and colourful schemes are possible.

A crowded room is usually disturbing in effect; a few pieces of essential furniture placed so that one may move freely, and plain, almost empty, walls at once give a sense of spaciousness and ease. Quiet colour also helps greatly. Furniture and fabrics, of which the design seems to strain upward, are not as restful as those which make more use of the horizontal line. Similarly, doors and windows which cut up the walls into a number of vertical sections and counteract a spacious effect should not be strongly contrasted with them in colour, or this tendency will be increased. A diffusion of interest should be aimed at rather than too great a concentration round, say, the fireplace. This is usually the focus of the room, but now that small and unassuming grates and gas and electric fires are used it has not the decorative importance that it had in, for instance, the Elizabethan interior.

A badly proportioned room is usually amenable to treatment. A too lofty ceiling becomes apparently lower if it is made darker than the walls, and these are divided horizontally. This may be done either with a dado rail, or with a picture rail with frieze above of the same colour as the ceiling. The horizontal line should be repeated in the furniture and hangings, and verticals avoided as far as possible. A room which is so low as to have a depressing effect may be improved by an opposite process. The ceiling should be light, and a vertical tendency introduced by means of mouldings applied to the walls to form narrow panels or by a striped wallpaper; curtains should reach to the floor although windows may not. The apparent height of a room is also affected by the height of the furniture. When the latter is low and the pictures are hung so as to be on a level with the eye when one is sitting down, the walls will seem higher. The reverse also holds.

Doors which are badly spaced on a wall should be painted to match it so that attention is not drawn to them. Similarly, awkwardly shaped and spaced windows may have curtains of the same colour as the wall. An unpleasant chimney-piece may be covered with a casing as described in Chapter III, Section 5. Alternatively, it could be completely boxed-in to form a cupboard and an electric fire fitted elsewhere in the room. Houses built in Victorian times frequently have skirtings and door and window surrounds with excessively wide and clumsy mouldings. If the woodwork is painted with a " scumbled " finish the pattern of light and shade will be broken up and the mouldings made less obtrusive.

Dark colours and matte surfaces absorb light and, if greatly used, make a room seem smaller and darker. Pale walls with a glossy varnished surface give a light and spacious effect; in this connection mirrors are also useful, particularly when placed opposite a window to pick up light from outside.

The psychological effects of colour are important, although they vary considerably with different people. To take extremes: large areas of scarlet are hot, restless, and violently stimulating. Deep blue soothes, but is cold and may become depressing. Northerly rooms, without direct sunlight, need a preponderance of warm colour to prevent a chilly and dispiriting effect. For these, colours such as pink, terra-cotta, or tangerine should be made use of, as they tend towards red and have some of its stimulating quality without being as strident. Yellows also suggest sunlight and warmth. Pale blues and greens are restful, but, unless there is warm colour to counteract their coldness, are most suitable for sunny rooms.

The aspect of the room, together with the colour of the furniture, will provide useful limitations when planning the colour scheme. It should be remembered that the relative quantities of the colours in a room are as important as their actual nature. For instance, the warm reddish colour of mahogany furniture may be admirably brought out by contrasting it with walls of turquoise blue or duck's-egg green. On the other hand, the relatively greater amount of blue or green would overpower the warm colour of the wood and the total effect would be cool. For a sunless room this would be unsuitable, and further warm colour would have to be introduced into curtains or carpet. An alternative treatment for such a room would be to have walls pale cream or peach colour, which are warm and yet contrast slightly with the red of mahogany, and to use smaller quantities of blue or green to prevent the effect becoming too hot.

Schemes in two contrasting colours, with everything in the room tending to either one or the other, can be completely satisfying and are easier to manage and more restful than a riot of colours. There are two approaches to a scheme of this sort; say in blue and brown. One is to use the colours in nearly equal quantities; brown furniture against blue walls, blue rugs on a brown floor, fabrics patterned in blue and brown. In this case neither colour predominates, but they are used one against the other to give a lively contrasted effect. The alternative method is to have the room in tones and variations of one colour with small touches of the other used for accents. For instance: furniture of natural unpolished oak, oatmeal coloured walls, fabrics the same but patterned in a darker tone, chocolate brown carpet. Clear pale blue pictures, cushions, or china will break the monotony of the brown, and bands of the same colour may be used to underline, as it were, architectural features such as the window or door architraves, skirting, and cornice.

A true contrast in colour is obtained by putting together two pure complementary colours; yellow and violet, for instance. The woods, fabrics, etc., used in furnishing are rarely quite pure in colour, so that this is not often possible. When it is, as in a painted scheme, such violent contrasts should be sparingly used. A subtler and more restful contrast is obtained when the colours have a common element; lilac and turquoise blue, for example, both contain blue, but one colour is warm in effect and the other cool. Similarly, pale green and the cream colour of sycamore both contain yellow, but here again there is a contrast of coolness and warmth. Many interesting arrangements are possible with warm and cool greys.

Variations of tone, the degree to which colours tend towards light and dark, can be used to give interest to a scheme which has no marked colour contrast. Contrasts of texture and surface are also valuable in this connection; curtains of rough tweed on a wall of identically the same colour will appear to contrast with the former if it has a glossy varnished surface to pick up reflected colour from the room. Attractive and restful schemes are possible with almost neutral browns, greys, black, and white. The woods and fabrics for such a scheme should be chosen for their texture and tone rather than for their colour. Any positive colour in pictures, flowers, or ornaments will be given a quite unusual value.

Fig. 1. An enclosed Mahogany Bookcase with cupboard at either end [Fig 4 (5)]

CHAPTER III

FURNITURE FOR THE LIVING-ROOM AND DINING-ROOM

Section 1.—Bookcases and Book-Tables

This section illustrates a variety of treatments for open and enclosed bookcases and also for book-tables. Fixed shelves should range in height from 7" to 14" and up to 10" in width; they should not be above 3' 0" long, or the weight of the books will tend to cause sagging. When very thick shelves are used, an appearance of lightness may be given by planing a bevel about 2" wide on the under side at the front and thus enabling the edge to show any desired thickness.

Open Bookcases.—Fig. 2 (1-8) shows open bookcases suitable for solid oak or walnut; alternatively, in the case of Fig. 2 (1, 2, 5) mahogany could be used. Fig. 2 (1) has a lap-dovetailed carcase, the arched top being built up with band-sawn sections. The shelves are connected to the ends by slip-dovetails or, if the construction

PLATE I

BOOKCASE IN WEATHERED OAK

Sir Ambrose Heal   *Heal & Son Ltd.*

BOOKCASE AND CUPBOARD UNITS IN "VENESTA" PLYWOOD

Venesta Ltd.

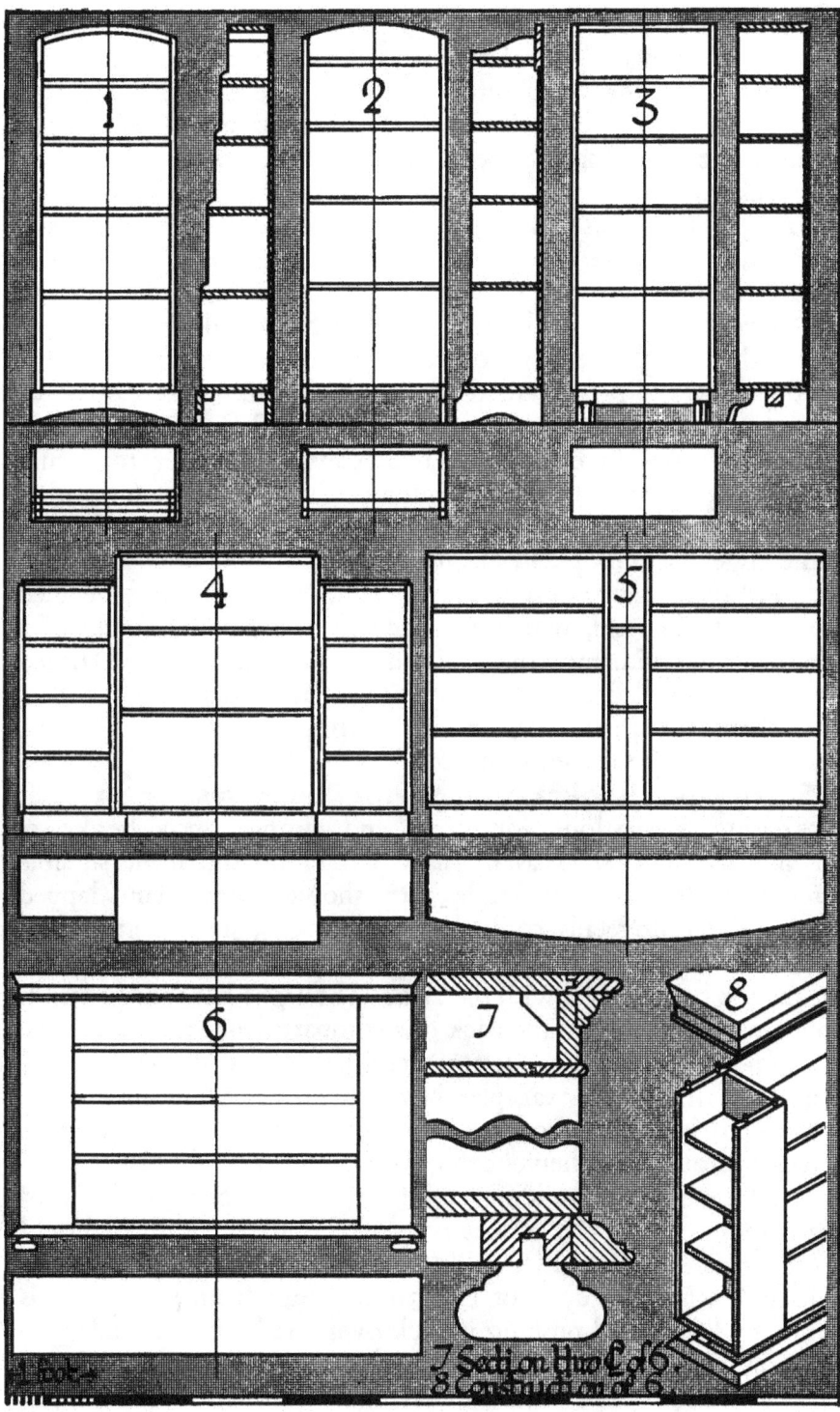

Fig. 2. Open Bookcases

is being "featured," by a series of small through-tenons. The plinth is "boxed-up" separately, and has fillets at front and back for screwing up into the bottom. The carcase should be rebated to take a back of $\frac{3}{8}''$ ply. In Fig. 2 (2) the ends are the full height of the bookcase, the shelves being fixed as in the previous example. The back rail is $\frac{5}{8}''$ thick and lap-dovetailed between the ends. Fig. 2 (3) has a carcase similar to Fig. 2 (1) and is screwed to two shaped feet connected by a tenoned rail. Fig. 2 (4) consists of three dovetailed carcases screwed to a "break-fronted" plinth; they have false tops set back $\frac{1}{16}''$. The front rails of the plinth below the wings are slip-dovetailed to the cross rails, which are themselves slip-dovetailed to the back rail. The carcase of Fig. 2 (5) should be through- or lap-dovetailed for oak or walnut and secret-mitre dovetailed for mahogany. In order to ensure accurate alignment of the bow front, it is advisable to fasten together the five boards for top, bottom, and shelves, and to shape and finish all the edges in one operation. Fig. 2 (6) has adjustable shelves in front and fixed shelves at either end. The latter are slip-dovetailed into separate carcases, which are screwed to a base consisting of a tenoned frame with moulding mitred round three sides, the turned feet being dowelled into this. The frieze is "boxed-up" with a mitre-clamped top and bottom, as shown in the section Fig. 2 (7), and is dowelled to the end carcases.

Small Open Bookcases and Unit Bookcases.—Fig. 3 (1-18) gives some suggestions for small and simple open bookcases and also for unit bookcases. Oak would be the most suitable material. The external angles are shown with plain lapped joints, but lap-dovetails could be used. Fig. 3 (1) is designed to stand at the side of an easy-chair and should be about 2' 0" high, so that the top comes level with the arm. The right-hand end extends above this top and forms the back of a compartment for small books. Fig. 3 (3-7) show various arrangements of shelves for small bookcases; the first three examples have cupboards with flush doors of veneered laminated board. In Fig. 3 (6) the vertical divisions run right through, the shelves being fixed as in Fig. 3 (2). Fig. 3 (9, 10) are unit bookcases for building up into any formation; they are 1' 6" square and 1' 6" by 3' 0" respectively. The adjustable shelf should be on "pins," detailed in Fig. 4 (8). Fig. 3 (9) has a glazed door on hinges, while the door of Fig. 3 (10) hangs from pivots and is opened by lifting and pushing it back over a rail tenoned under the top; Fig. 3 (8) shows it in the closed position. The top edge is rounded and the pivots made by driving in thick screws and cutting

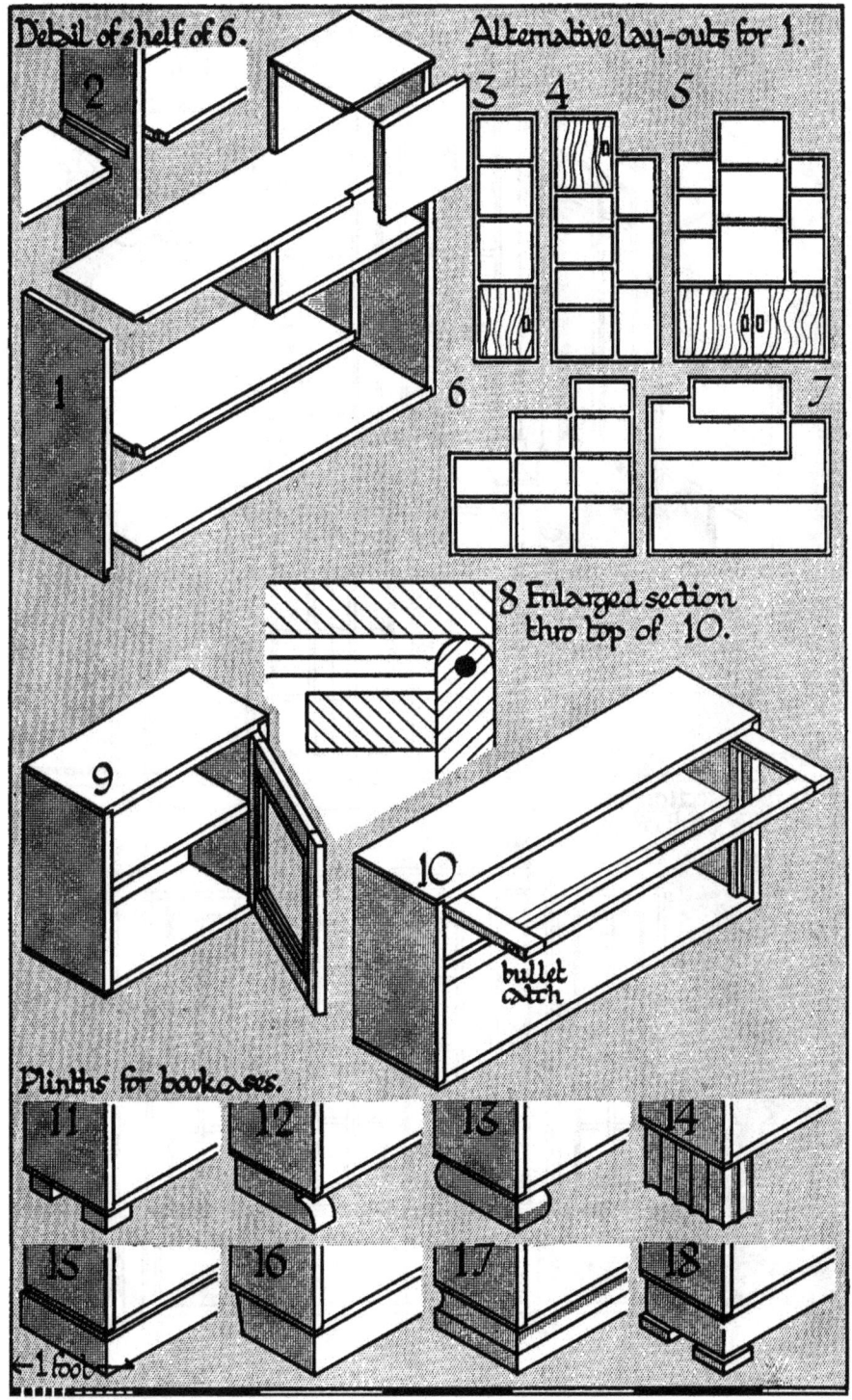

Fig. 3. Small Open Bookcases and Unit Bookcases

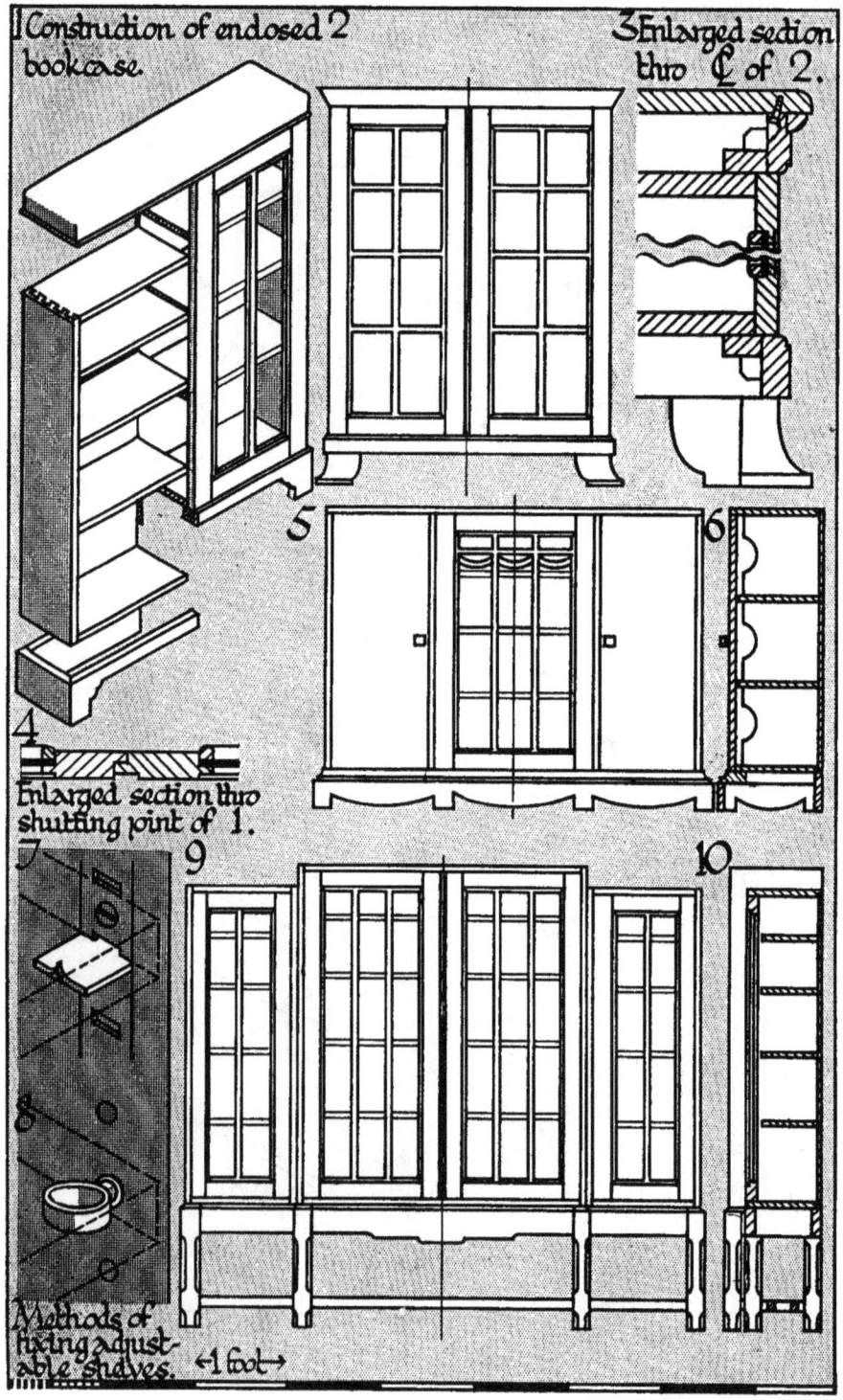

Fig. 4. Bookcases with glazed doors

PLATE III

"PLAN" BOOKCASE AND CUPBOARD UNITS IN UNPOLISHED OAK

Serge Chermayeff, F.R.I.B.A.

PLATE IV

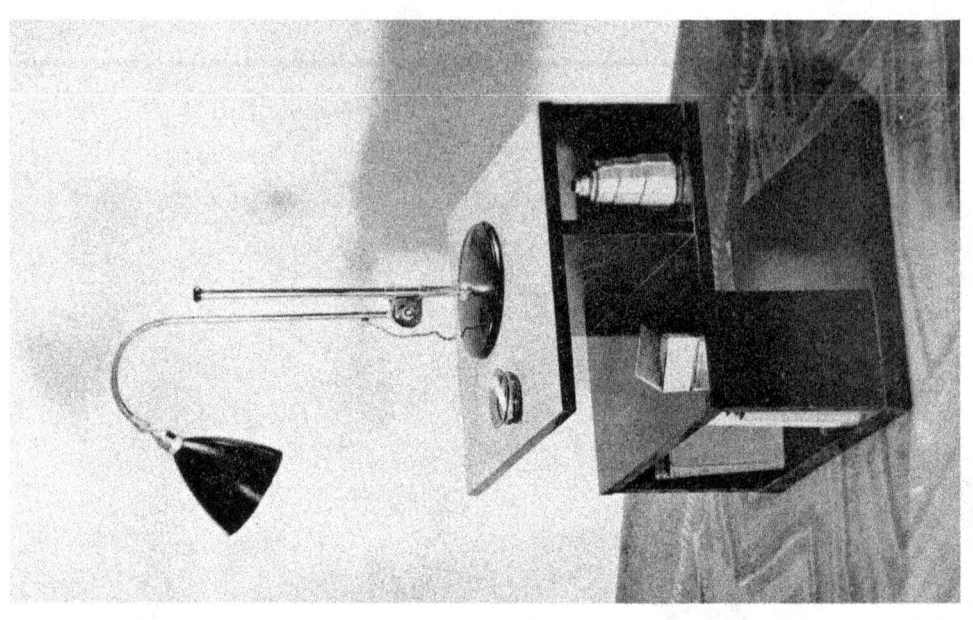

BOOK-TABLE IN FIGURED BIRCH WITH TOP OF FIGURED TEAK
Heal & Son Ltd.

BOOK-TABLE WITH BLACK CELLULOSED FINISH
The Bath Cabinet Makers Co. Ltd.

off the heads. These slide in stopped grooves cut in the carcase ends, the door being put in from behind before the back of the unit is fitted. The bookcases on this page are shown without plinths; various alternatives for these are detailed in Fig. 3 (11-18). Fig. 3 (15-18) are "boxed-up" and could be cross-banded with a wood contrasting with that of the carcase.

Bookcases with Glazed Doors.—Fig. 4 (1-10) shows bookcases enclosed by barred and glazed doors. Fig. 4 (1) illustrates the construction of a typical example for mahogany. The carcase is lap-dovetailed and screwed to the plinth and frieze, the latter being "boxed-up" with a flush top of veneered laminated board. The doors are framed up with the glazing bars set $\frac{1}{16}''$ below the face, and there is a corresponding rebate on the edges of the stiles and rails as shown in the section Fig. 4 (4). Fig. 4 (2) is similar in construction, but has an overhanging top and shaped feet. Feet of this type are dealt with in Fig. 3 of the section on "Sideboards." Mahogany would be suitable for Fig. 4 (5); it is made with a dovetailed carcase which has slip-dovetailed divisions to form cupboards at the ends. These could be fitted with shelves and divided for the storage of gramophone records, as shown in section in Fig. 4 (6). The plinth has a cavetto moulding mitred round three sides of the top. Fig. 4 (9) would also make an attractive display cabinet and could be in solid oak or walnut. It consists of three lap-dovetailed carcases screwed to a stand with a "breakfront," the centre carcase being deeper than the wings, as seen in the section Fig. 4 (10). The front rails of the stand below the wings are tenoned into the cross rails, and these are tenoned to a continuous back rail. Fig. 4 (7) shows the Tonks' Patent Strip for adjustable shelves; it is grooved into the carcase ends at back and front, and the shelves are supported by metal clips which fit into the slots. Fig. 4 (8) details an alternative method of fixing, in which rows of holes are bored 1" between centres and fitted with brass "pins." Two holes are bored at each end of the shelf to slip over the "pins" and thus lock it in position. It is desirable that the shelves in enclosed bookcases should line with the horizontal glazing bars, as in Fig. 4 (2), but when adjustable shelves are used the doors may be made with vertical bars only, as in Fig. 4 (1, 5, 9).

Book-Tables.—Fig. 5 (1-13) shows examples of book-tables; if made about 2′ 0″ high they could be also used for low tea-tables. Fig. 5 (1) consists of four uprights into which an X-shaped stretcher is dovetailed, the top being screwed to this and the shelf housed below and pocket-screwed or bracketed. Both top and shelf should

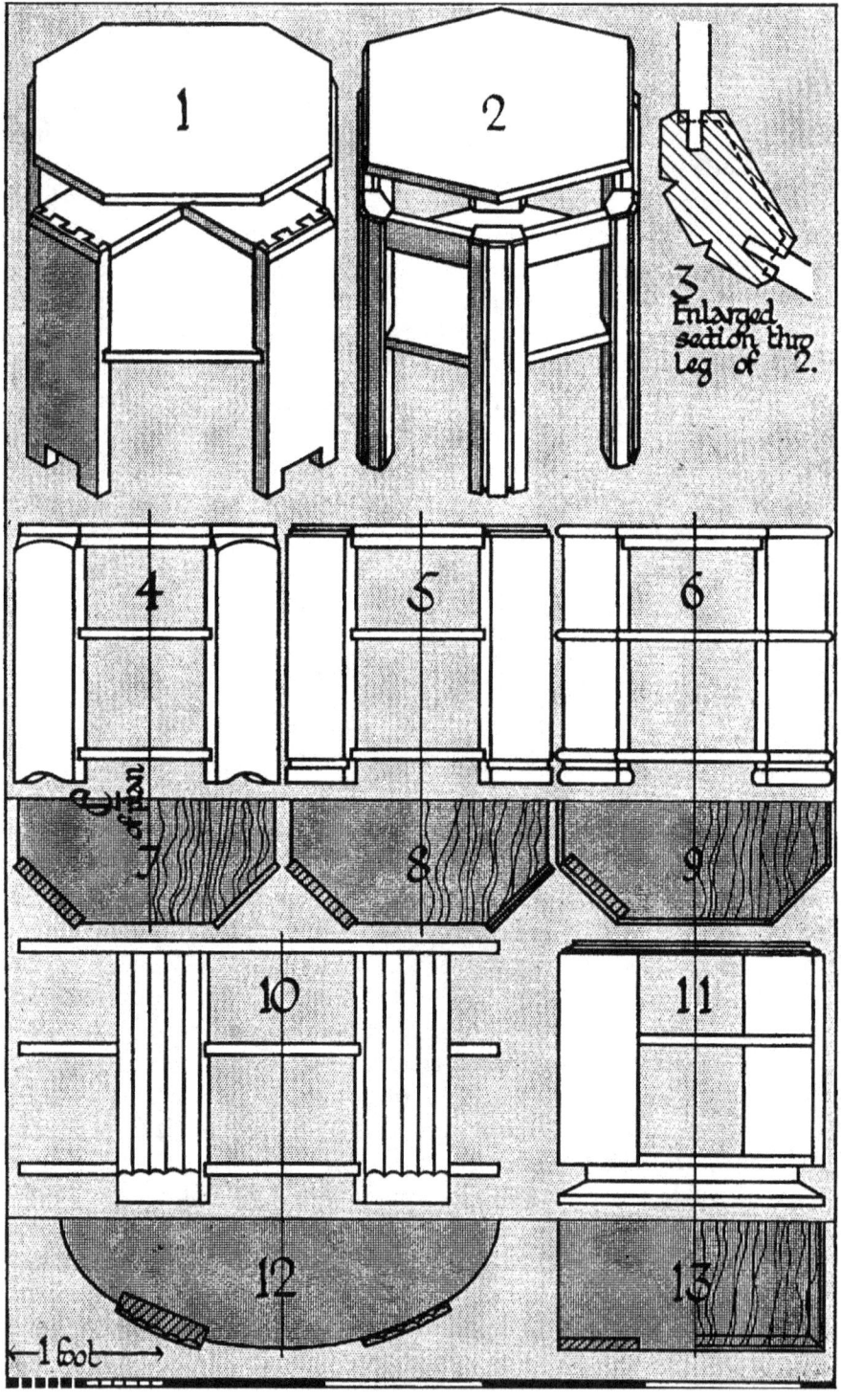

Fig. 5. Book-Tables

preferably be of veneered laminated board with clamped edges. Fig. 5 (4, 5, 6) are constructed in the same way as the first example, but have a third shelf and show alternative detail. Fig. 5 (6) has a half-round moulding applied to the edges of the shelves and moulded feet dowelled to the uprights. Fig. 5 (2) is framed up with six legs and tenoned rails, as detailed in Fig. 5 (3), the dotted line indicating the housing of the shelf. The elliptical example, Fig. 5 (10), has a construction similar to that of Fig. 5 (1), but the stretcher beneath the top is only half the width of the uprights. Fig. 5 (11) has four flat uprights, 6" wide, which are dowelled to the top and bottom. The plinth is "boxed-up" separately and screwed from below.

Section 2.—Boxes and Caskets

Tea-Caddies, Cigarette-Boxes, etc.—Fig. 1 (1-10) illustrates small shaped boxes for cigarettes or for use as tea-caddies. They would also be suitable for glove or handkerchief boxes, and could be in finely figured walnut or mahogany, used either in the solid or as veneers.

Fig. 1 (1-5) embody rather similar technique; it is customary in such work to complete the assembly and veneering of the box before cutting off the lid, in order to ensure an exact register. Fig. 1 (6) shows a method of through-dovetailing the box with one of the pins made wider to allow for the cutting and trueing up of the lid. Fig. 1 (7) shows an alternative method in which four pieces are mitred round a soft-wood core and fixed temporarily with panel-pins. Saw kerfs are then made in a dovetail form to receive keys of veneer, and after gluing on the bottom the core is removed.

The shaped lid of Fig. 1 (2) may either be worked from the solid or built up with layers of veneer in a caul, as in Fig. 1 (8); if it is to be veneered, a caul must be used in either case. The shaped ends of Fig. 1 (5) are planed up from the solid and the sides lap-dovetailed into them. The raised panel on the lid of this example could be formed with a rebating plane or applied; the latter method would simplify veneering. An enlarged section through Fig. 1 (4) is shown in Fig. 1 (9), the cavetto moulding on the lid being worked after assembly. The lining is of $\frac{3}{16}$" stuff and projects $\frac{1}{8}$" below the lid, the ends are butted against the sides and the top inch mitred; there is no necessity for the mitre to be the full depth of the box. Fig. 1 (10) shows a box-hinge which has a stop to prevent it opening beyond a right angle.

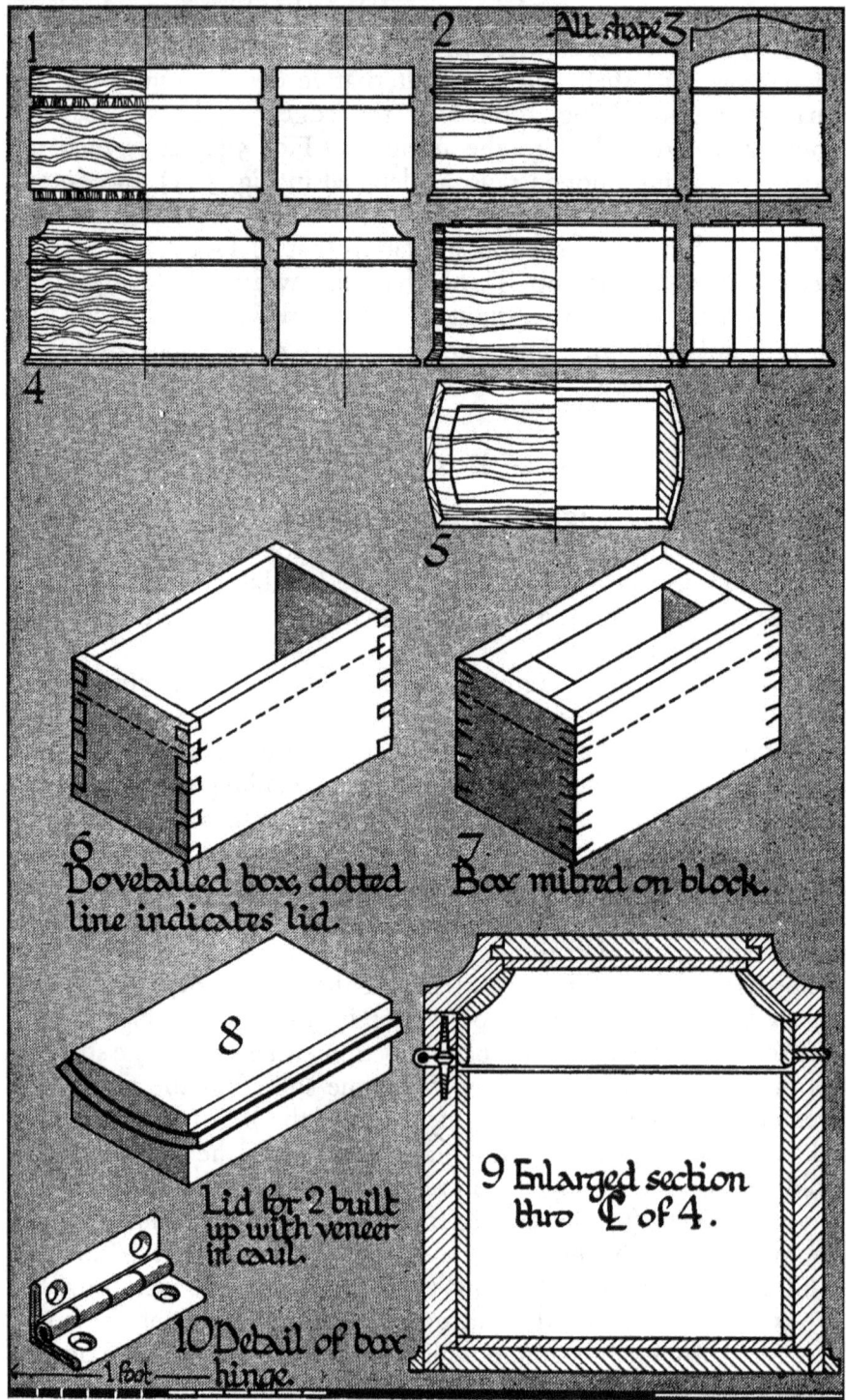

Fig. 1. Tea-Caddies and Cigarette-Boxes

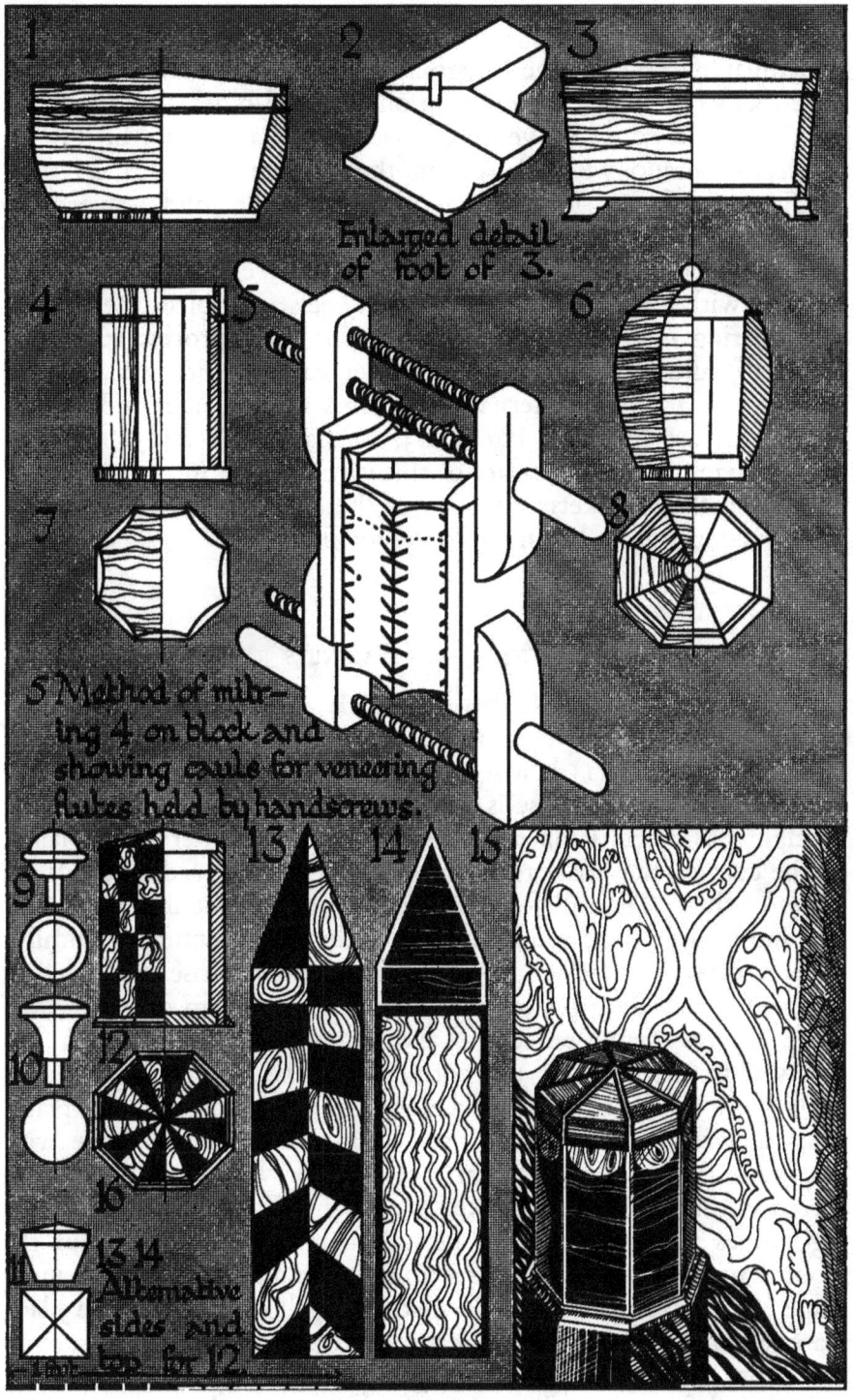

Fig. 2. Caskets

Caskets.—Fig. 2 (1-15) gives some suggestions for small caskets for similar purposes to the foregoing, but of a more frankly decorative character. They are built up on a shaped block, as previously described, and could be veneered with macassar ebony, bird's-eye maple, or zebrano, with inlays of mother of pearl, ebony, and ivory.

Fig. 2 (3) has a shaped lid worked from the solid; two cauls will be needed for veneering it; one to fit the curve from front to back and the other for the long curve of the front elevation. Fig. 2 (4) is fluted with a round plane after it has been assembled, the process of veneering is shown in Fig. 2 (5). The same process applies to Fig. 2 (6) and (12), but in the former case the lid is made and veneered separately. Alternative patterns for the sides and top of Fig. 2 (12) are given in Fig. 2 (13, 14), and Fig. 2 (15) shows a further suggestion for a casket of this type. Fig. 2 (9, 10, 11) detail knobs for these caskets; they could be made in ebony or ivory, the turned examples having a dowel for fixing.

Section 3.—Cabinets

Hanging Corner Cabinets with Concealed Lighting. —Fig. 2 (1-6) shows hanging corner cabinets for the display of china, etc. Fig. 2 (1) is a section through Fig. 2 (2) showing the construction. The carcase is semi-elliptical in plan, and is built up of eight flat pieces rubbed-jointed together and afterwards planed to the curve; the pilasters are cross-banded and glued to the front edges of this. The rail for the cornice is slip-dovetailed across the top and is faced with solid wood with the grain running vertically. The carcase is dowelled to a laminated board base to which is screwed a moulding grooved to take a false bottom of ply. Two lamp-holders with reflectors and low-consumption bulbs are screwed to the back of the cornice rail, the light being diffused by a piece of frosted glass and flooding down through the plate-glass shelves. These fit into grooves in the carcase and line with the glazing bars. Ventilation holes to prevent overheating are bored in the top and are masked with bent pieces of tin so that the light does not escape. The glazing bars project $\frac{1}{8}''$ beyond the door frame, which has a corresponding raised margin on its inner edge. This example could be made in mahogany, with the black parts ebonized and the interior veneered in a lighter wood such as sycamore or maple; alternatively, it could be silvered. Fig. 2 (3) is intended for oak, and consists of five posts, as shown in the plan

Fig. 2 (6), with rails tenoned between them at top and bottom. The door is between the two front posts. The frame is grooved to take a bottom of laminated board and the top, also of laminated board with clamped edges, is pocket-screwed to the rails. Concealed lighting could be arranged as in the previous example. These cabinets should be hung by slotted screw-plates in the back coinciding with screws driven into the wall. If this is very uneven, scribing pieces screwed to the sides will ensure a close fit.

Built-in Display Cabinets.—Fig. 3 (1-9) illustrates display cabinets for building into a corner or recess. Fig. 3 (1) has a framed front which is fitted into a corner of the room and reaches from floor to ceiling. It is scribed to the skirting, a length of which is carried across the bottom. There is a glazed door above and a panelled door below. The shelves are of ply and rest on fillets screwed to the wall, the two bottom shelves being also fixed to the framing. This consists of two uprights with rails tenoned between; the arch should be of laminated board. After fitting to the wall a $\frac{1}{2}''$ bead is worked round the edge, and it is fixed by nailing to two grounds made of 2″ square stuff with one corner bevelled

Fig. 1. China Cabinet built into a corner [Fig. 3 (1)]

Fig. 2. Hanging Corner Cabinets with concealed lighting

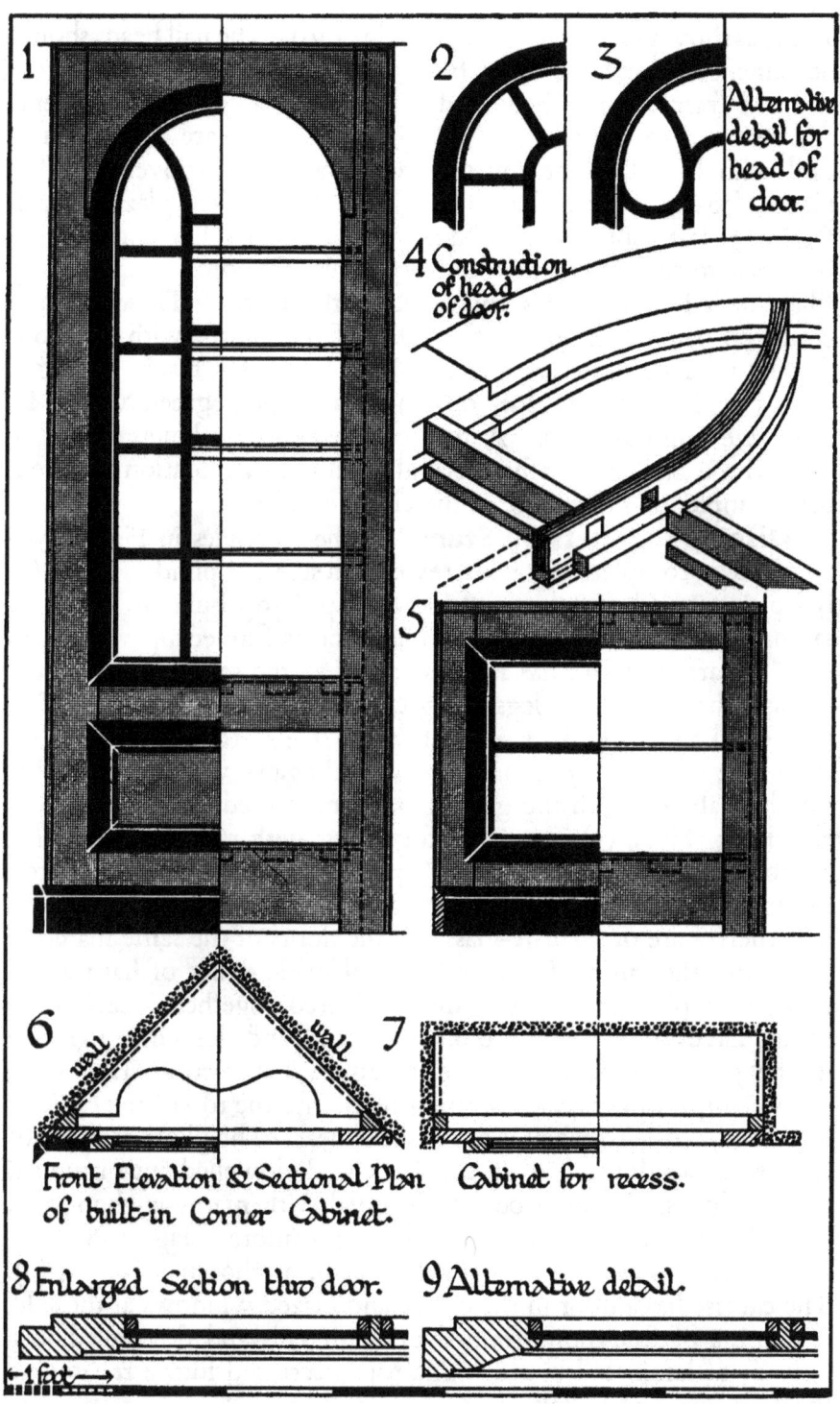

Fig. 3. Built-in Display Cabinets

away, as shown in the sectional plan Fig. 3 (6). The nail heads should be punched in and the holes filled with putty. The doors have a tenoned frame, the arched head being made up of three segments and tenoned to the stiles, as in Fig. 3 (4). Arcs are built up in a caul with five strips of saw-cut veneer, and are grooved into flat pieces, bow-sawn to shape, to form the curved glazing bars. Fig. 3 (5) is a cabinet for building into a recess. The construction is similar to that of the previous example; the top is supported by fillets nailed to the sides and back of the recess. These cabinets could be painted to match the walls of the room, with the door frames in a contrasting colour. Pale pink and black, primrose yellow and turquoise blue, or white and apple green would be attractive combinations. A pair of the corner cabinets could be used as the basis of a rather formal scheme of decoration; placed, for example, on either side of the chimney-piece.

Display Cabinets on Stands.—The examples in Fig. 4 (1-9) are made as complete carcases screwed to a stand or plinth. Fig. 4 (1) is lap-dovetailed together and has a shaped top built up of band-sawn sections, as in Fig. 4 (4). The stand is framed up with posts of 2" square stuff and has fillets screwed to the rails to support the carcase, the tops of the legs being cut down level with these. The face of the glazing bars is flush with a $\frac{1}{16}$" rebate worked on the inside edge of the door frames. Mahogany would be suitable for this cabinet, with the glazing bars and the edges of the carcase ebonized. Fig. 4 (5) consists of four posts with rails slip-dovetailed at front and back and ends of $\frac{3}{4}$" laminated board. The flush top fits into a rebate and the ends are grooved to take the bottom. The shelves are of $\frac{1}{4}$" plate-glass and the doors of the same material. The latter slide in an E-section channel made either of hard wood or of two pieces of brass channel soldered together. Each door should have a finger-grip ground at the end, and closes into a groove in the post to give a dust-proof joint. The section, Fig. 4 (7), shows lamps for concealed lighting fitted into the top of the cabinet, which is lined with asbestos to resist the heat. The plinth is made of four rails lap-dovetailed at the back and dowelled into rounded corner blocks. It could be cross-banded with macassar ebony and the cabinet itself veneered in oak or sycamore. Fig. 4 (8) is in walnut and has the sides splayed in plan, as shown in Fig. 4 (9). The carcase has a door in the centre and glazed windows at the side. It consists of four posts framed up with rails and dovetailed to a bottom of laminated board. The top is screwed into a rebate and the rails grooved to take a $\frac{1}{2}$" flattened bead. The door stiles are

DISPLAY CABINETS ON STANDS

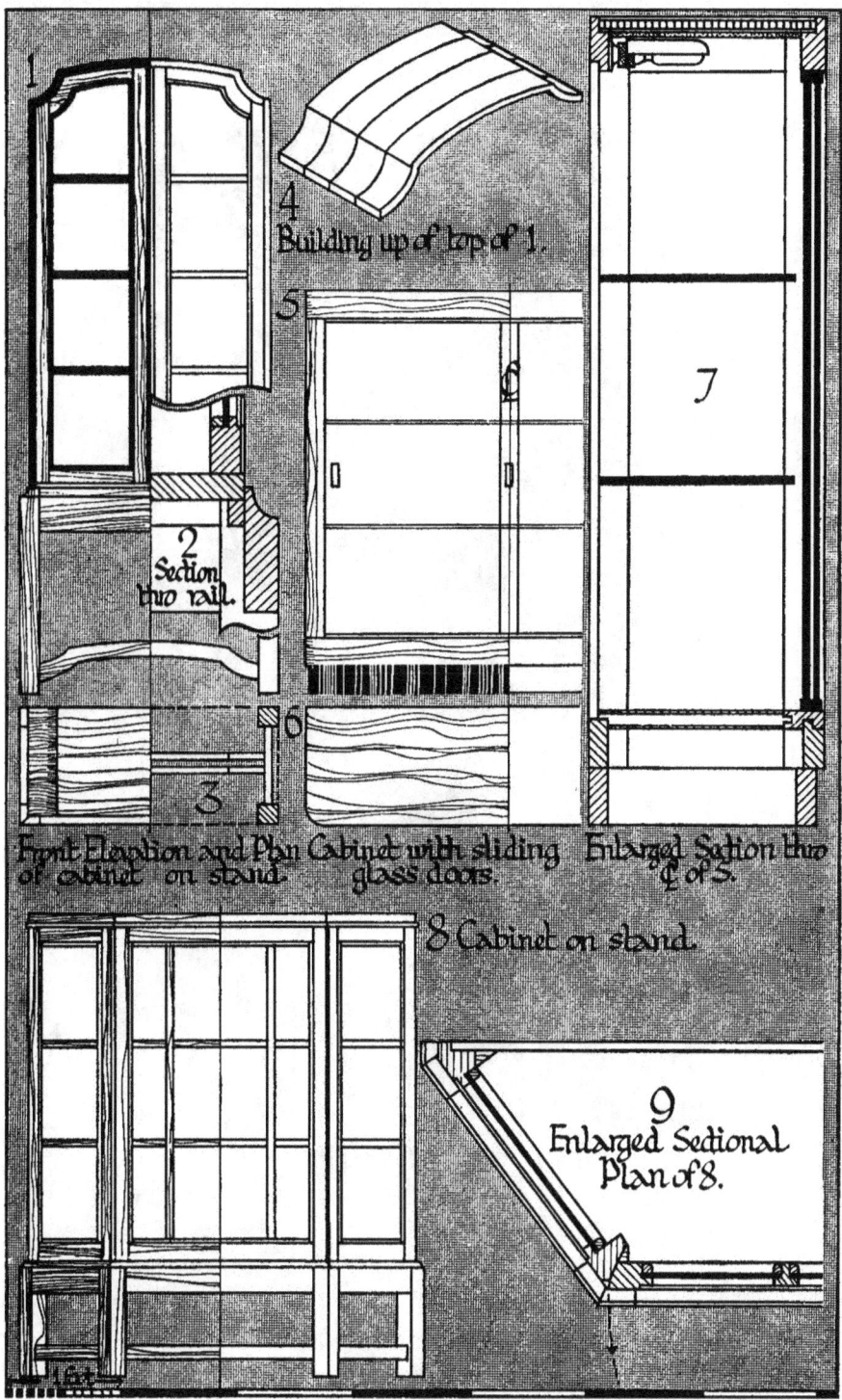

Fig. 4. Display Cabinets on stands

Fig. 5. Small Enclosed Cabinets

CABINET IN WALNUT WITH ROSEWOOD STAND

Gordon Russell Ltd.

PLATE VI

WEATHERED OAK DINING CHAIRS

Sir Ambrose Heal   *Heal & Son Ltd.*

DINING CHAIRS FINISHED IN VERMILION CELLULOSE WITH BLACK UPHOLSTERY

The Bath Cabinet Makers Co. Ltd.

bevelled so that a complete post is formed when the door is closed, the joint being concealed by a $\frac{3}{16}''$ rebate. The stand is framed up with posts of the same section as those of the upper part which drops into it, as in the example in Fig. 4 (1).

Small Enclosed Cabinets.—Fig. 5 (1–6) gives some suggestions for small decorative cabinets on stands; the interior could be fitted as a cocktail cabinet, or have trays or shelves for storing music, etc. They consist of a lap-dovetailed carcase screwed to a tenoned stand, the shaped corners beneath the rail of the latter being made as in Fig. 4 (3) of the section on sideboards. The block feet of Fig. 5 (1, 4) are made separately and fixed by dowels. The doors are of $\frac{3}{4}''$ laminated board with clamped edges. The drawer of Fig. 5 (5) fits into a separate lap-dovetailed carcase screwed between the cupboard section and the stand. The drawer sides are slip-dovetailed into the front and overhang the carcase ends; similarly, the doors above are hinged over the ends. Fig. 5 (6) has the division for the drawer slip-dovetailed between the ends and a false top fixed by secret-screwing. It is veneered in stripy walnut, with handles and edgings of black-stained hornbeam. Fig. 5 (1, 4, 5) are in mahogany or American white wood, with a painted finish, the two latter examples being decorated in coral pink, blue, and apple green on a ground of a pale colour such as ivory or vellum. The bolder pattern suggested in Fig. 5 (1) could be carried out in strongly contrasted colours such as maroon and lime green or deep blue and fawn. Alternatively, the decoration could be confined to the carcase edges, Fig. 5 (3) giving some suggestions for running patterns for these.

Section 4.—Chairs

This section comprises suggestions for simple arm and single chairs in oak, walnut, and mahogany. The construction of the frame shown in Fig. 5 (3) applies to both types. The back and front are tenoned together separately and are then joined by the side rails, the tenons of which are cut with a splayed shoulder to give the taper of the seat. "Horns" of an inch or so are left on the front legs to prevent splitting of the mortises during assembly. Brackets should be screwed across the angles of the seat to obviate "racking" and the tenons mitred for the same reason.

The height over the seat should be 1' 6" and to the top of the back about 2' 10". This should have a rake of about 2" at the side and the bottom of the leg be set slightly beyond, also the seat should

Fig. 1. Dining Chairs in mahogany [Fig. 3 (2)]

slope back slightly in elevation. The usual overall width for the seat of a single chair is 1′ 6″ tapering to 1′ 3″; arm-chairs are about 2″ wider.

Single Chairs with Loose Seats.—The examples in Fig. 2 (1-10) are in oak or walnut and have a loose stuffed seat fitting into a rebate as described in the section on "Stools." The construction of Fig. 2 (1) is shown in Fig. 5 (3). The top rail of the back is cut out of the solid and, as it is flush with the uprights, could be dovetailed down into them instead of being tenoned. The legs should be tapered on the outside faces only so that the tenons may come up squarely. Fig. 2 (2) has a splat hollowed to fit the back. The ogee-shaped splats of Fig. 2 (6) are tenoned at both ends, the top rail being in one piece with the centre splat tenoned up into it. Fig. 2 (8, 9, 10) show a very simple type of back consisting of a $\tfrac{3}{8}$″ panel tenoned between the uprights.

Arm-Chairs with Loose Seats.—Fig. 3 (1-7) shows chairs made on similar lines to the preceding examples but with the addition of arms. Fig. 3 (1) is in oak, the horizontal rails being

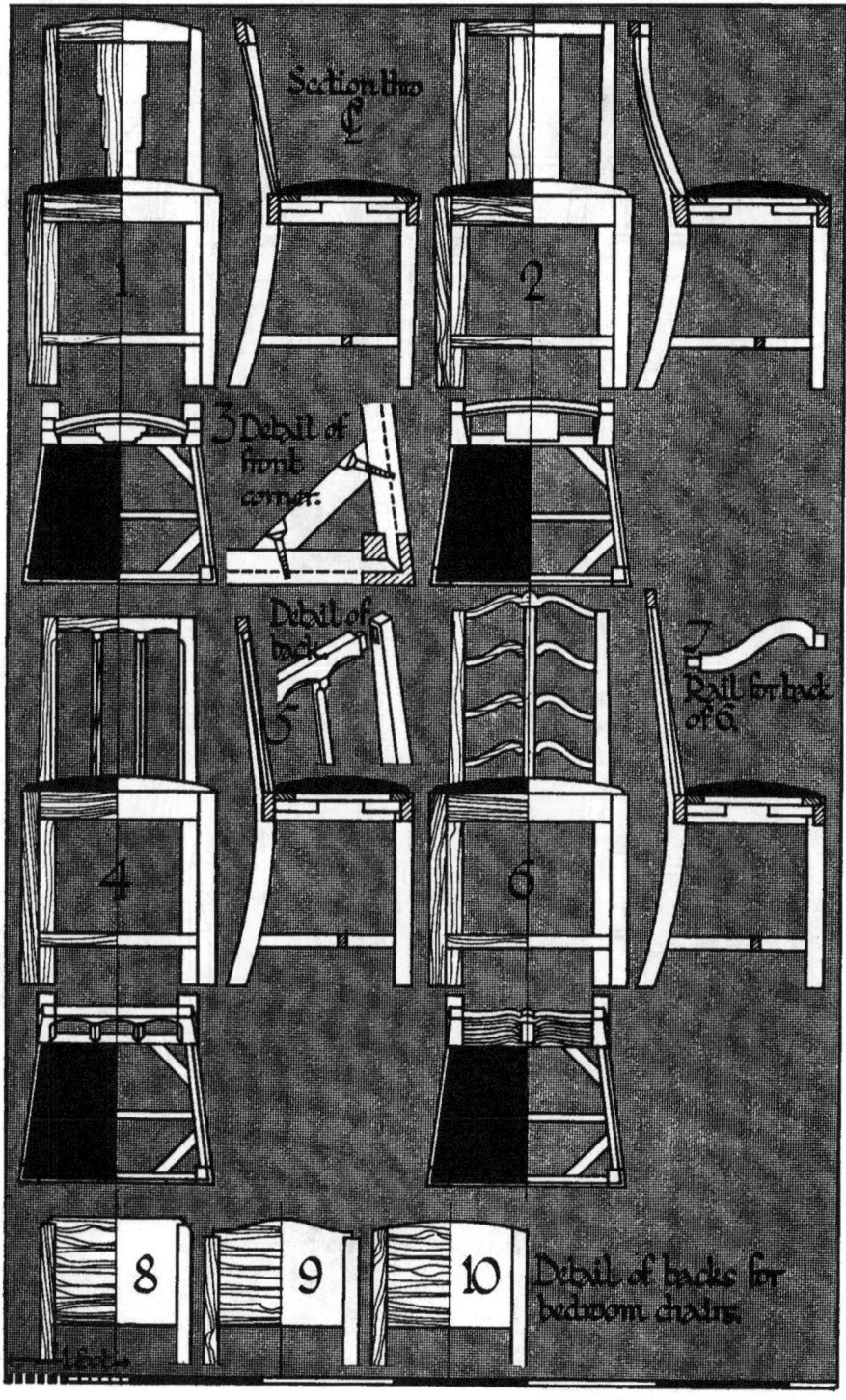

Fig. 2. Single Chairs with loose seats

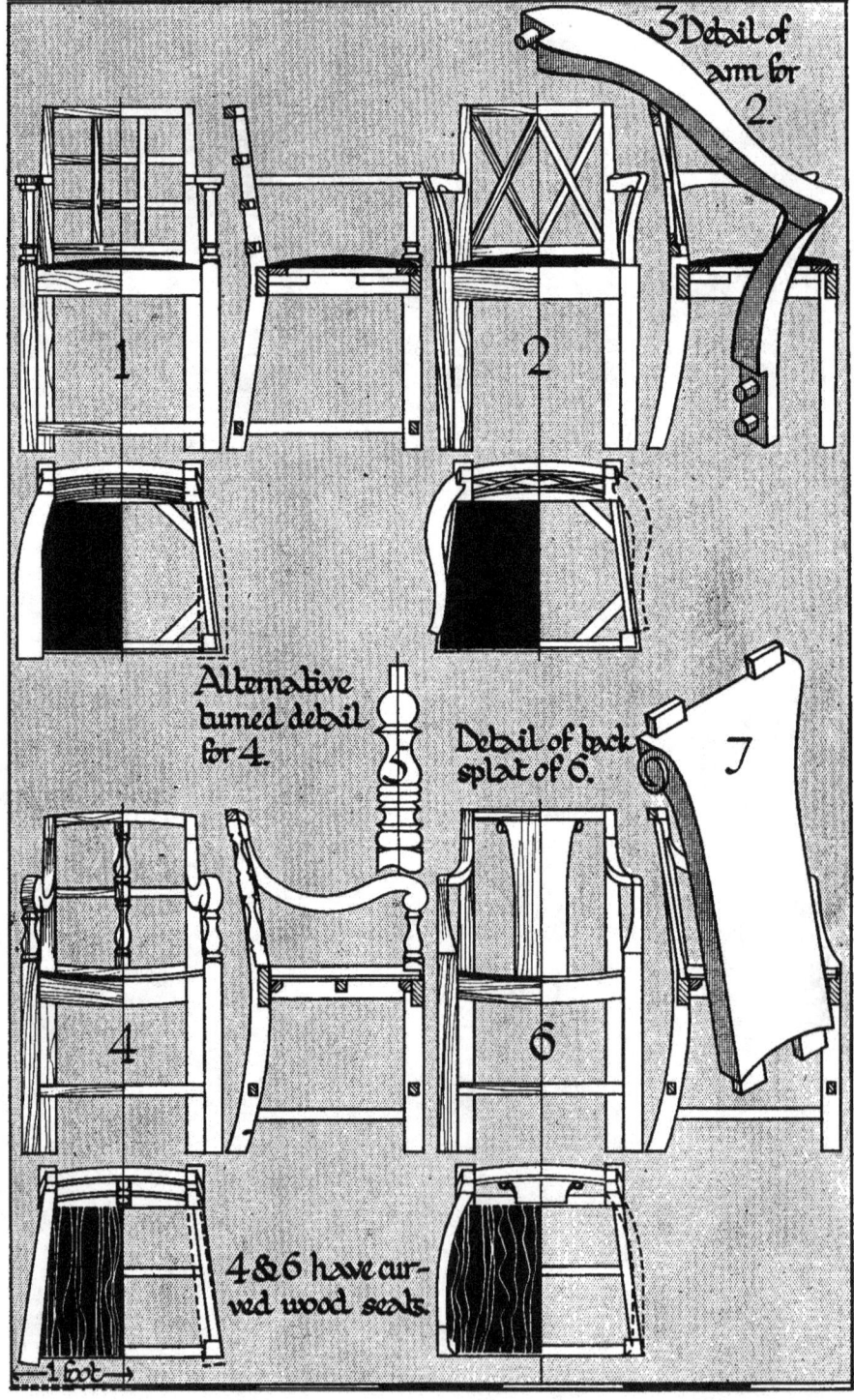

Fig. 3. Arm-Chairs with loose seats

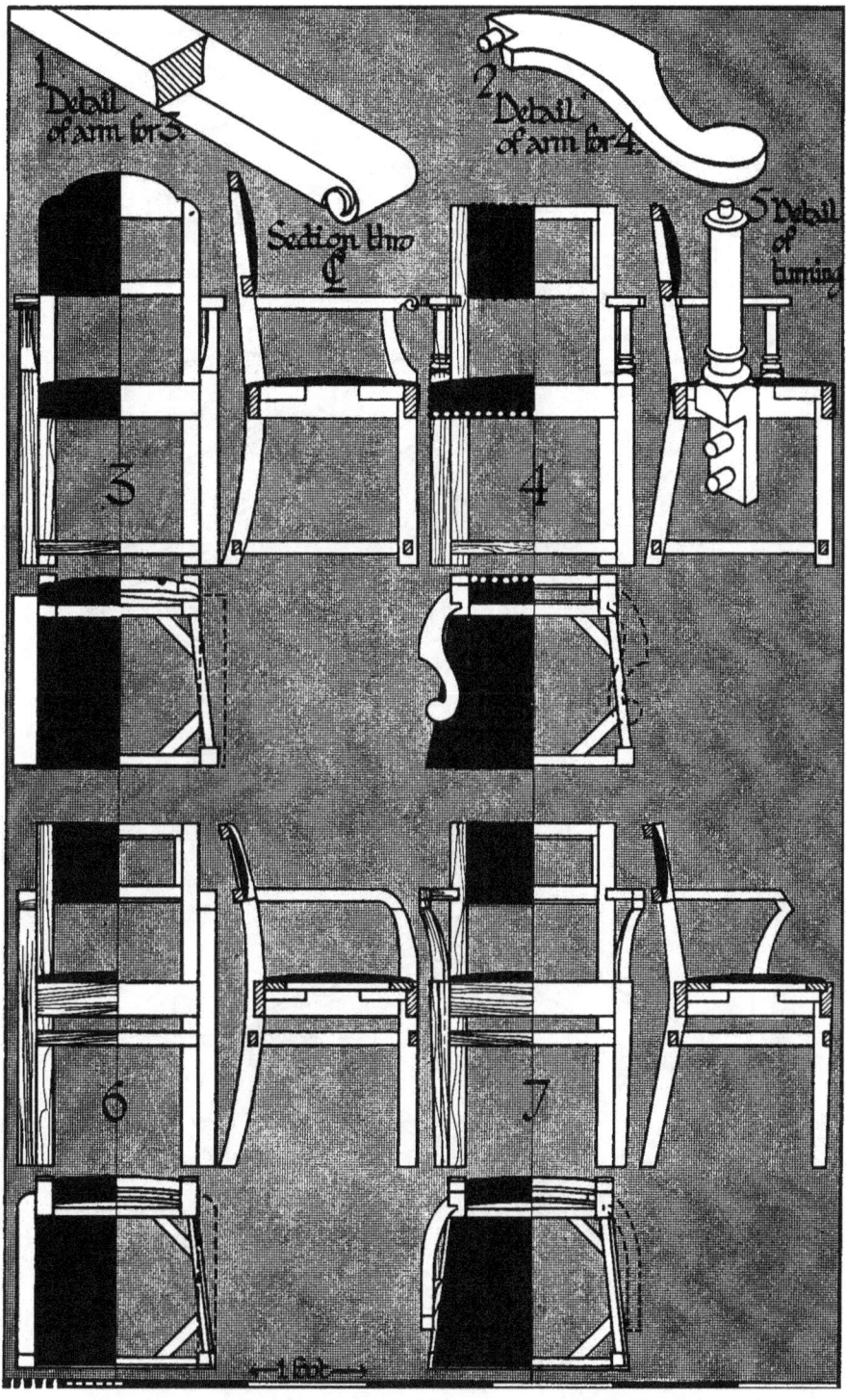

Fig. 4. Arm-Chairs with upholstered seats and backs

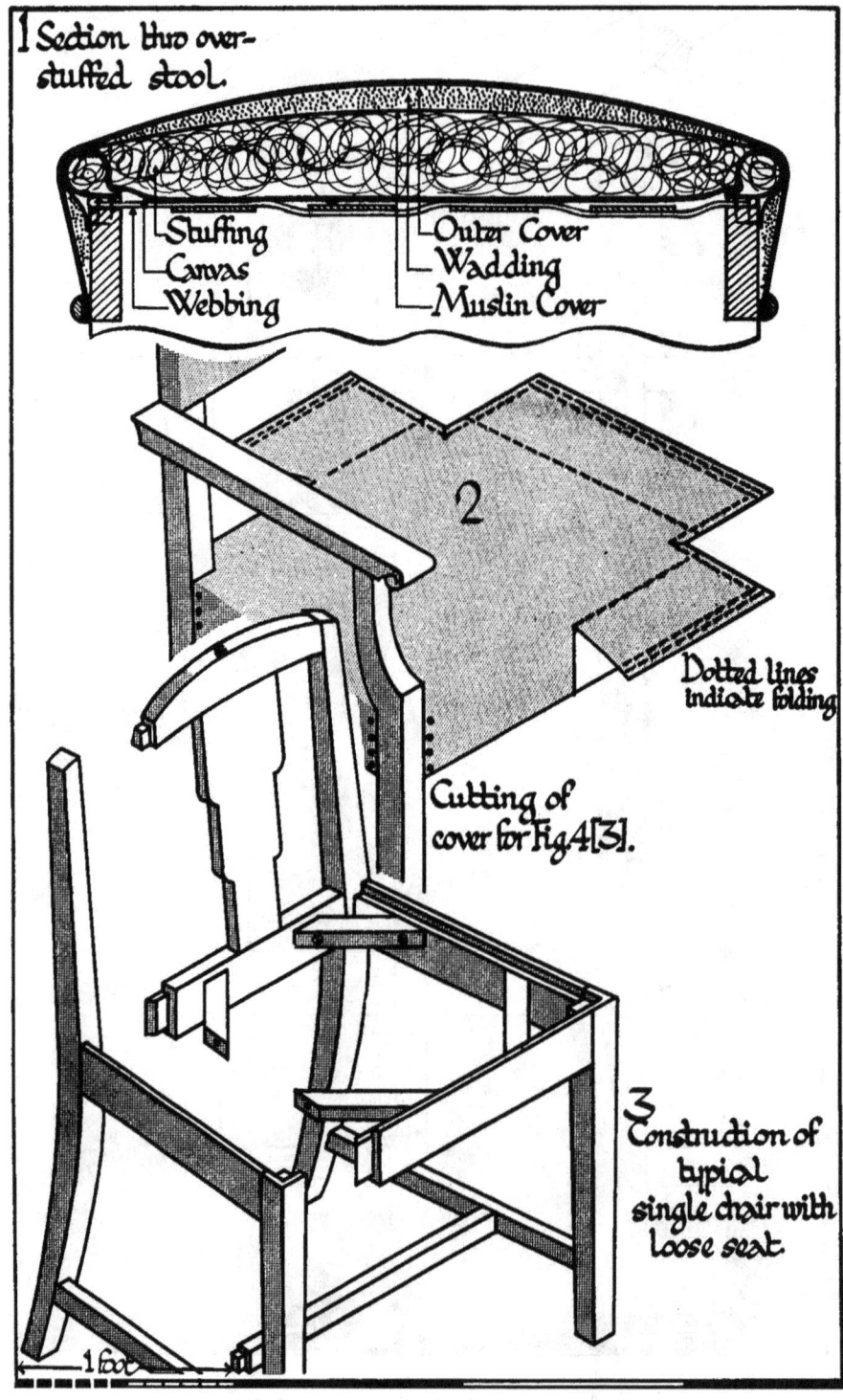

Fig. 5. Constructional details for chairs in Figs. 2 and 4, and for upholstered stool

PLATE VII

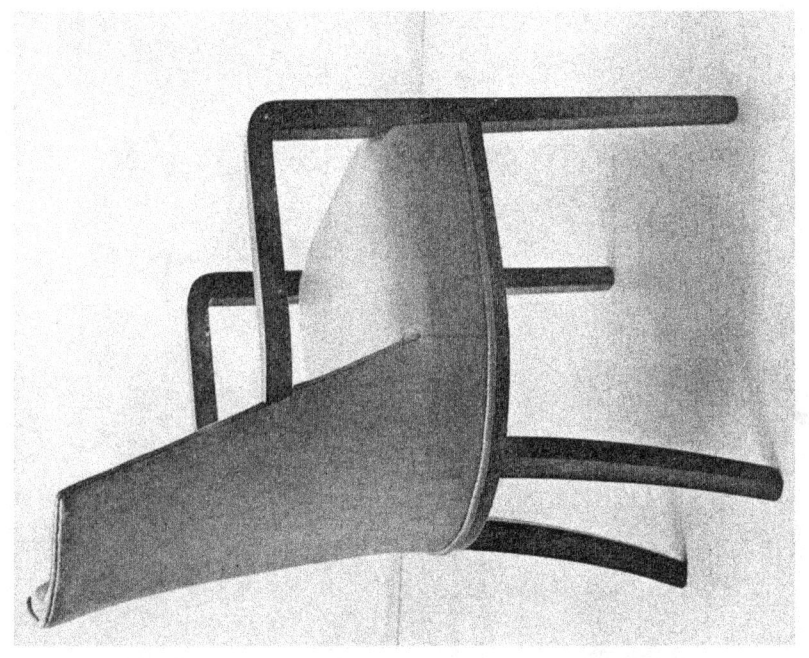

DINING CHAIR IN ROSEWOOD WITH LEATHER UPHOLSTERY

Serge Chermayeff, F.R.I.B.A.

OCCASIONAL CHAIR WITH FRAME OF WAXED BIRCH

The Rowley Gallery Ltd.

PLATE VIII

A FIREPLACE TREATMENT IN PLYWOOD FACED WITH INDIAN WHITE MAHOGANY;
THE WALLS ARE LINED WITH THE SAME MATERIAL

Philip Evans Palmer, A.R.I.B.A. *Venesta Ltd.*

curved in plan and halved to the verticals. The arm is dowelled into the turned upper part of the leg and is tenoned into the back. Fig. 3 (2) could be made in mahogany or walnut; the arm consists of two pieces shaped with a bowsaw and spokeshave and dowelled together. Fig. 3 (4) has a turned back splat with a dowel at either end for fixing, the horizontal rails being tenoned into the square block in the centre. The arm is dowelled in front and notched and dowelled into the back. Fig. 3 (6) has arms fixed in the same way and the part of the leg above the seat is shaped into a curve. Beech or ash would be appropriate for these last two examples, and they could have "saddle" seats of a contrasting wood such as elm instead of the loose seats. The wood should be thoroughly wetted on the under side to assist in pulling it down to the curve; alternatively, a series of sawcuts may be made from front to back.

Arm-Chairs with Upholstered Seats and Backs.—The examples in Fig. 4 (1-7) are in oak and have seats and backs stuffed and covered with fabric or leather. The construction is as previously described, the arms being dowelled at front and back. Fig. 4 (4, 6, 7) have a strip screwed inside the uprights of the back to which are tacked the horizontal pieces of webbing.

The seats of Fig. 4 (3, 4) are made with a rolled edge as described in the section on "Stools." Fig. 5 (2) shows the cutting of the cover; it is pulled down over the rails and tacked to the under side. Mitres are cut at the corners, leaving enough material for turning under and tacking on either side of the legs. The back is also webbed and stuffed and the cover tacked to the edges of the frame, the heads of the tacks being concealed with a strip of gimp. Fig. 4 (4) has the cover carried over the legs and fastened with round-headed nails. Fig. 4 (6, 7) are shown with loose seats, the back is stuffed as in the previous examples, and the cover tacked to the front of the frame. The back should have a filling of material to conceal the unsightly appearance of the webbing.

SECTION 5.—CHIMNEY-PIECES

Chimney-Pieces to Fit over Tiled Fireplace Surround. —Fig. 1 (1-9) shows simple chimney-pieces to fit over the tiled surround of the fireplace. If possible, the opening should be slightly under a square in height and the baseblocks should line with the flat of the skirting.

Fig. 1 (1) consists of a tenoned frame of $1\frac{1}{2}''$ stuff with a moulded shelf planted on and screwed from behind. Fig. 1 (3) also has a tenoned frame; the uprights have a stopped bevel on the inside, and there is a shallow sinking 1" from the outer edge. Fig. 1 (5) is adapted from a Wren chimney-piece. Two ends, 5" wide, are lap-dovetailed to a horizontal rail to form a three-sided frame. A cavetto moulding, mitred to return to the wall, is planted on top of this to take the mantel-shelf, as shown in the section Fig. 1 (6). The baseblocks are made separately and screwed from behind. Heavy bolection mouldings, as in this example, should have the mitres connected by " coach " bolts, as otherwise shrinkage may cause unsightly joints. Fig. 1 (8) has a flat tenoned frame, as in the examples in Fig. 1 (1, 3). The fluted faces of the pilasters are rebated into sides 4" deep to form three-sided boxes without ends, the baseblocks being made as separate boxes. The flutes at the top of the pilasters are then planed away and the corner squares glued on. These are $\frac{1}{4}$" thick, project $\frac{1}{8}$" over the pilaster face, and have a hole to form the circular sinking. The back frame is screwed on from behind.

Fig. 1 (9) gives sections for wood kerbs which are made by mitreing together three pieces of moulding.

Fig. 1 (4) is a back view of Fig. 1 (1) and shows how it is fixed. Screws are driven into wall-plugs to project $\frac{1}{4}$" from the wall face, corresponding holes with slots above being bored in the frame of the chimney-piece. When this is driven down into position the screw heads enter the slots and hold it firmly to the wall.

Wood chimney-pieces built up of several members should have these screwed through the back as reinforcement. Also, it is important to note, particularly with new brick or plaster work, that all the back parts should be painted two coats of colour containing red lead to obviate swelling caused by temporary dampness.

Surrounds for Fitted-in Gas or Electric Fires.—Fig. 2 (1-6) shows surrounds for fitted-in gas or electric fires. They are " boxed-up " in construction and may be made to fit over and conceal existing fireplaces which are unpleasant in appearance and impracticable to remove. The fire is mounted in a panel of asbestos or building board which is screwed to the surround from behind Ventilation up the chimney-flue or by other means should be provided. Fig. 2 (4) details the fitting of a Ferranti flush type electric fire.

Fig. 2 (1, 2, 3, 5) are all made with a front facing of three pieces tenoned together and planted on a frame. This frame forms the sides and top and is lap-dovetailed on the ends. In Fig. 2 (1) the under edge of the horizontal facing piece is rebated and the ends

CHIMNEY-PIECES OVER TILED SURROUND

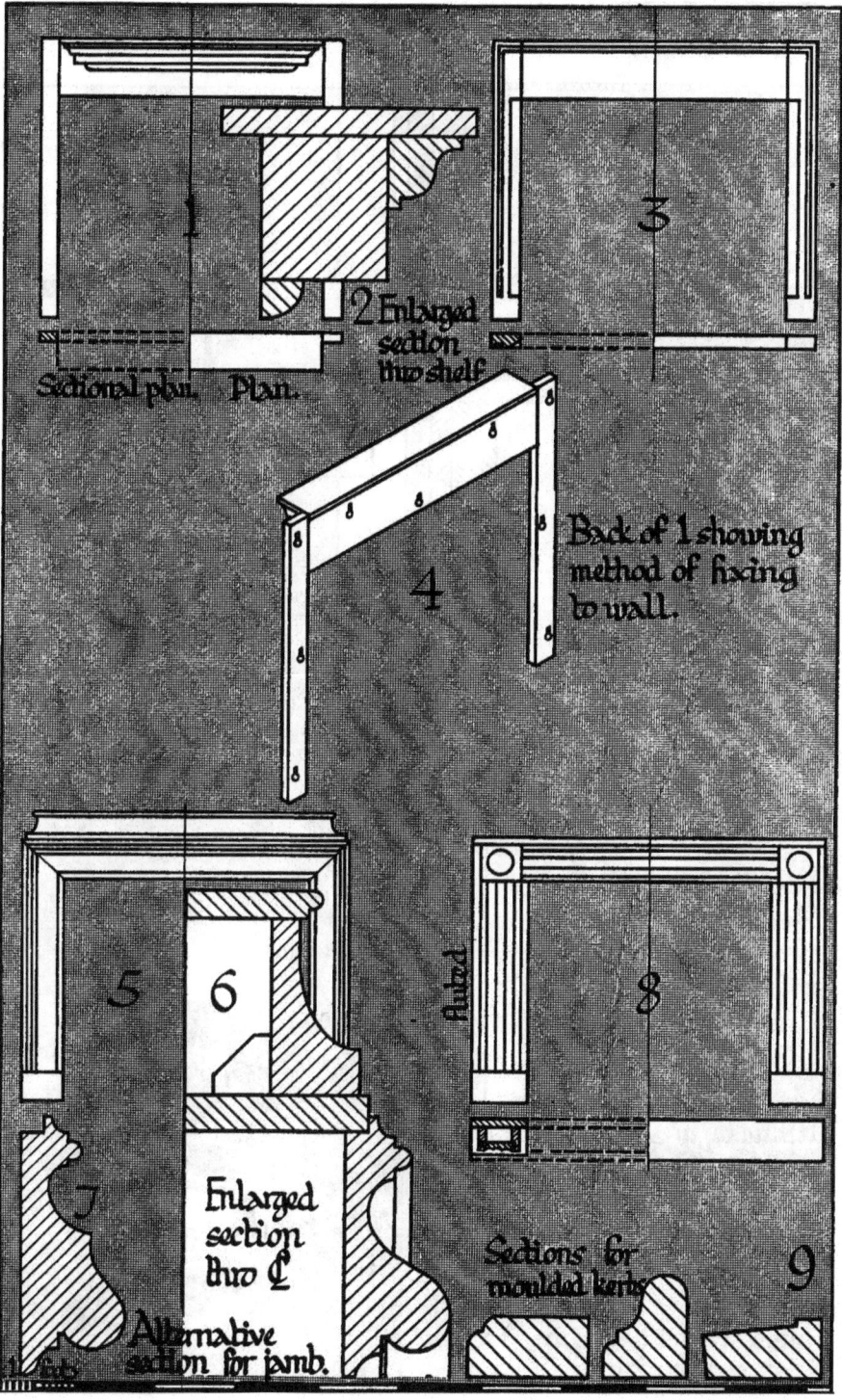

Fig. 1. Chimney-Pieces to fit over tiled surround of fireplace opening

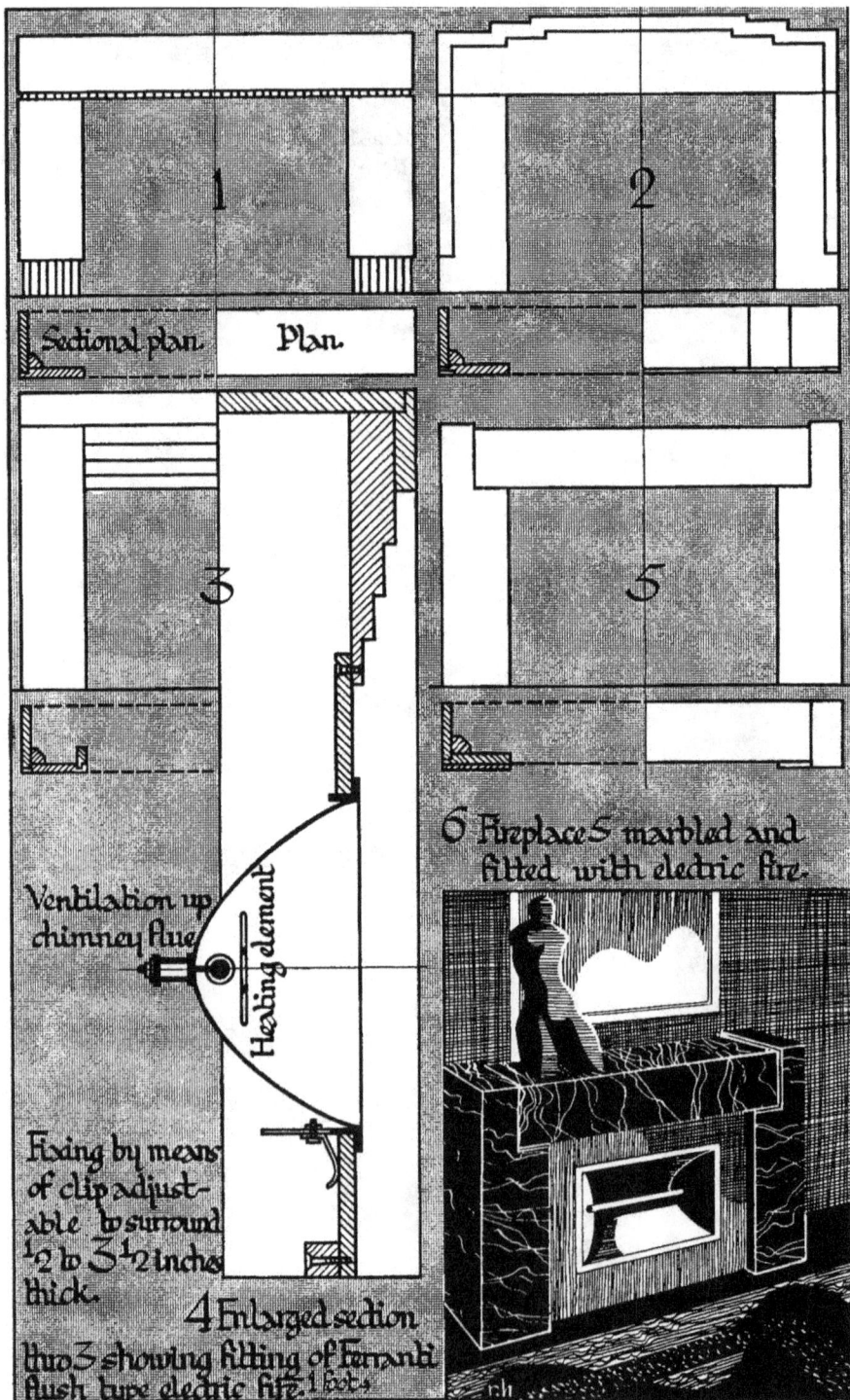

Fig. 2. Surrounds for fitted-in gas or electric fires

grooved to take the band of vertical flutes. All the fluting for this example may be made from one piece of 8" board, working with the grain. Two pieces are cut from this and mitred for each baseblock, and narrow strips are glued in the rebate to form a continuous band. The mantel-shelf in Fig. 2 (2) has three steps glued to it to correspond with the stepped top of the facing piece. The vertical steps in Fig. 2 (3) are made from one piece 2" thick, which is dowelled between the uprights, as shown in the enlarged section Fig. 2 (4). Fig. 2 (5) has a second facing piece glued to the first to form the L-shaped breaks at the top, and the mantel-shelf is faced at the ends to continue this break.

Section 6.—Clocks

It must be impressed that the first step in making a clock-case is to consider the type of movement required and to relate the design, construction, and interior sizes to this. The designs for long-case, mantel, and wall clocks given in this section provide for the fitting of well-defined trade types of movement which are shown in Fig. 5 and briefly described below.

Clock Movements

English Grandmother Movement.—This is shown in Fig. 5 (2, 3) and is suitable for the cases in Fig. 2; it may also be obtained with a metal dial which will necessitate revision of the woodwork detail of the front of the case, the method of fixing remaining the same. The movement is wound from the front and regulated by adjusting the length of the pendulum by means of the nut provided. The striking action is shown in Fig. 5 (1, 4), and consists of a steel coil weighted with a block. This is struck by a hammer projecting from the back of the movement, the hammer being shown at the point of impact. In order to ensure a good tone the coil must be left quite free, its only point of contact with the case being where the vertical spindle is gripped by a collar on a plate screwed to the back of the case. The movement proper is fixed by bolting through a "seat-board" supported by two bearers; a slot is cut in this and in the bottom of the hood to allow for the swing of the pendulum.

German Grandmother Movement.—This closely follows the English type and is suitable for the same cases. It is usually made with a chiming attachment, the notes being produced by

Fig. 1. Long-Case Clock with painted finish [Fig. 2 (1, 4)]

hammers striking a series of hanging metal rods. These are either fixed direct to the side of the case or to packing pieces.

Timepiece Movement.—A movement of this type may be used with a wood dial as for the cases in Figs. 6 and 9, or, alternatively, may be obtained with a metal dial and glazed bezel for types as in Fig. 8. It is an eight-day movement, and, as it is wound, regulated, and set from the front, the case may have a " screwed-in " back as distinct from a hinged door.

Fig. 5 (6) shows the movement used with a wood dial; it is fixed by screwing through three lugs attached to the metal dust-cover. With a metal dial, fixing is by screwing through the square dial-plate as in Fig. 5 (7, 8). The square or circular bezel is hinged to a metal frame of the same thickness as the front of the case and screwed inside an opening cut in it.

Drum or Barrel Timepiece.—This is an eight-day movement of Swiss origin and is contained in a metal drum about 3″ in diameter with a glazed bezel fixed to the front. It is operated entirely from the back, which is closed by a hand-tight metal cover. This movement is particularly suitable for small block cases as it simply slips into a circular hole cut through the centre, as in the lower half of Fig. 5 (5), and is

LONG-CASE CLOCKS

Fig. 2. Long-Case Clocks

fixed by screwing through the side of the drum. The upper half of Fig. 5 (5) shows it in a boxed case; small blocks to receive the fixing screws must be glued to the sides of the opening in the back.

English Bracket Movement.—This is the best timekeeper of the movements described and operates by pendulum; it is the one usually chosen for first-class work. It may be obtained with either a circular or square dial and glazed bezel, and is suitable for an upright rectangular case of the type shown in Fig. 8 (2); this should be fitted with a hinged door at the back. The movement is placed upon a "seat-board," and is secured by two brackets which are screwed through the case, as shown in the plan Fig. 5 (9). The dial fits inside a metal frame screwed inside the opening and the bezel is hinged to the wood front of the case.

French Pendulum Movement.—This type functions for either eight or fifteen days and is usually fitted with a striking attachment. It includes a dial and glazed bezel, and is suited to cases of the same type as the preceding example. Winding and regulation are from the front, further regulation being effected by adjusting the pendulum. The dial and bezel are fixed to the movement, which is inserted through a hole in the front of the case, as shown in Fig. 5 (10). A similar hole is cut in the back to take a rim with a hinged metal cover. The movement is fixed by two metal straps, which are threaded to receive screws projecting from the back rim. When these screws are tightened, the front and back flanges are drawn together so that they bed firmly on the wood case. The striking action is independent of the movement and consists of a coil, similar to that in the English grandmother movement, mounted on a vertical spindle screwed through the bottom of the case.

Electric Movements.—These operate upon two systems; in the first type the movement is connected with a mechanically driven master clock, while in the second the impulses are communicated from frequency meters at the electric supply stations. In both cases the movements are usually contained in small rectangular boxes and are particularly suitable for wall clocks of the type shown in Fig. 9. For mantel clocks a movement of the second type may be obtained, which is similar in shape and size to a barrel timepiece and is supplied complete with dial and bezel.

CASE CONSTRUCTION

In making cases with wood dials, as in the examples in Figs. 2, 8, and 9, the dial must be of such a thickness that the centre-pin

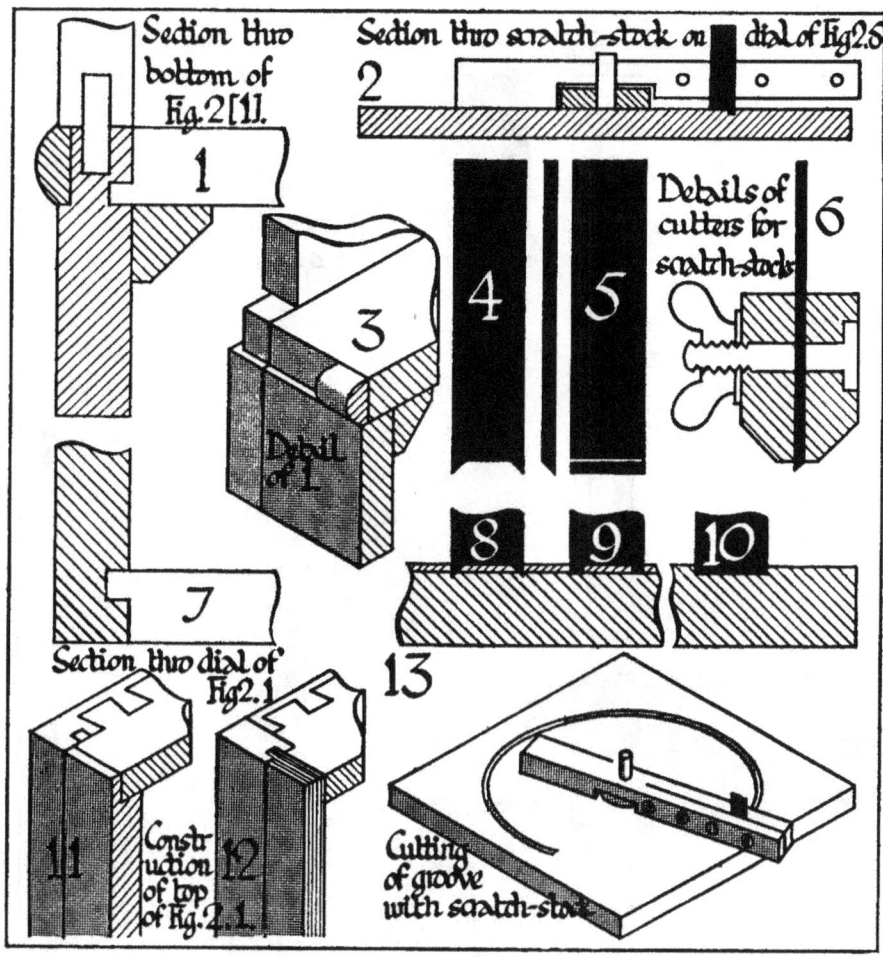

Fig. 3. Constructional details for Fig. 2 (1) and method of cutting groove for inlaid dial with scratch-stock

and sleeve of the movement project sufficiently to enable the hands to be fixed. This may alternatively be done by recessing the back of the dial to admit the movement. The hands shown for dials of this type should be cut from sheet brass and either bronzed or chromium plated. They should be made as light as possible or counterbalanced to avoid affecting the movement; this may be assisted by filing away the under side so that it is tapered in section.

Long-Case Clocks.—Fig. 2 (1-6) shows three types of long-case clock. Fig. 2 (1) is for painting and consists of a carcase lap-dovetailed at the top and with a tenoned division. It is dowelled to a " boxed-up " plinth, which is rebated for a half-round moulding,

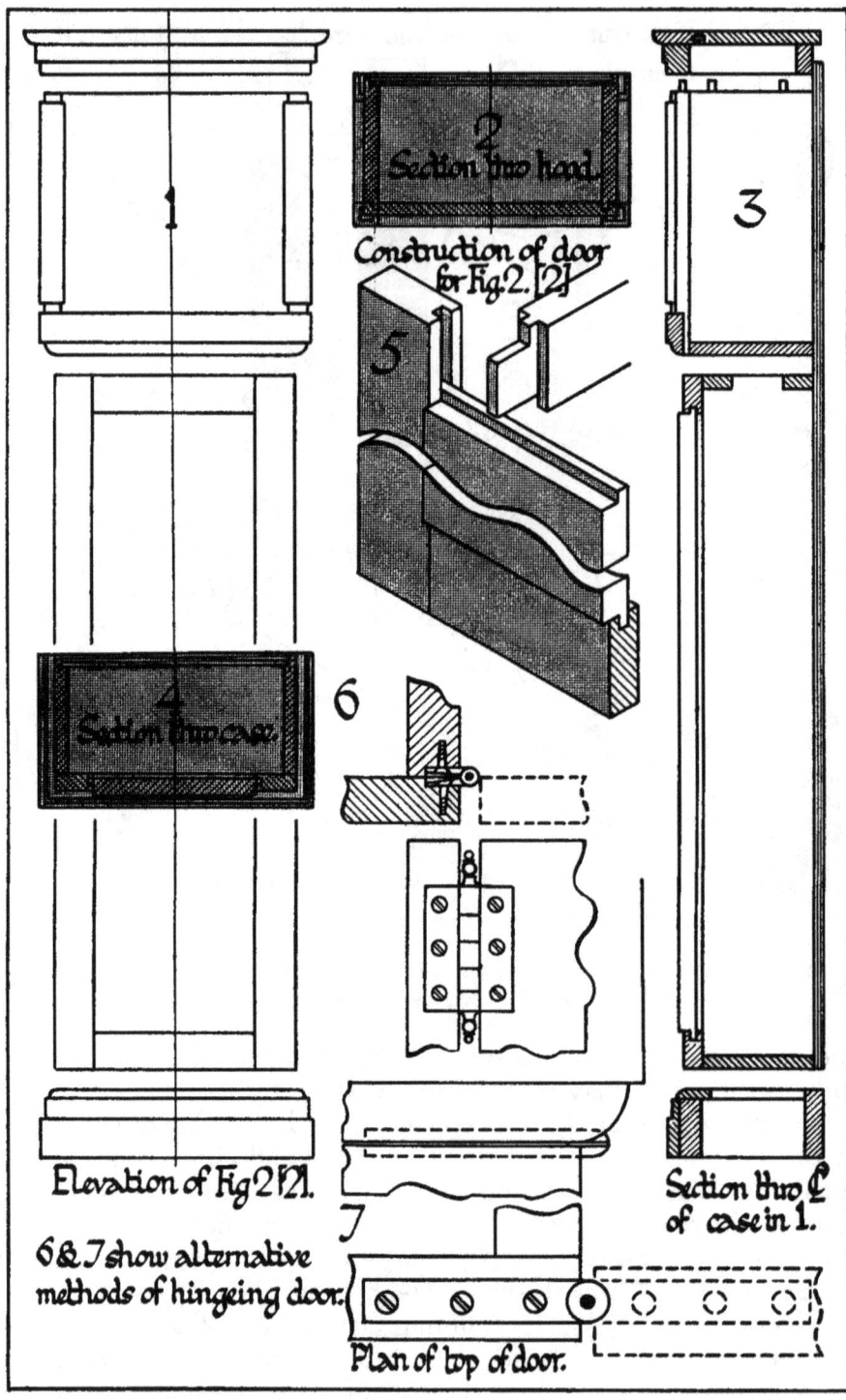

Fig. 4. Constructional details for Fig. 2 (2)

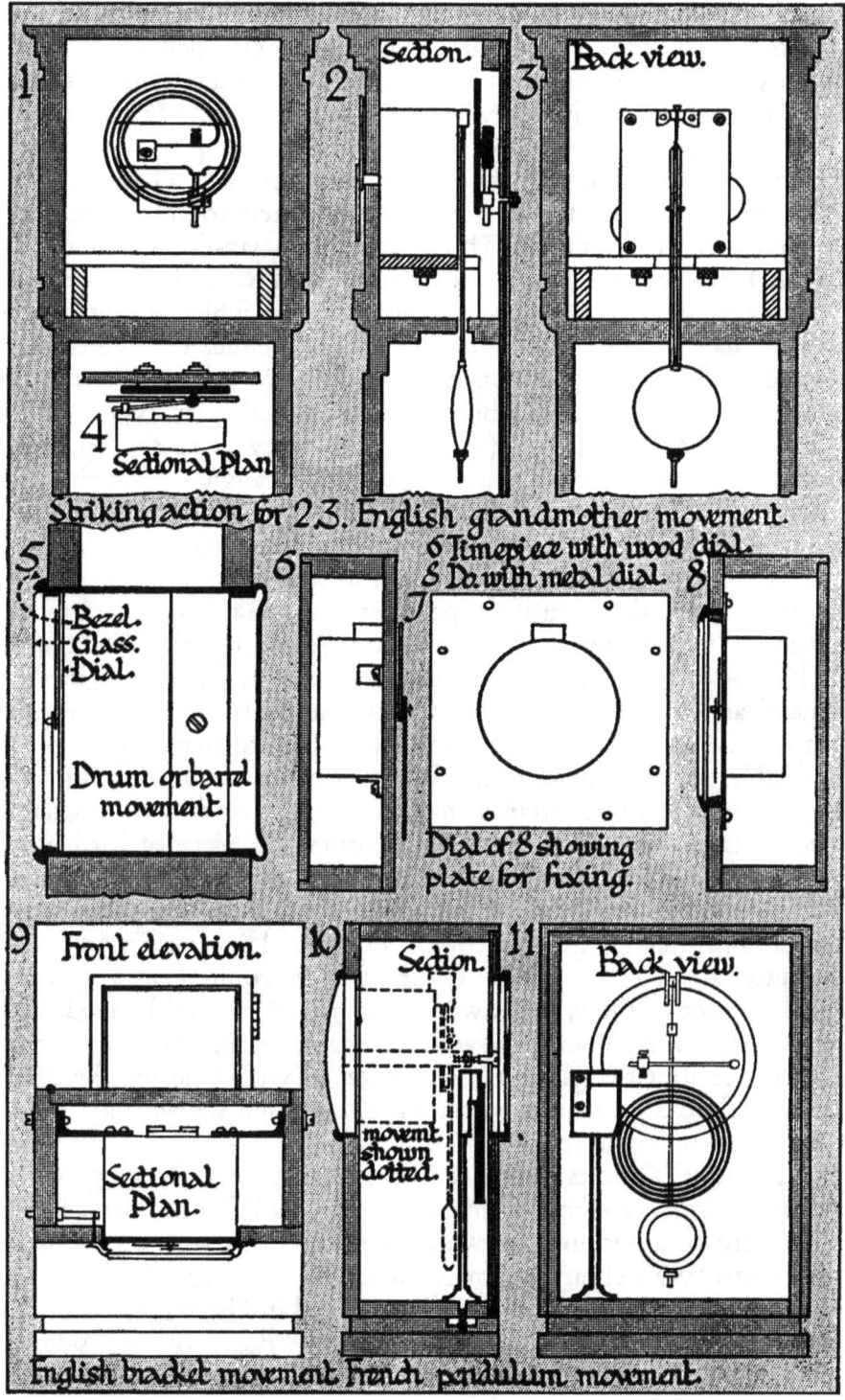

Fig. 5. Clock Movements

as shown in Fig. 3 (1, 3). The dial-board may either be of solid wood, as in Fig. 3 (11), or of ply with clamped edges, as in Fig. 3 (12). The door is of laminated board with a tongued clamp, and the back is of ply, screwed into a rebate. Fig. 2 (2) is intended for mahogany with inlays of ebony and is made up of four separate components: plinth, shaft, hood, and cornice. The plinth is "boxed-up" with the base moulding mitred round the top and is screwed to the shaft. This consists of a lap-dovetailed carcase with a panelled door, and is in turn screwed to the hood, the latter having a dovetailed bottom and an open top which is dowelled to the cornice section. The door may be hung either with butt-hinges fitted with "acorn" terminals, as in Fig. 4 (6), or with centre-pin hinges. These are less obtrusive than the former type and are fitted as shown in Fig. 4 (7); they are screwed to the hood and plinth, and the free wings opened to a right angle so that the door may be slipped between them. Fig. 2 (3) is suitable for oak, and consists of a through-dovetailed carcase on a tenoned stand. It has a panelled and hinged dial-board so that the movement may be adjusted from the front if a type other than the grandmother movement is fitted. The dials for these examples are shown in Fig. 2 (4-6). The ring marking the hours in Fig. 2 (4, 6) is fretted out in sheet metal and has thin bolts soldered to the back for fixing by nuts inside the case. The figures for Fig. 2 (5) are made up of pieces of inlay, as detailed in Fig. 9 (9). The rings are made with lines of ebony glued in a circular channel. This is made with a scratch-stock, as shown in Fig. 3 (2). It consists of a piece of hard wood slotted to hold a cutter made of a piece of saw steel and is centred by a dowel working in a block glued to the dial. Fig. 3 (9) shows a cutter for making grooves for a double inlaid line, and Fig. 3 (5, 10) a cutter for a wider band. If the band is required on a veneered dial a cutter of the type shown in Fig. 3 (4, 8) should be used; this forms two vee-section grooves and enables a ring of veneer to be lifted out after the glue has been softened with a heated file. The cutters should be sharpened on an oilstone and set with a "burr" similar to that of a scraper.

Mantel Clocks with Wood Dials.—Fig. 6 (1-15) shows cases for mantel clocks with wood dials and fretted metal hands. They are veneered in light woods, such as stripy walnut, maple, or amboyna, with ebony or macassar ebony used as contrast. The construction of Fig. 6 (7) is further detailed in Fig. 7 (1-4); the dial could either project, as in Fig. 7 (3), or be flush with the sides, as in Fig. 7 (4). Fig. 6 (11), if small, may be cut out of a solid block;

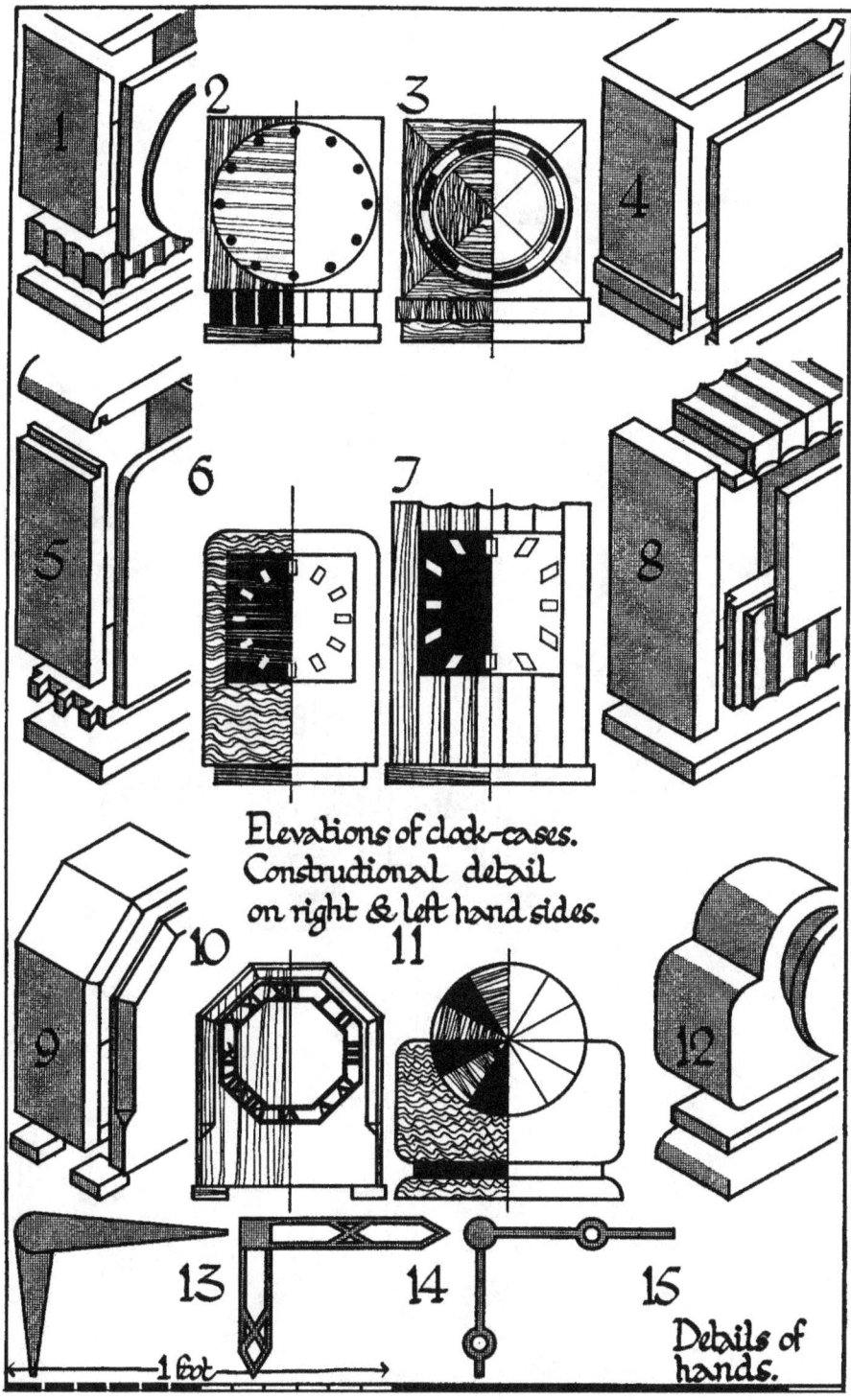

Fig. 6. Mantel Clocks with wood dials

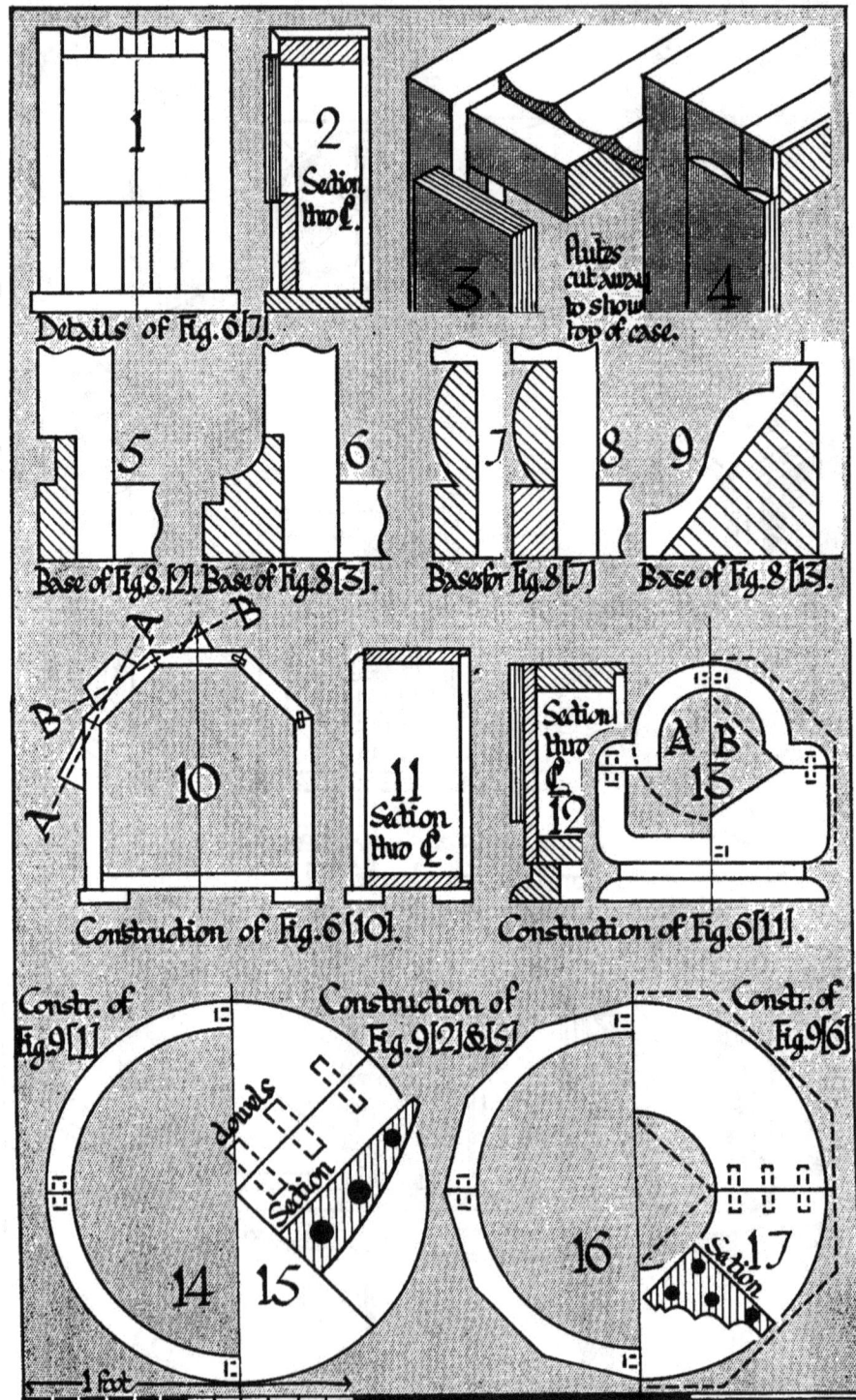

Fig. 7. Constructional details for Figs. 6, 8, and 9

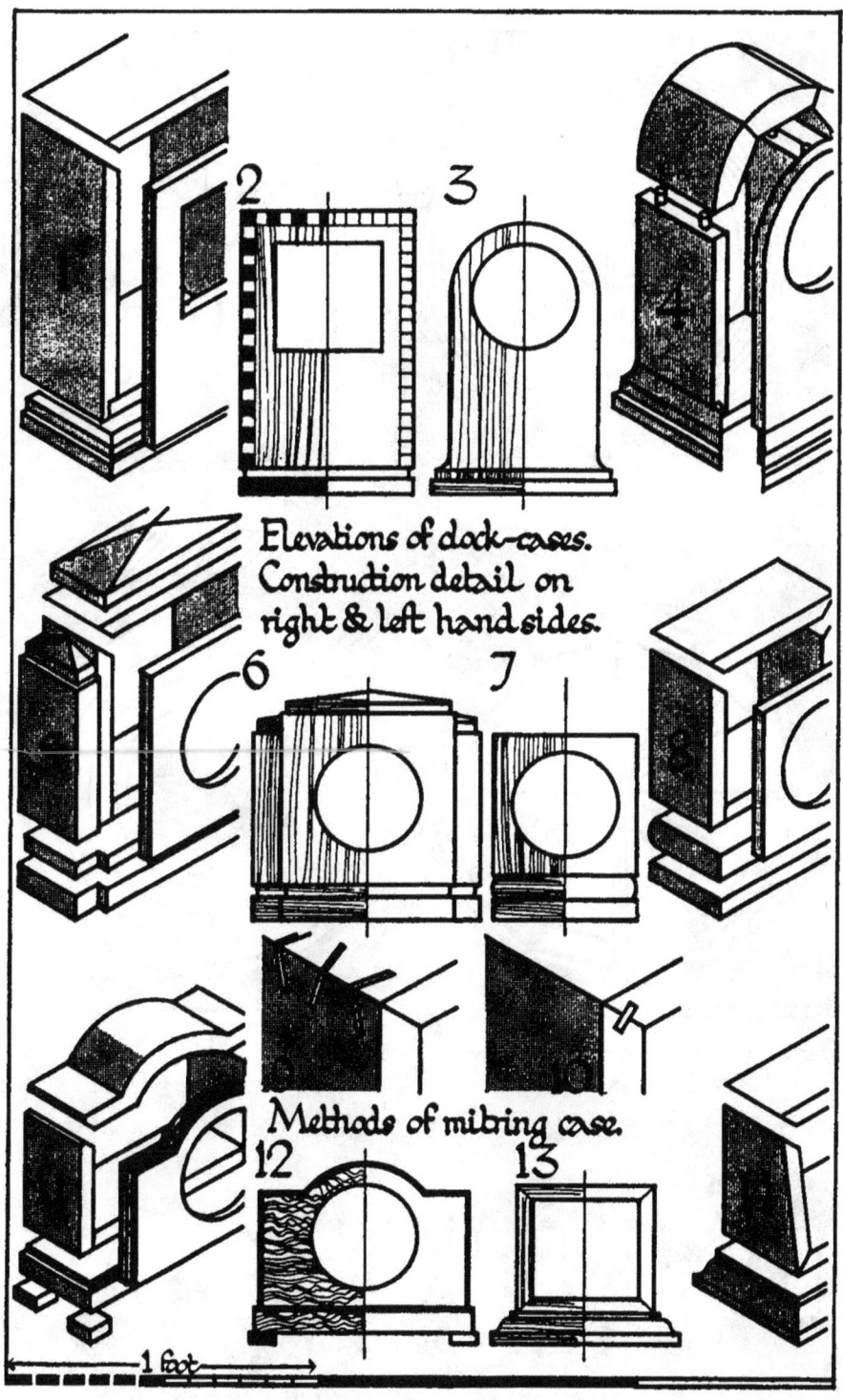

Fig. 8. Mantel Clocks for fitting with movement with metal dial and glazed bezel

48 CLOCKS

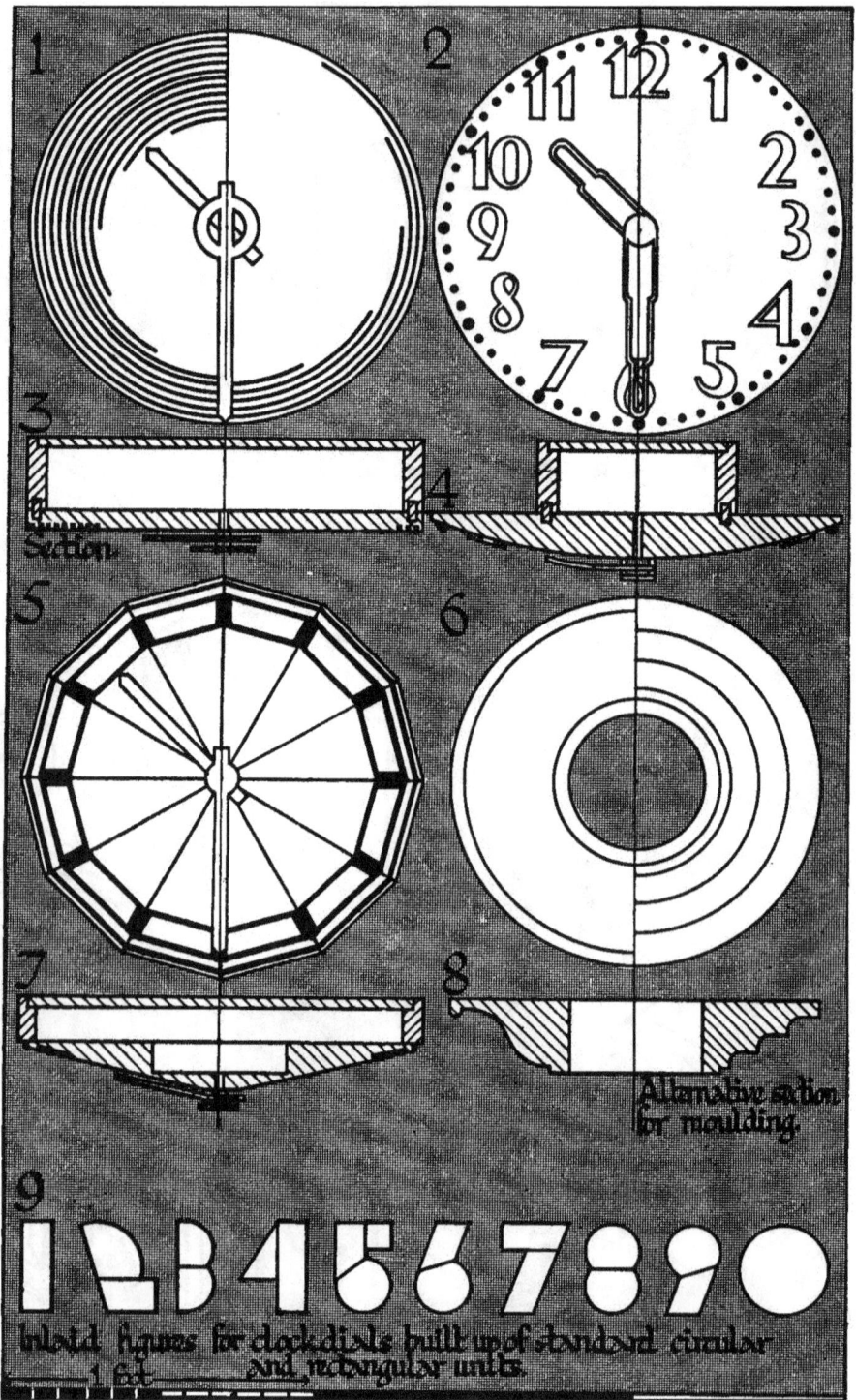

Fig. 9. Wall Clocks

alternatively, it may be built up from shaped sections dowelled together as in (A) or (B) of Fig. 7 (13). The remaining examples are "boxed-up" with a lap-dovetailed bottom. In the case of Fig. 6 (10) blocks should be glued at right angles to the lines A, A and B, B in Fig. 7 (10) to assist in the cramping up.

Mantel Clocks for Metal Dial and Bezel.—Fig. 8 (1-14) shows cases for mantel clocks to be fitted with a movement complete with metal dial and glazed bezel. They are "boxed-up" as in the preceding examples, with the joints at the top either mitred and keyed, as in Fig. 8 (9), or mitred and tongued, Fig. 8 (10). To simplify the construction the bases are shown solid; for small work this is the most convenient method, but for larger examples the case should be grooved and the mouldings mitred round as in Fig. 7 (5-9).

Wall Clocks.—Fig. 9 (1-9) shows four alternative types of wall clock. Fig. 9 (1, 5) consist of a rim built up of four dowelled segments, as shown in Fig. 7 (14, 16), dowelled or butt-glued to the dial. Fig. 9 (2, 6) are turned, the construction of the block being shown in Fig. 7 (15, 17); the first example has a lap-dovetailed box to contain the movement dowelled to the back of the dial. Fig. 9 (1, 5) have inlaid dials, the lines on the former being dealt with as described for the dial of Fig. 2 (5). The figures and divisions for Fig. 9 (2) may be either painted or fretted out of thin metal and fixed by pins. An alternative treatment is given in Fig. 9 (9); the figures are inlaid and are built up of straight sections cut from a strip and of circular sections of two diameters, the latter being cut from cylinders turned with the grain running across the length.

SECTION 7.—HANDLES, HANDHOLES, AND KNOBS

Fig. 1 (1-23) gives some suggestions for handles, handholes, and knobs for the drawers and cupboards of pieces dealt with in the other chapters. Fig. 1 (1-7) shows sections for strip handles; they are moulded in lengths, from which pieces are cut off as required and squared at the ends. Fig. 1 (8-13) are similar, but the ends also are moulded. For Fig. 1 (14) a disc is turned to the section and is then cut in half to form two handles. The other shaped handles, Fig. 1 (15-17), are made by gluing together blocks for as many handles as are required and planing them all to shape in one operation; paper should be put between them while gluing up so that they may afterwards be separated. The handholes in Fig. 1 (18, 19)

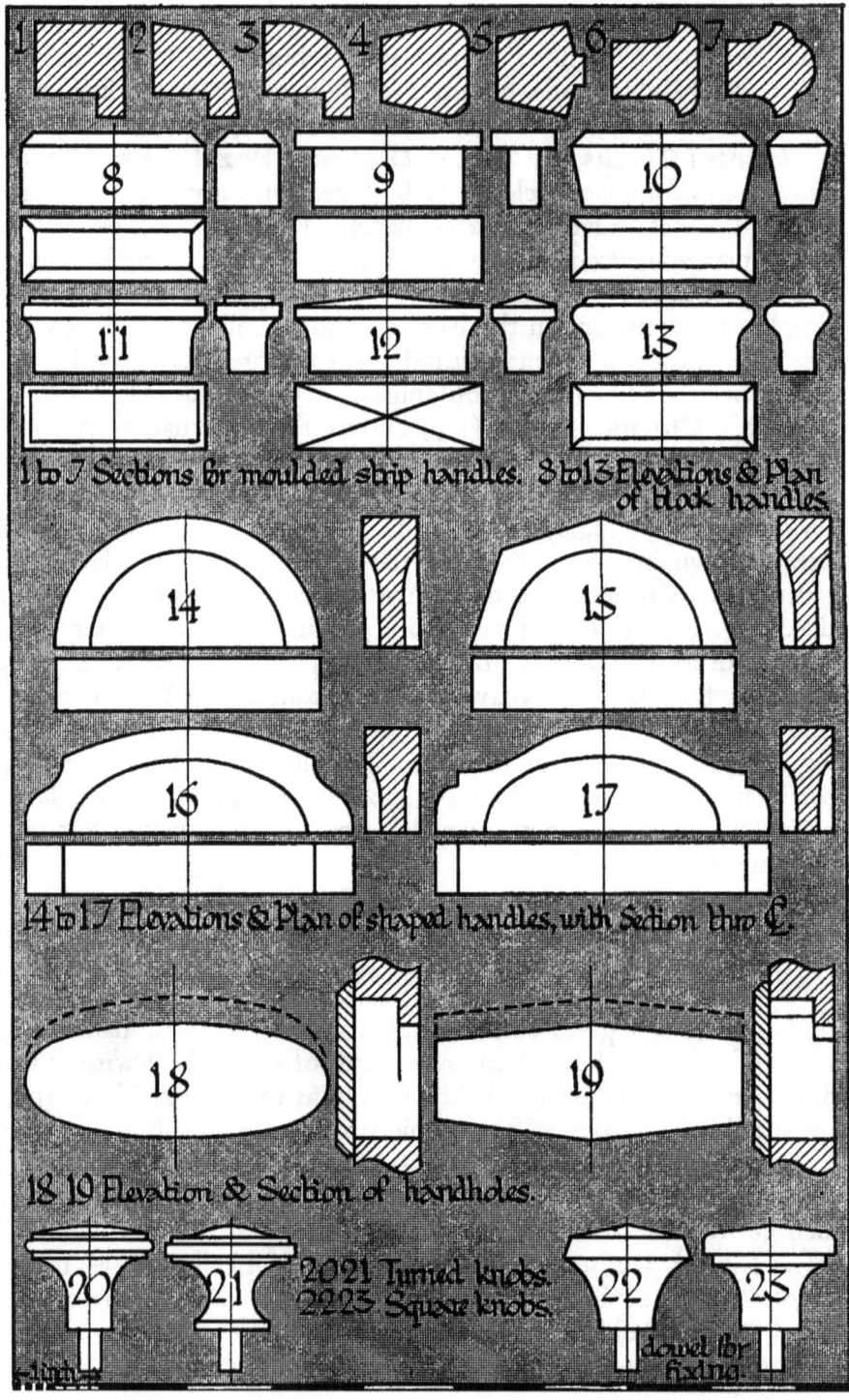

Fig. 1. Handles, Handholes, and Knobs

consist of a hole cut right through the drawer front with the top edge rebated to give a grip for the fingers. A piece of thin wood should be screwed over the hole at the back. The knobs in Fig. 1 (20, 21) should have a dowel for fixing turned on the bottom, and the moulded knobs, Fig. 1 (22, 23), are bored for a dowel. The handles above may be fixed in the same manner or by gluing and screwing from the back of the drawer front or door.

Section 8.—Lighting Fittings

This section gives some suggestions for electric lighting fittings to be made in wood. Fittings of the floor standard, table standard, and ceiling pendant types are dealt with and are completed by the addition of lamp-holders, etc., as detailed below. It is desirable that these should be obtained first so that proper provision may be made for fixing them.

Floor standards may be arranged to give either a downward light for reading, etc., an upward light to illuminate the room by reflection from a highly varnished or silvered ceiling, or to combine both these functions. For a downward light the standard is fitted with an ordinary lamp-holder, with switch incorporated as in Fig. 2 (12), which has a collar tapped to screw over a metal conduit which fits in the hole through the column. Table lamps are fitted in the same way. For an upward light, a shallow bowl reflector, finished in bronze or chromium, is slipped over the lamp-holder and fixed by screwing down the ring at the base; a standard of this type is shown in Fig. 1. The fitting in Fig. 2 (11) consists of a bowl reflector with one lamp inside to throw light upwards and two lamps below reflecting downwards off the side of the bowl. Each has a separate switch so that the fitting may be used for either or both purposes. The shade for a standard of this type is made with a wire ring which rests in the bowl, no other fixing being necessary.

The table lamps in Fig. 3 (13, 14) and the pendant in Fig. 4 (2) are intended for candle lamps. Either the small flame-shaped lamps or the 10" cylindrical type may be used; the former will require a special holder. Fig. 4 (5, 6) show pendant fittings with strip-lights. These have a contact at either end which fits into a porcelain holder, as detailed in Fig. 4 (9).

Standard Lamps.—Fig. 2 (1–12) shows four types of floor standard suitable for oak or walnut. They are made about 5′ 0″ high

LIGHTING FITTINGS

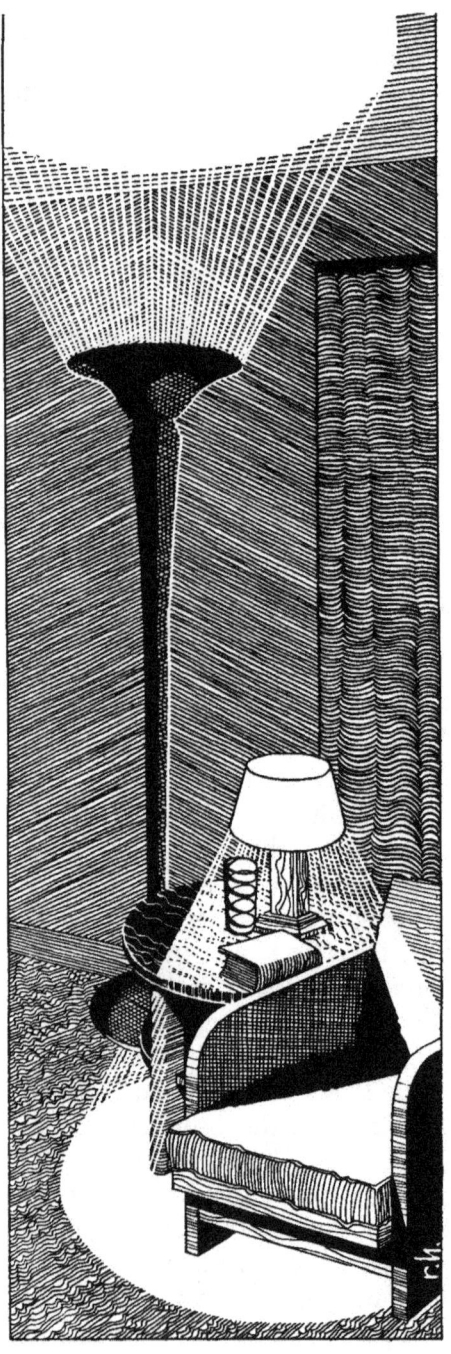

Fig. 1. A Standard Lamp for reflected lighting and a Table Lamp [Fig. 2 (1) and Fig. 3 (1)]

overall; if used for ceiling lighting they should be higher so that the rim of the bowl is well above the eye level. The column is tenoned through the base and is built up in two pieces, as shown in Fig. 2 (5). One of these is grooved to take the flex, and a length of string should be inserted during assembly so that the flex may be tied to it and pulled through. Fig. 2 (1, 2) are turned, the base of the latter being made in two pieces glued together, as shown in the section. Fig. 2 (3) is veneered in walnut or, alternatively, in macassar ebony; the base consists of eight mitred and tongued sections rebated for a top of laminated board. The column of Fig. 2 (4) is "boxed-up" with four lengths of 1" stuff and is tenoned through an X-shaped base. These standards are weighted with a block of lead, shown solid black in the sections, screwed to the under side of the base. The latter, except in the last example, should be fitted with three small turned feet to prevent rocking on an uneven floor.

Table Lamps.—The construction of the table standards in Fig. 3 (1-16) is similar to that of the floor standards, except that a short column may be bored to take the flex instead of being built up. Fig. 3 (2) has a square centre column with four buttressing

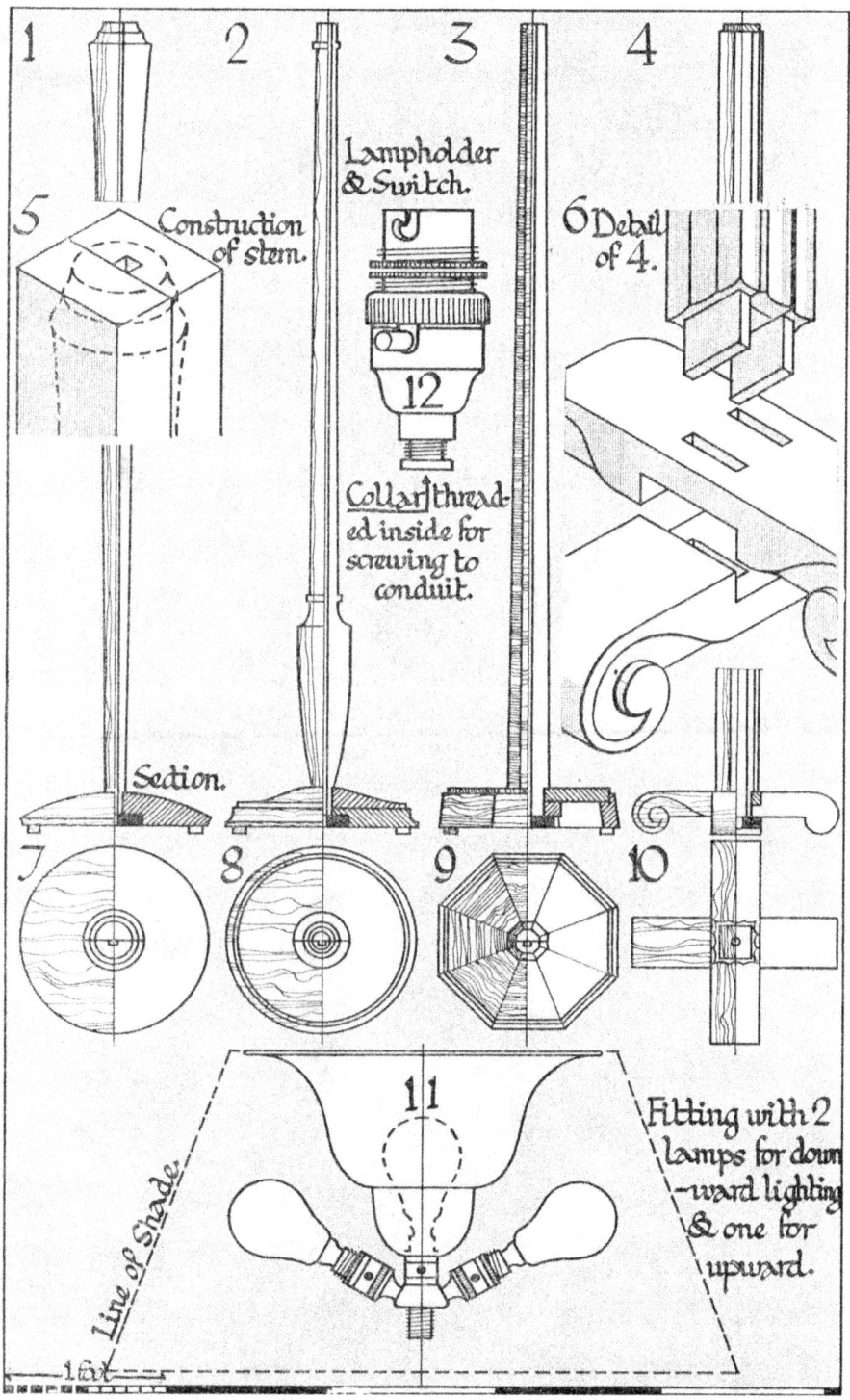

Fig. 2. Standard Lamps

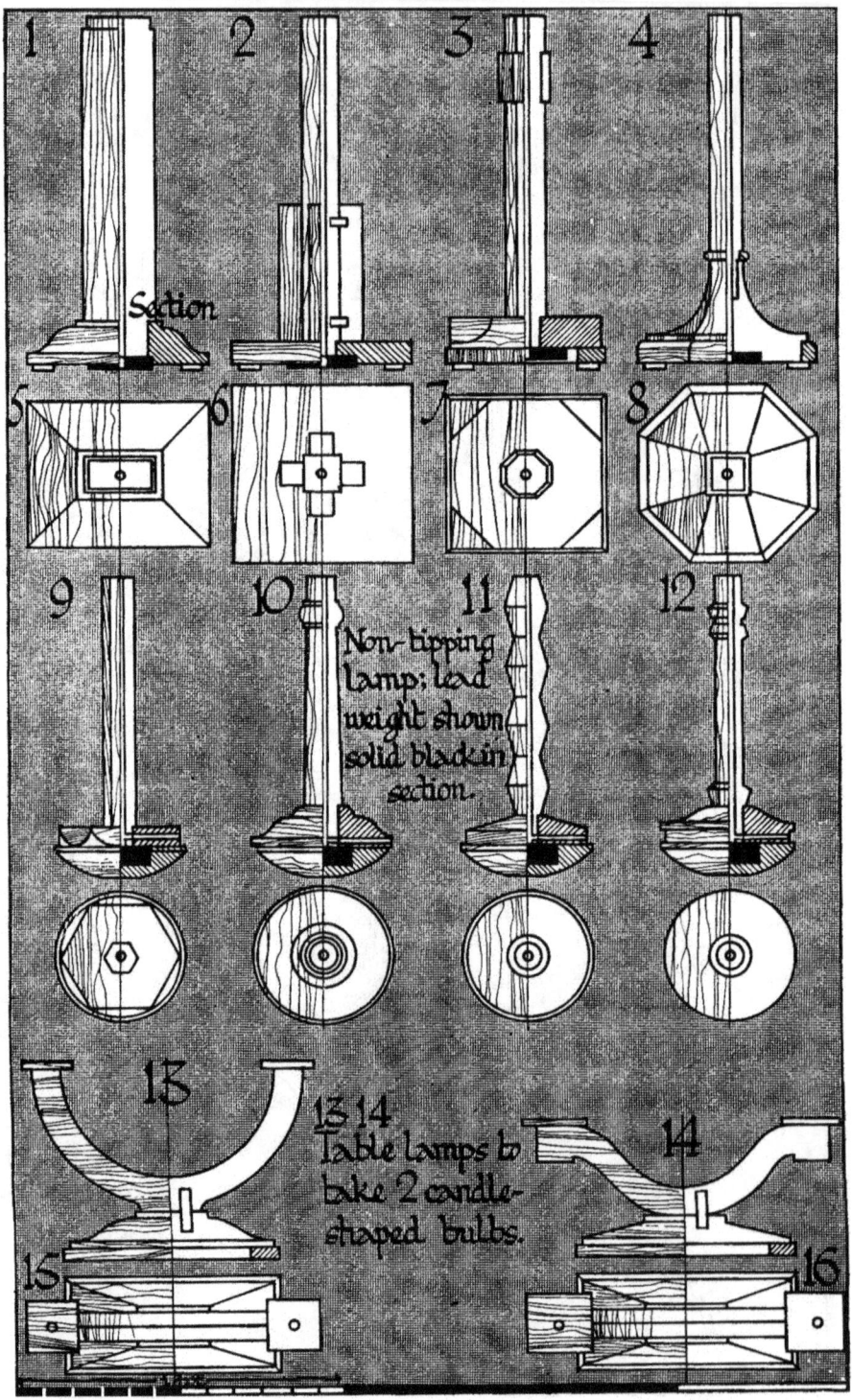

Fig. 3. Table Lamps

CEILING PENDANTS

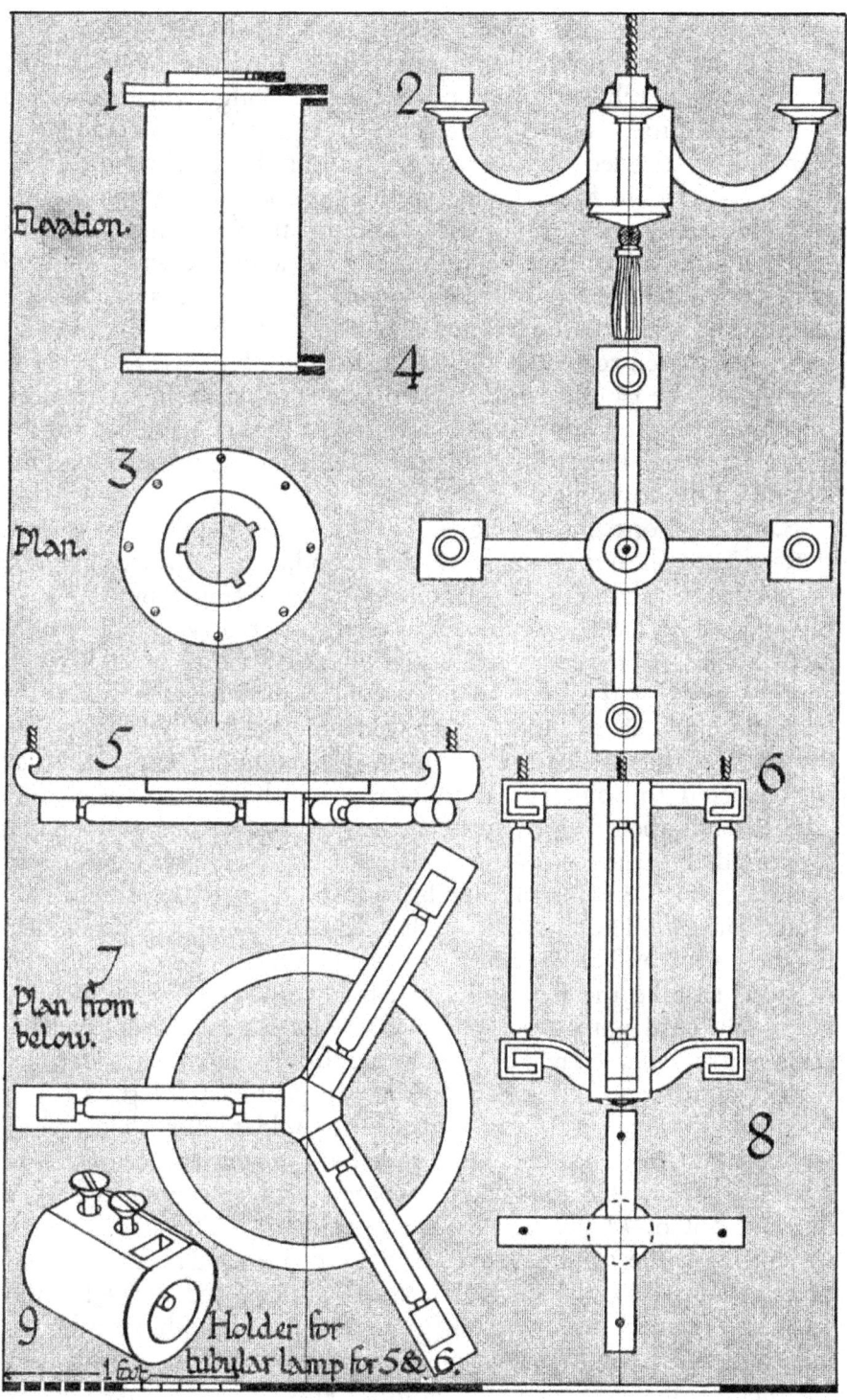

Fig. 4. Ceiling Pendants

pieces dowelled to the sides. The cross-banded step of Fig. 3 (3) is made with a mitred frame screwed to the base from below; the column is rebated all round for the necking, which is mitred and glued into position. The base of Fig. 3 (4) is octagonal in plan and is tenoned to a square column at the level of the bead. Fig. 3 (9-12) give four alternative designs for a non-tipping lamp with turned detail. The base is made in two parts dowelled together, the lower part being a sector of a sphere and weighted with lead. If the lamp is pushed over it simply rocks on this and springs up again to the vertical position; the bottom should be slightly flattened so that it will stand firmly. Fig. 3 (13, 14) show fittings to take candle lamps. The arms are made in two pieces, which are roughly cut to shape and one of them channelled for the flex. They are then glued together, the shaping finished, and the base fixed by dowelling.

Ceiling Pendants.—Fig. 4 (1-9) illustrates pendants of various types. They should be made in hard wood, with a gilded, silvered, or painted finish. Fig. 4 (1) consists of four rings cut out in $\frac{3}{8}''$ ply and connected by a cylinder of oiled paper or vegetable parchment. This is pinned to the inside edges of the two inner rings, another piece of the same material being sandwiched between the bottom rings before they are screwed together. Three screws are driven into the side of the block on the ceiling to which the flex is connected to coincide with slots cut in the top of the fitting. The latter is then slipped over the screws and turned so that it is supported by the screws, the lamp hanging down inside the cylinder. Fig. 4 (2) is a four-light chandelier to be fitted with candle lamps. The arms are each made in two pieces channelled for the wiring and are tenoned to a turned centre-block. The latter is bored to take the flex and has a hole through the centre for a heavy silk cord with tassel below. The blocks on the ends of the arms are screwed from above, and are fitted with a turned collar which slips over and conceals the lamp-holder. Fig. 4 (5) is designed to take four strip-lights, the holders for these being screwed to flat rails arranged radially. They are tenoned or dowelled into a hexagonal centre-block, and are connected by a ring cut out of $\frac{1}{2}''$ ply and halved over them. The scrolled ends are cut from the solid and are fixed by dowels. The rails should have an open channel cut in the top to carry the wires for the necessary connections. Fig. 4 (6) is also fitted with strip-lights, and consists of two X-shaped pieces, each made of two rails halved together, bridled over a centre column. This is bored to take the flex and the arms made in halves and channelled as previously described. The lamp-holders are sunk flush into holes bored in the scrolls.

SECTION 9.—RADIO AND RADIO-GRAMOPHONE CABINETS

In making cabinets for wireless sets it is desirable that the set be obtained first and the cabinet made to fit it. The examples illustrated are shown 1′ 3″ wide by 1′ 8″ high by 9″ deep inside, these sizes being based on the average general-purposes set and loudspeaker. For a radio-gramophone cabinet, 2′ 0″ wide by 1′ 6″ deep inside will be found adequate to take the motor turntable and the control knobs, while a height of 3′ 0″ will obviate undue stooping in changing records.

Table Model Radio Cabinets.—Fig. 1 (1-10) shows radio cabinets designed to be placed on a table or stand. They are shown in walnut, with black-stained hornbeam, macassar ebony, and sycamore used as contrast. The carcase is lap-dovetailed, with a front of laminated board either butt-glued or rebated and afterwards veneered. The grille for the loudspeaker opening is made separately and is screwed from behind. Fig. 1 (3) is an exception in that the front is framed up with solid wood. The grille consists of a frame, $\frac{3}{8}$″ square in section, with the vertical bars halved into it, the horizontal bars being of black-stained hornbeam and notched over the others, as in the section Fig. 1 (1). The black bands are continued by flush inlays of hornbeam, and a strip of the same wood is mitred and glued into a rebate at the bottom of the cabinet. Fig. 1 (4) has a separate plinth pocket-screwed from below; the curved bars in the grille of this example are dowelled to the centre division and to the outside frame. The front and sides of the top of the carcase of Fig. 1 (5) are rounded and a false top $\frac{1}{4}$″ thick glued on to form the double ovolo moulding. The construction of Fig. 1 (6) is shown in Fig. 2 (1), the top being hollowed to admit the chassis of the loudspeaker. Fig. 1 (7, 9) each have a facing of $\frac{1}{4}$″ ply to form the step on front and sides, the top edges being clamped. Fig. 2 (2) gives the construction of the latter example. The ring for the loudspeaker opening is turned from black-stained hornbeam; the wood is held by gluing to a block screwed to the face-plate of the lathe. Fig. 1 (7) has a similar ring, but with the bottom rebated to lap over the raised facing.

Before the grilles of these cabinets are screwed into position the aperture should be covered with a piece of silk, stretched as tightly

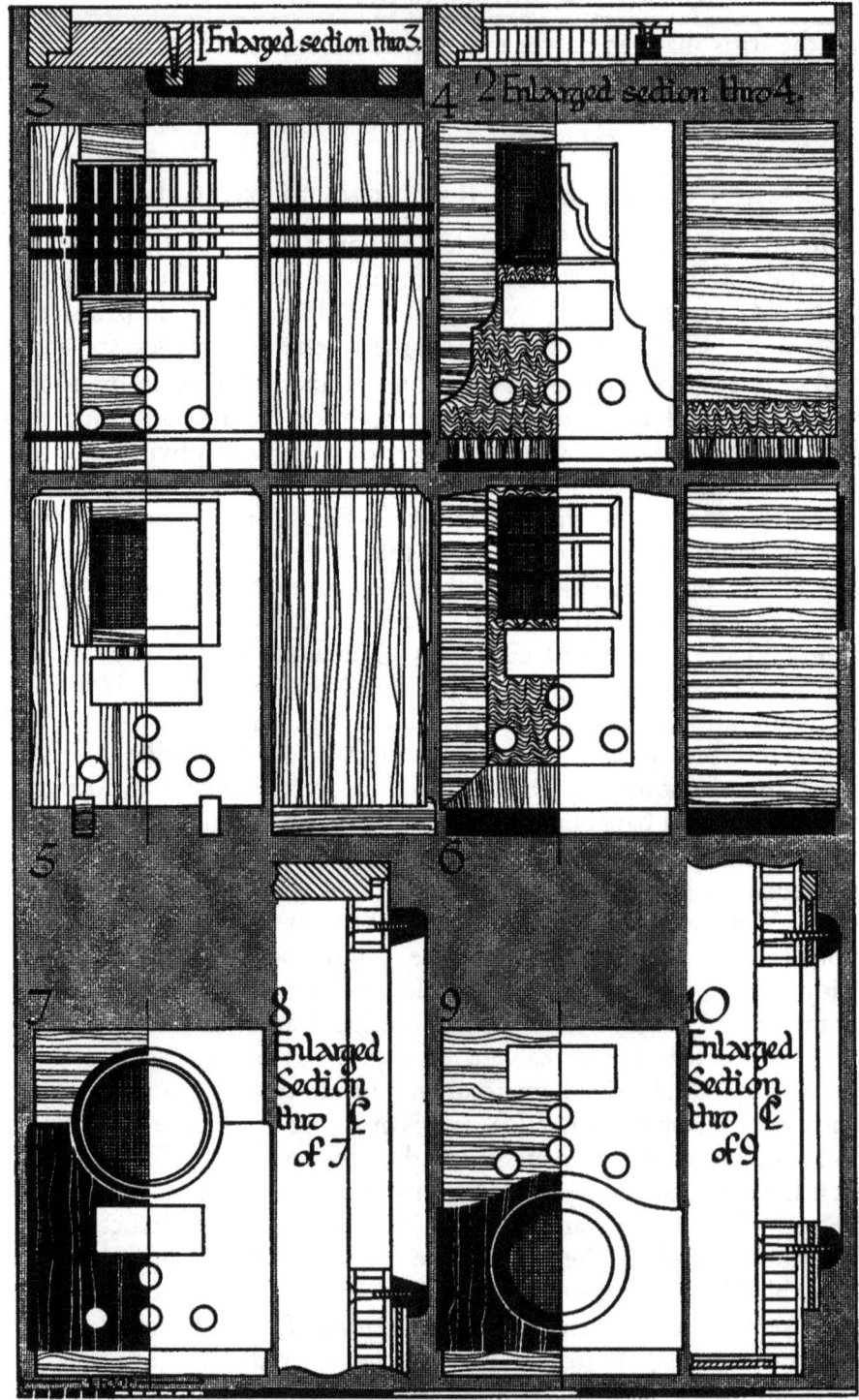

Fig. 1. Table Model Radio Cabinets

CONSTRUCTIONAL DETAILS

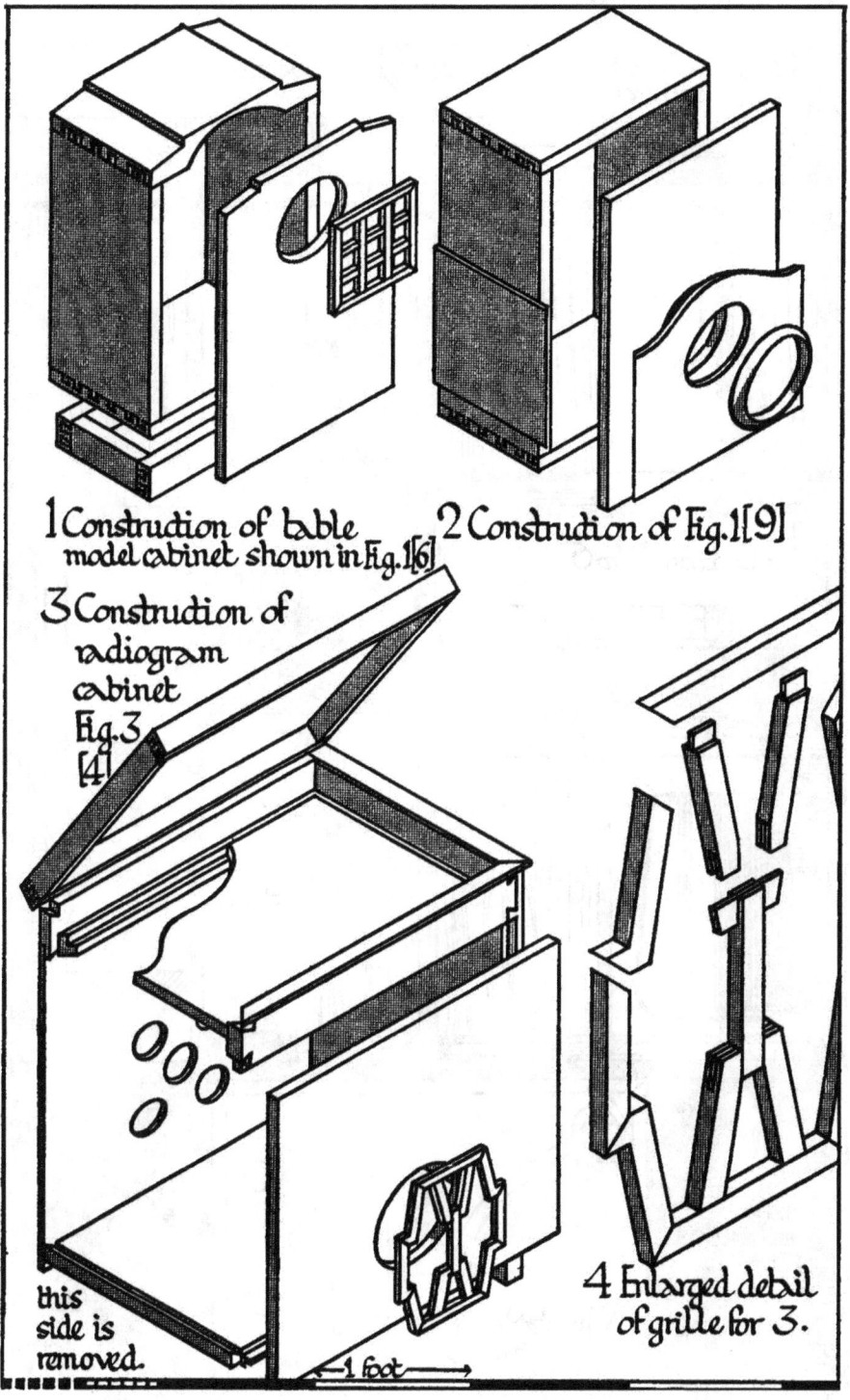

Fig. 2. Constructional details for Radio and Radio-gramophone Cabinets in Figs. 1 and 3

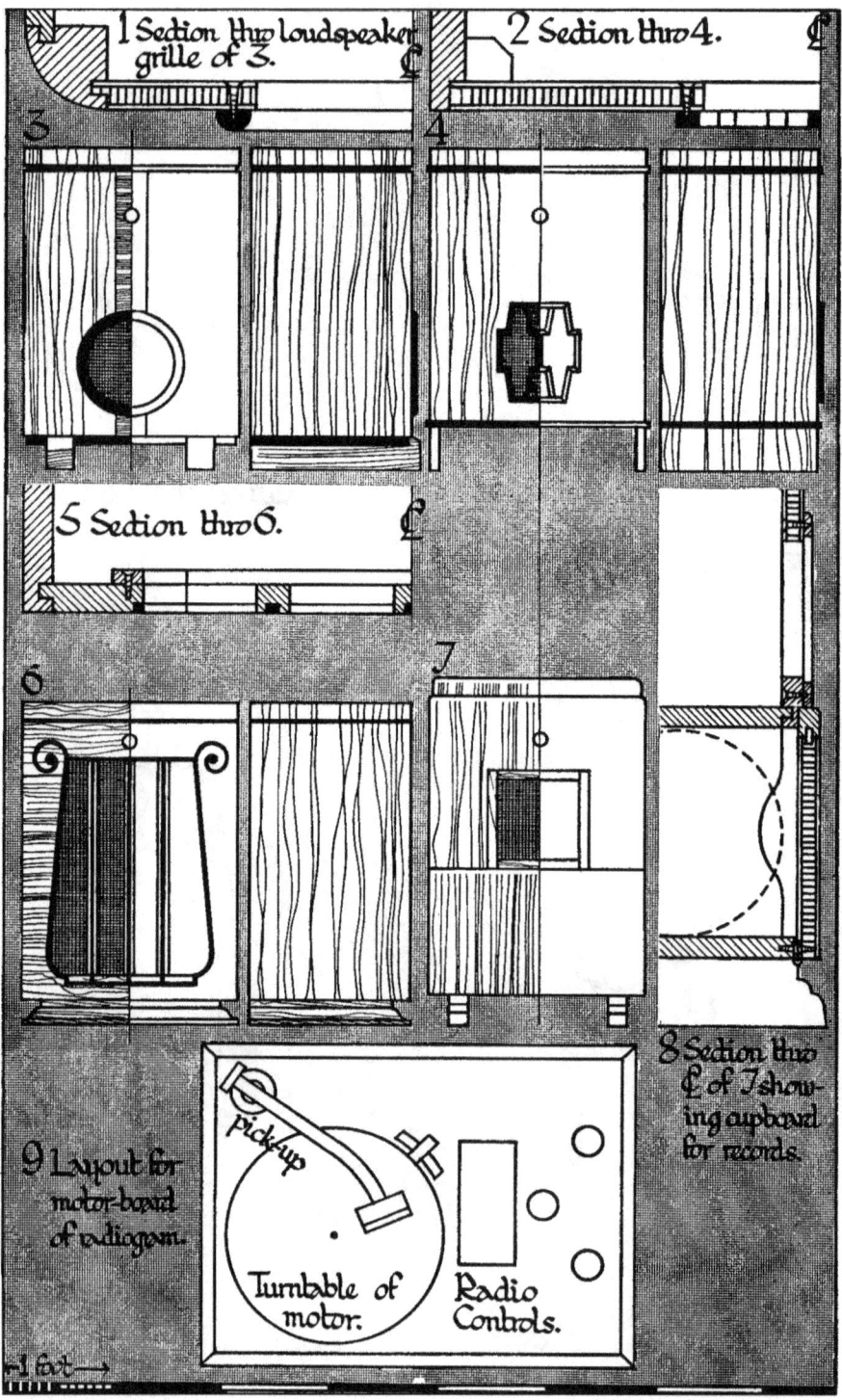

Fig. 3. Console type Radio-gramophone Cabinets

as possible and glued at the edges. The carcase is rebated to take a ply back, which has a ring of $1\frac{1}{2}''$ holes centred on the loudspeaker and also covered with material. The inside of the cabinet may be lined with "Celotex" to reduce resonance.

Console Type Radio-gramophone Cabinets.—Fig. 3 (1-9) shows console type radio-gramophone cabinets. They could appropriately be made in walnut or mahogany. Fig. 3 (3) has sides of $\frac{7}{8}''$ stuff tongued into corner posts, which are afterwards rounded as in the section Fig. 3 (1). The bottom is lap-dovetailed to the ends and fits into a rebate in the front. The lid is made separately, the sides being dowelled into shaped corner blocks in front and lap-dovetailed at the back; they are rebated for a flush top of ply. It is hinged with a piano-hinge, and should be fitted with a stay to hold it open. The motor-board is dropped in from above and is screwed to four rebated fillets. Fig. 3 (9) gives a lay-out for this, all the controls being under the lid except the volume-control, which is outside in the centre. The construction of Fig. 3 (4) is shown in Fig. 2 (3). The bottom is slip-dovetailed between the ends, which are joined at the top by 4" rails at back and front. The front is of $\frac{3}{4}''$ laminated board and fits into a rebate. The grille is built up as shown in Fig. 2 (4), the corners being mitred and keyed. Fig. 3 (6) is intended for a set with twin loudspeakers. The ends are lap-dovetailed into the bottom and a moulded plinth screwed from below. The front is framed up and veneered and the lyre inlaid with black-stained hornbeam. Fig. 3 (7) has a cupboard below for gramophone records, as in the section Fig. 3 (8). The carcase is dovetailed as in the preceding example, but with a shelf slip-dovetailed between the ends 1' 1" up from the bottom. The front is of laminated board, with a 2" rail tongued across the bottom of the loudspeaker aperture.

SECTION 10.—SIDEBOARDS

This section shows various treatments for sideboards, ranging from simple sideboard-dressers to more advanced " buffet " and fitted types. The dresser type is of value, particularly in a " cottage " scheme, in that the upper part provides space for china, etc., and enables this to be displayed as a decorative feature. In a scheme of " unit " furniture a sideboard may be assembled with a drawer unit, detailed in " Chests of Drawers," Fig. 1 (9), flanked by shelf or cupboard units.

Fig. 1. A Buffet Sideboard in walnut [Fig. 4 (6)]

Sideboards usually range from 3' 6" to 5' 0" wide and should be about 3' 0" high by 1' 6" deep overall.

Sideboard-Dressers.—Fig. 2 (1-10) shows three alternatives for sideboard-dressers; solid oak, chestnut, elm, or teak could be used, and decorative use made of through-dovetails and tenons. The lower part of Fig. 2 (1) consists of a dovetailed carcase with a solid division forming two cupboards with drawers above. This is dowelled to the shelf section, which has a "break-front" as in Fig. 2 (2). The curved tops may either be cut from the solid or built up, and are dovetailed to the uprights, the shelves being tenoned. Constructional detail for the shaped feet is given in Fig. 3 (1); they are made with a dovetailed angle to which the moulded pieces are mitred and applied, and may be fixed either by pocket-screwing or by dowelling, as in (A) and (B) of Fig. 3 (2). Fig. 3 (3, 4) show an alternative foot with shaped sides glued to a 3" block and screwed up into a base moulding. Fig. 2 (3) has a lower carcase similar to that of the preceding example, but with a framed false top screwed from below, as in Fig. 2 (9). The upper

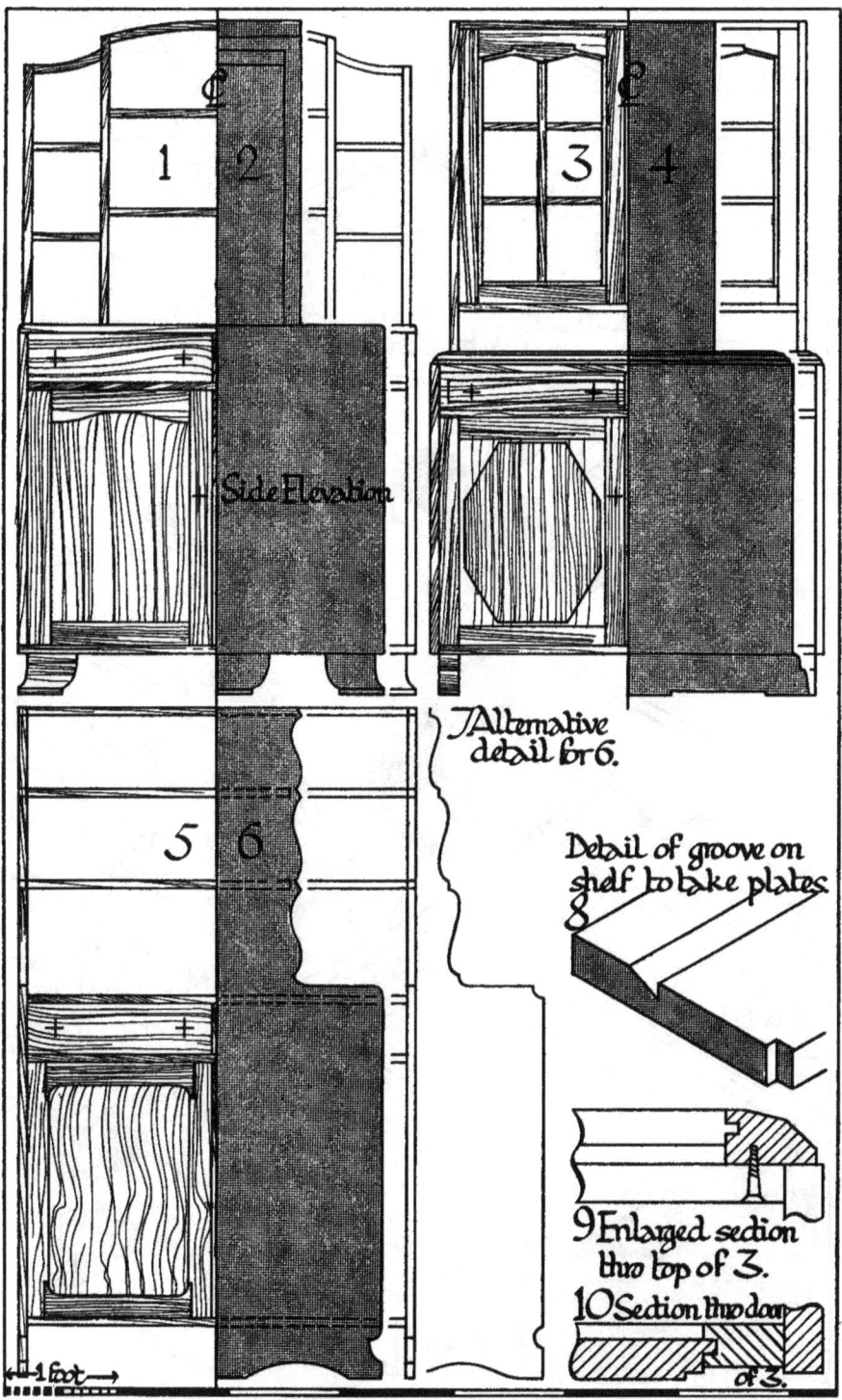

Fig. 2. Sideboard-Dressers

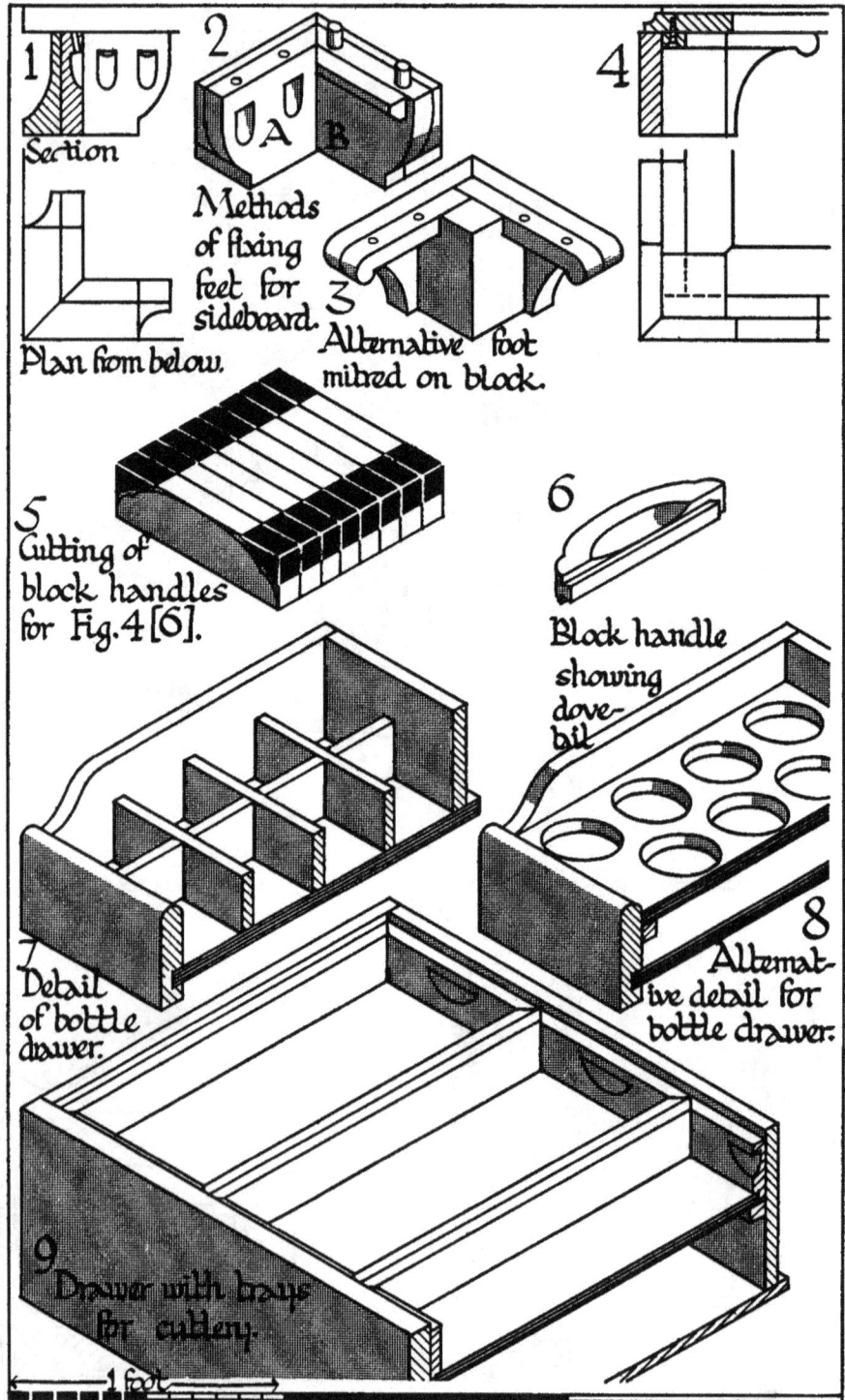

Fig. 3. Constructional details for Sideboards in Figs. 2, 4, and 5

PLATE IX

SIDEBOARD IN ENGLISH WALNUT AND ROOT ASH WITH OAK HANDLES
Gordon Russell Ltd.

SIDEBOARD IN ENGLISH WALNUT
Heal & Son Ltd.

PLATE X

SIDEBOARD IN AUSTRALIAN WALNUT

Maurice Adams Ltd.

Maurice Adams

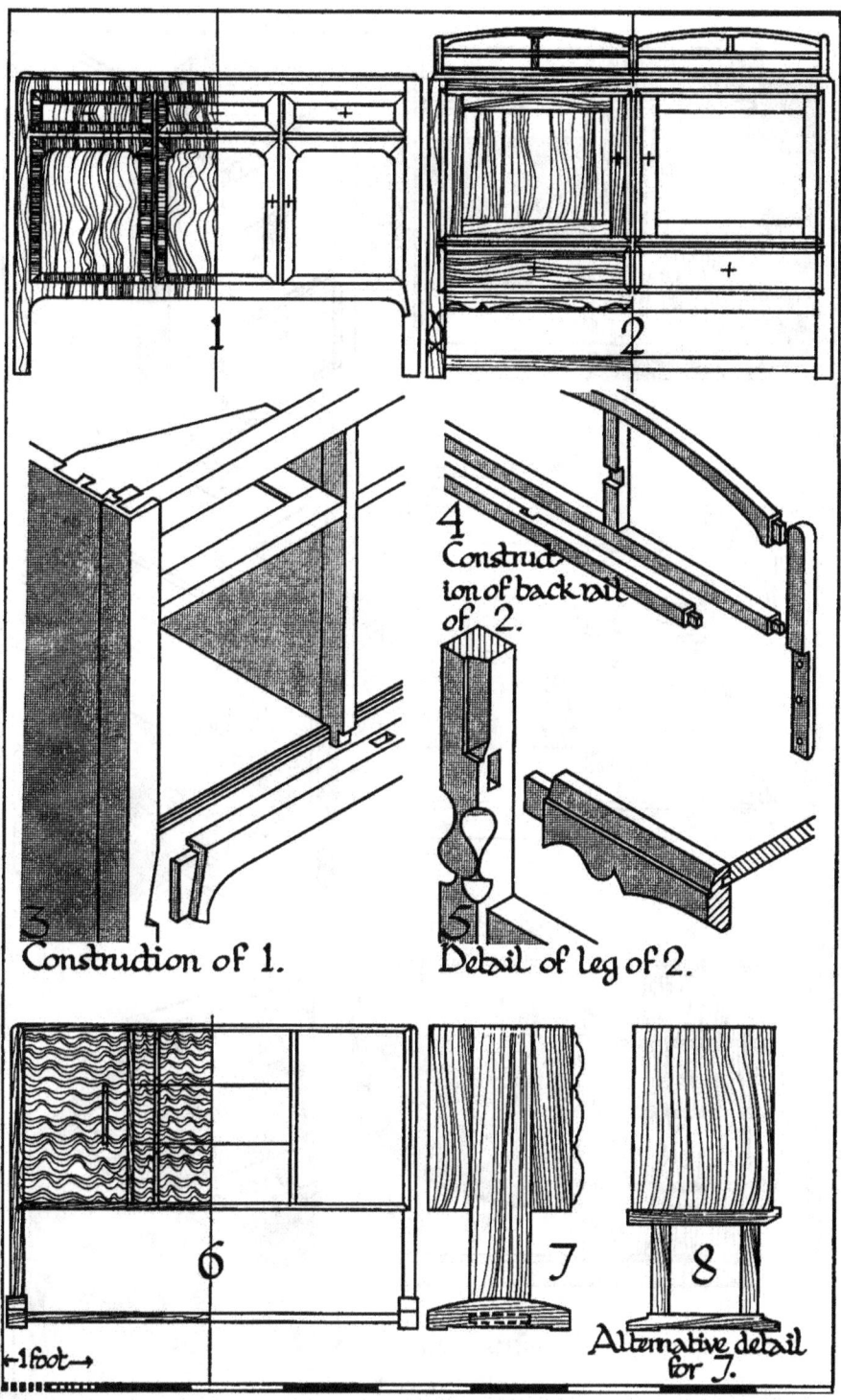

Fig. 4. Buffet Sideboards

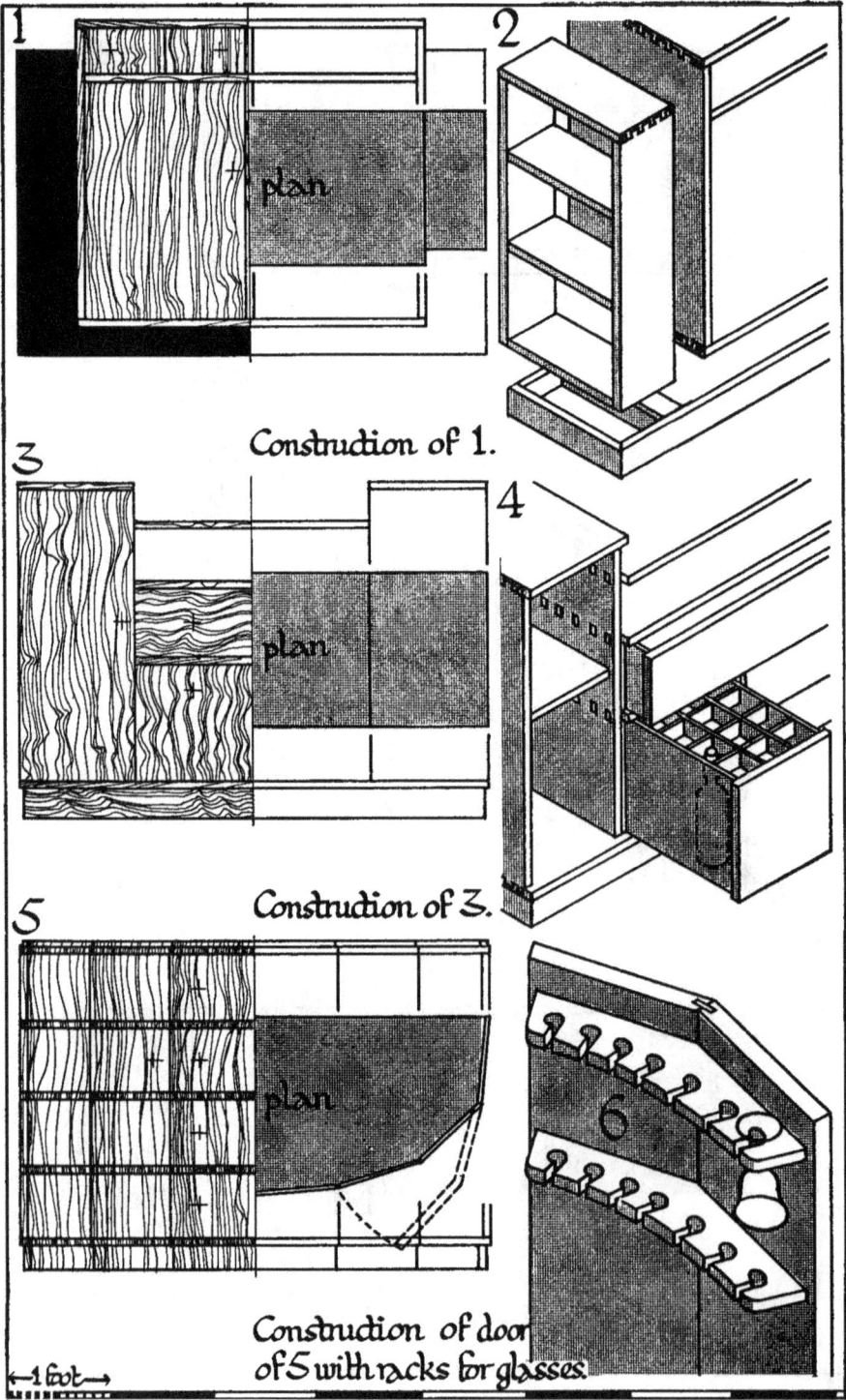

Fig. 5. Fitted Sideboards

PLATE XI

SIDEBOARD IN MACASSAR EBONY AND WALNUT; THE FITTED INTERIOR IS SHOWN IN PLATE XII
Serge Chermayeff, F.R.I.B.A.

PLATE XII

INTERIOR FITTINGS OF SIDEBOARD IN PLATE XI

Serge Chermayeff, F.R.I.B.A.

carcase is enclosed by two glazed doors which have a raised margin flush with the bars to harmonize with the raised panels of the doors below. The shaped ends of Fig. 2 (5) are continuous, the horizontal carcasing members being tenoned between them and the top dovetailed. All these examples should have the ends and top wider than the interior members to allow for rebating for a back of ply or matched-jointed boards.

Buffet Sideboards.—Fig. 4 (1-8) shows three types of "buffet" sideboard. Fig. 4 (1, 2) are framed up with posts and rails and are suitable for mahogany and oak respectively. The construction of the former is detailed in Fig. 4 (3). It consists of four 2" posts connected by tenoned lower rails and dovetailed top rails and grooved to receive the ends. The carcase is divided by two ends tenoned between the rails and the false top is screwed from below. The doors are of laminated board with mitre-clamped edges and are veneered with a cross-banded margin and inlaid black line. Fig. 4 (2) is made in the same way and has a "gallery" for plates, etc., built up as in Fig. 4 (4) and screwed to the back. Fig. 4 (6) is made as a simple dovetailed carcase with slip-dovetailed or tenoned divisions, and is screwed to two "slab" ends which are tenoned into feet joined by a stretcher. Fig. 4 (8) shows an alternative stand consisting of two framed ends connected by rails. This example would be attractive if veneered with a pale wood such as maple or sycamore; the shaped handles provide a decorative feature and are arranged in vertical bands over the drawer fronts. The method of making these handles is detailed in Fig. 3 (5). The pieces of wood for them are glued together with paper between the joints so that they may afterwards be separated, the parts shown black are sawn off and the shaping finished by planing and glass-papering. They are then separated and the fingergrips cut with a gouge. The fixing may either be by means of slip-dovetails, cut as in Fig. 3 (6), or by gluing with dowels or screws.

Fitted Sideboards.—Fig. 5 (1-6) illustrates fitted sideboards with flush surfaces suitable for finely figured veneers of walnut, mahogany, macassar ebony, or Nigerian cherry. Fig. 5 (1) has bookcases at either end and is made with three lap-dovetailed carcases screwed to a "boxed-up" plinth with cross rails. This and the ends are veneered with a contrasting wood. The drawers are fitted with trays for cutlery as detailed in Fig. 3 (9), and one of the cupboards has a drawer divided to accommodate wine bottles as in Fig. 3 (7, 8). These are made like a wardrobe tray and slide on fillets. Fig. 5 (3) has cupboards at the ends, and in the centre a cutlery drawer with a deep "cellaret" drawer below. The doors are hinged over the carcase ends and the drawer sides slip-dovetailed into the fronts so that these may lap over and conceal the division in the centre. The eight-sided example, Fig. 5 (5), has drawers in the centre and cupboards at either side. The top and bottom are of laminated board with fillets mitred round the edges, and are dovetailed to the ends and tenoned to the divisions. The cupboard doors are made with two pieces tongued together at an angle and stiffened with "fiddle-board" racks for wine glasses dowelled to the inside.

Section 11.—Stools

Stools are usually made the same height and width as chairs but slightly narrower from front to back. A useful size is 1' 6" high and wide by 1' 0" deep overall. Stools for the fireside and for low dressing tables should be 3" lower.

Four-Legged Stools with Loose Seat.—Fig. 1 (1-9) gives suggestions for framed-up stools with legs tied by a cross stretcher. They are intended to be fitted with a loose seat as in Fig. 1 (9). The legs could alternatively be left square at the bottom and the stretcher replaced by four tenoned rails. Fig. 1 (1) shows the construction and Fig. 1 (2) the mitred tenons and corner blocks to prevent the frame "racking." An extra inch should be allowed on the leg above the mortise to resist the upward pressure of the tenon as it is driven home. These "horns" are afterwards sawn off and the tops of the legs levelled. The feet are separate and have a dowel to fit a hole in the upper part of the leg. The stretcher is fixed by driving these dowels through holes in the corner squares and up into the leg. The stretchers in Fig. 1 (8) are each made of two pieces cut one "inside" the other to reduce waste and dowelled along the centre line.

Upholstered Stools with Solid Ends.—The stools in Fig. 2 (1-10) have solid ends joined by slip-dovetailed rails. They would make attractive dressing stools and could either be veneered or have a cellulose finish with upholstery to match. Fig. 2 (1 and 3) are similar in construction, the ends being of $1\frac{1}{4}$" stuff. Fig. 2 (4) has a dovetailed base and a mitred plinth as shown in Fig. 2 (5). Fig. 2 (6) has a box seat and a loose cushion. The rails are grooved on the inside to take the bottom of the box and corresponding stopped grooves are cut in the ends. The hinged lid fits between distance-pieces to prevent scraping as it is raised, and there is a finger-hold cut in the front rail. Fig. 2 (7, 9) are heavier and stronger, as they

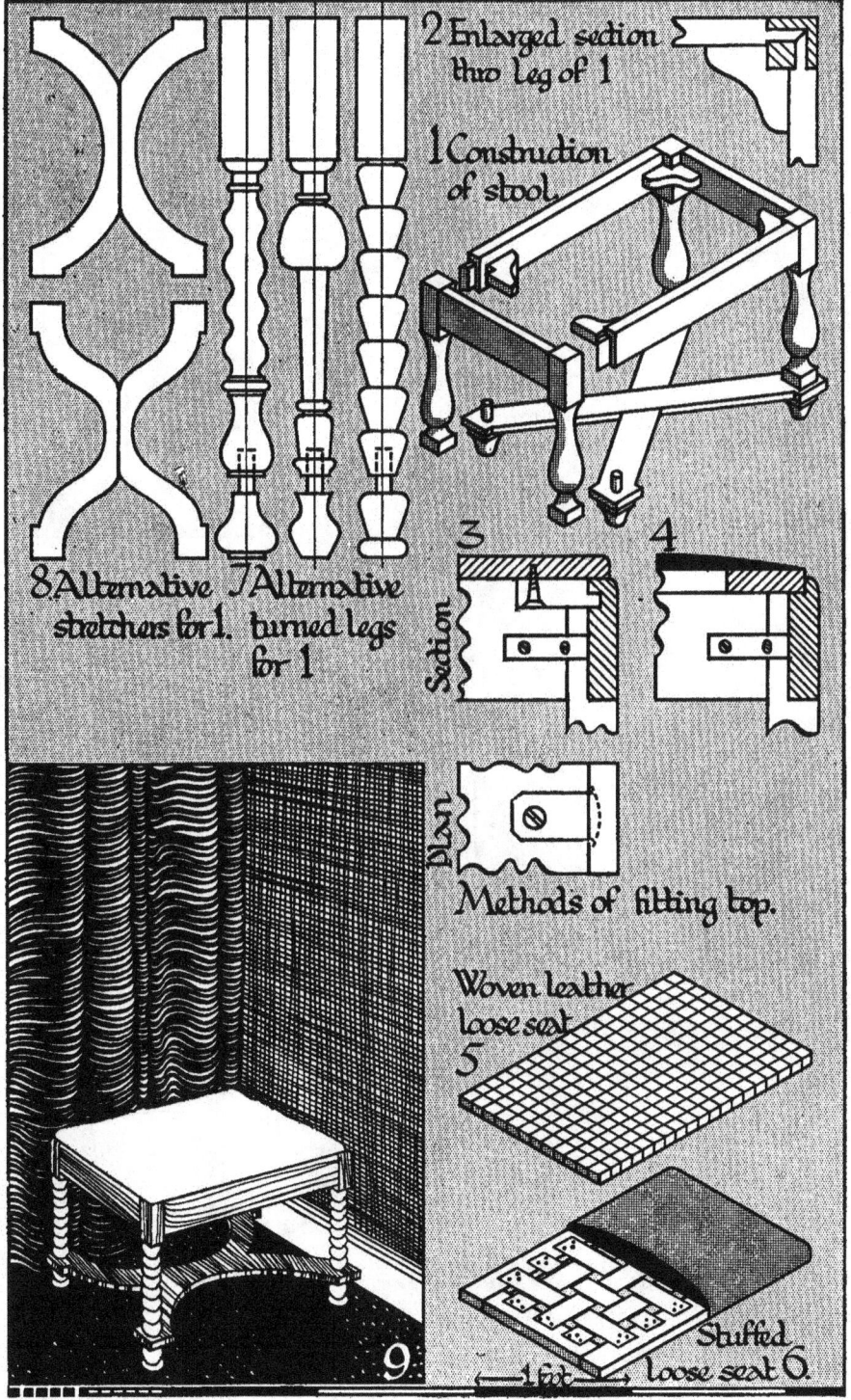

Fig. 1. Four-Legged Stools with loose seat

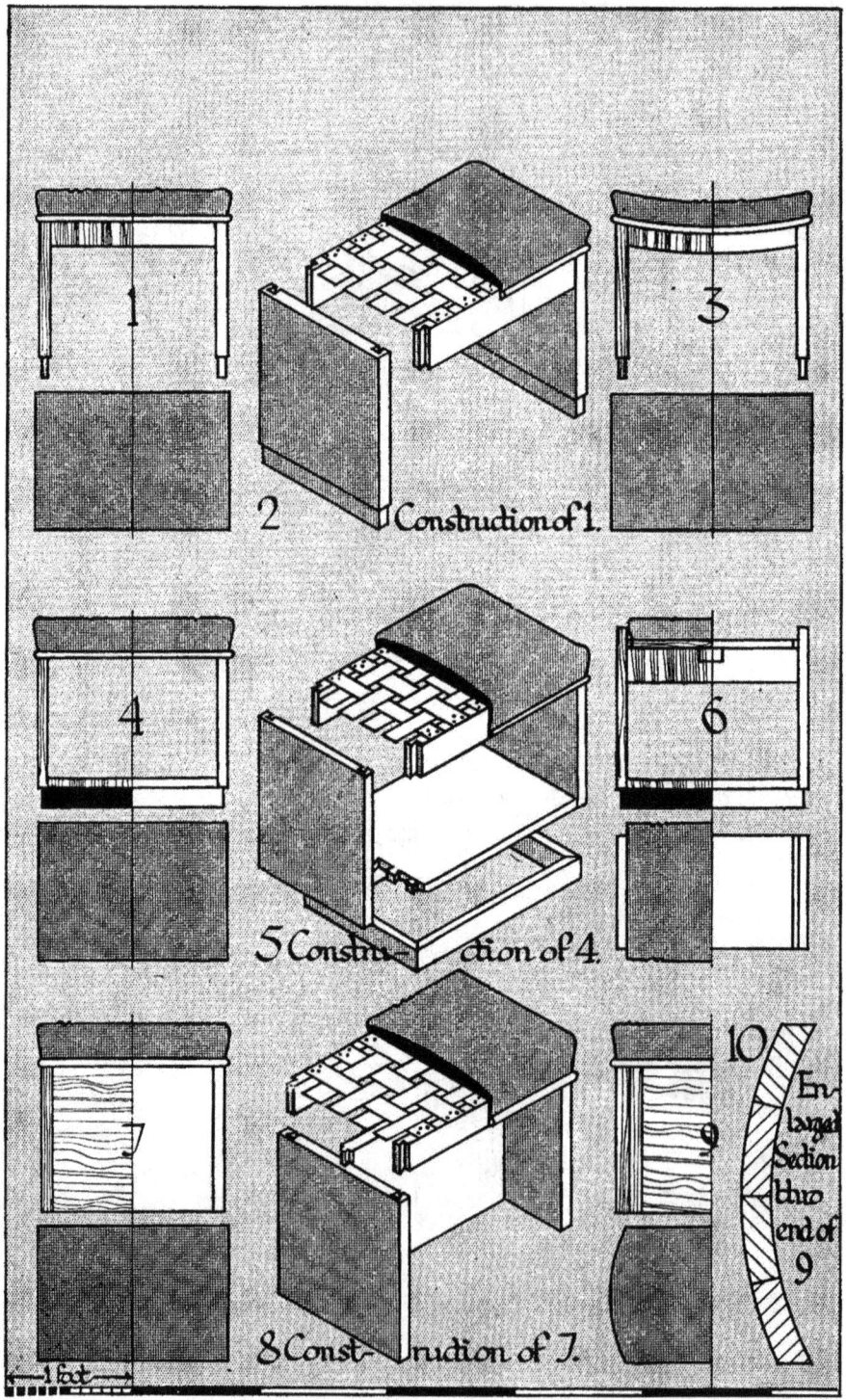

Fig. 2. Upholstered Stools with solid ends

PLATE XIII

DRAW-LEAF DINING TABLE AND SIDEBOARD IN ENGLISH OAK; THE DARKER
PANELS AND HANDLES ARE IN BROWN OAK

Crossley & Brown

PLATE XIV

DINING-ROOM FURNITURE IN AUSTRALIAN WALNUT

Maurice Adams *Maurice Adams Ltd.*

have a centre rail of veneered laminated board housed between the ends. Fig. 2 (10) is a detail of the end of Fig. 2 (9). It is built up of four flat pieces of wood, rather thicker than the finished size to allow for planing to shape. They are rubbed-jointed together in pairs, two pairs being jointed again to form each end, which is then planed to the curve, toothed, and veneered.

Seats for Stools.—A wood seat should be fixed with "buttons" which are screwed under the top, and when turned enter slots cut for them in the rails as shown in Fig. 1 (3). The top is stepped back $\frac{1}{8}$" to conceal any shrinkage that may occur.

The basis of a loose seat is a tenoned frame made to fit into a $\frac{3}{8}$" rebate round the top of the stool. This is shown in section in Fig. 1 (4); the rebate may be worked on the rails before assembly and the inside corners of the legs levelled down afterwards. Fig. 1 (5) shows a woven seat made by interlacing strips of leather and tacking them under the frame. The making of a stuffed seat is illustrated in Fig. 1 (6). Webbing is stretched tightly across the frame with a webbing stretcher, each strip being interlaced with the others and 3" longer than the inside size of the frame to allow the ends to be doubled over for tacking. Above the webbing is stretched a piece of canvas and about three-quarters of the stuffing sewn to this, the rest being packed in to smooth off the top. A muslin cover is stretched over the stuffing, next comes a layer of wadding, and finally the outer cover is mitred at the corners and tacked to the under side of the wood frame.

An over-stuffed seat, as in Fig. 2 (1, 3, 4, 7, 9), is made in the same way but has a rolled edge. This is made after the webbing has been stretched by tacking four strips of canvas round the outer edges of the wood frame. Stuffing is then placed on these strips and they are turned over and tacked again to form a stuffed tube 1" in diameter running round the top of the stool and projecting $\frac{1}{2}$" over it. As the solid ends of these stools prevent the cover being carried underneath, it is tacked to the faces of the rails, which are padded out with wadding. The tack heads are concealed with a strip of gimp or with a half-round bead covered with material. This type of seat is detailed in Fig. 5 (1) of the section on "Chairs."

SECTION 12.—TABLES

Figs. 1 to 5 of this section suggest treatments for dining tables of various types, while Figs. 6 and 7 show tea and occasional tables.

Fig. 1. A Dining Table in light and dark walnut with side tables to fit at either end [Fig. 2 (12)]

For a small room the most suitable dining table is probably either the four-legged type shown in Fig. 2 or the circular table with pedestal, as in Fig. 5. The former types are shown with two side tables to match; these are complete in themselves but may be added to the ends of the centre table when more accommodation is required. The refectory type of table, shown in Figs. 4 and 5, has considerable decorative possibilities but is best suited to a long and rather narrow room. The gate-leg tables in Fig. 6 are primarily intended for tea and card tables, but could be used as dining tables where space is limited. Dining tables are made 2' 6" high and 2' 0" of length allowed for each person; the rectangular examples should be about 3' wide.

Four-Legged Dining Tables with Side Tables at Ends.—Fig. 2 (1-12) shows four-legged dining tables with side tables, the latter being shown at the left of each plan and elevation. Mahogany or walnut would be suitable materials. In each case the centre table is framed up with tenoned rails, the tops being of solid wood and fixed by table plates. These are detailed in Fig. 4 (15),

PLATE XV

Betty Joel Ltd.

DINING-ROOM FURNITURE IN ENGLISH SYCAMORE

PLATE XVI

REFECTORY TABLE IN ENGLISH OAK

Heal & Son Ltd.

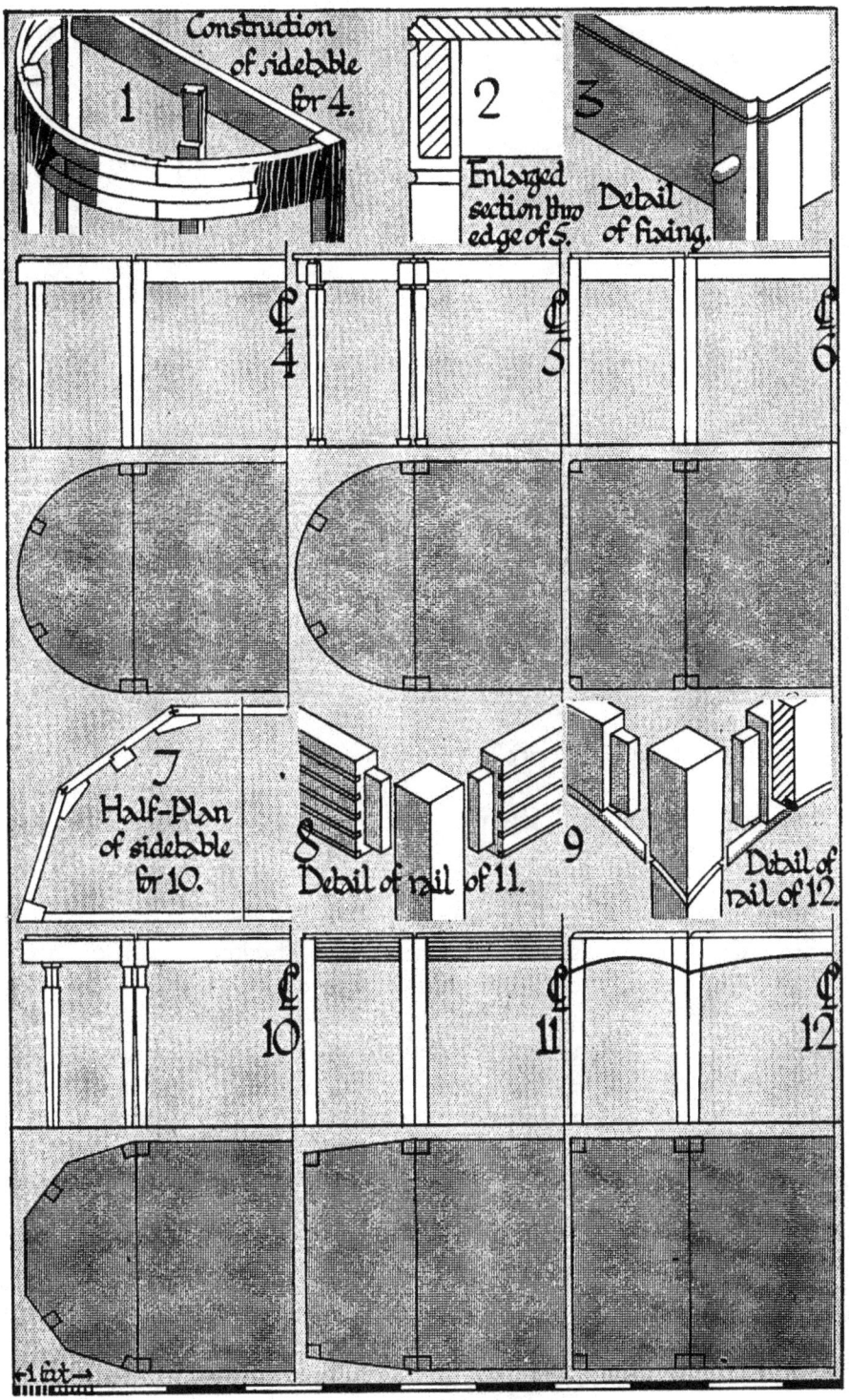

Fig. 2. Four-Legged Dining Tables with side tables to fit at ends

74 TABLES

Fig. 3. An elm Refectory Table and a Bench with the same detail [Fig. 4 (2)]

and are cut into the rails with the slot parallel with the direction of shrinkage of the top. The side table for Fig. 2 (4) has a semicircular end, the two inner legs being slip-dovetailed into this. It is built up, "brickwork fashion," in three layers. Segments to form the curve are bandsawn to shape, rather thicker than the finished size. The semicircle is then marked out on a base of stout ply and the first layer lightly glued to this. The top is trued with a trying plane and the second layer glued down, the joints being arranged to come in the centre of the segments below. The process is repeated for the third layer and the ply removed. Fig. 2 (3) details the leg of Fig. 2 (6) and shows the dowels which fit into holes in the back of the side table and ensure a level top when all three tables are together. The rails of Fig. 2 (11) are inlaid with lines of ebony or box. Fig. 2 (12) has shaped rails with a bead of black-stained hornbeam rebated to the under side, the legs being grooved so that this may be continued to the outer corners.

Refectory Tables with Solid Ends.—Fig. 4 (1-15) gives alternative treatments for a refectory table with shaped ends. It

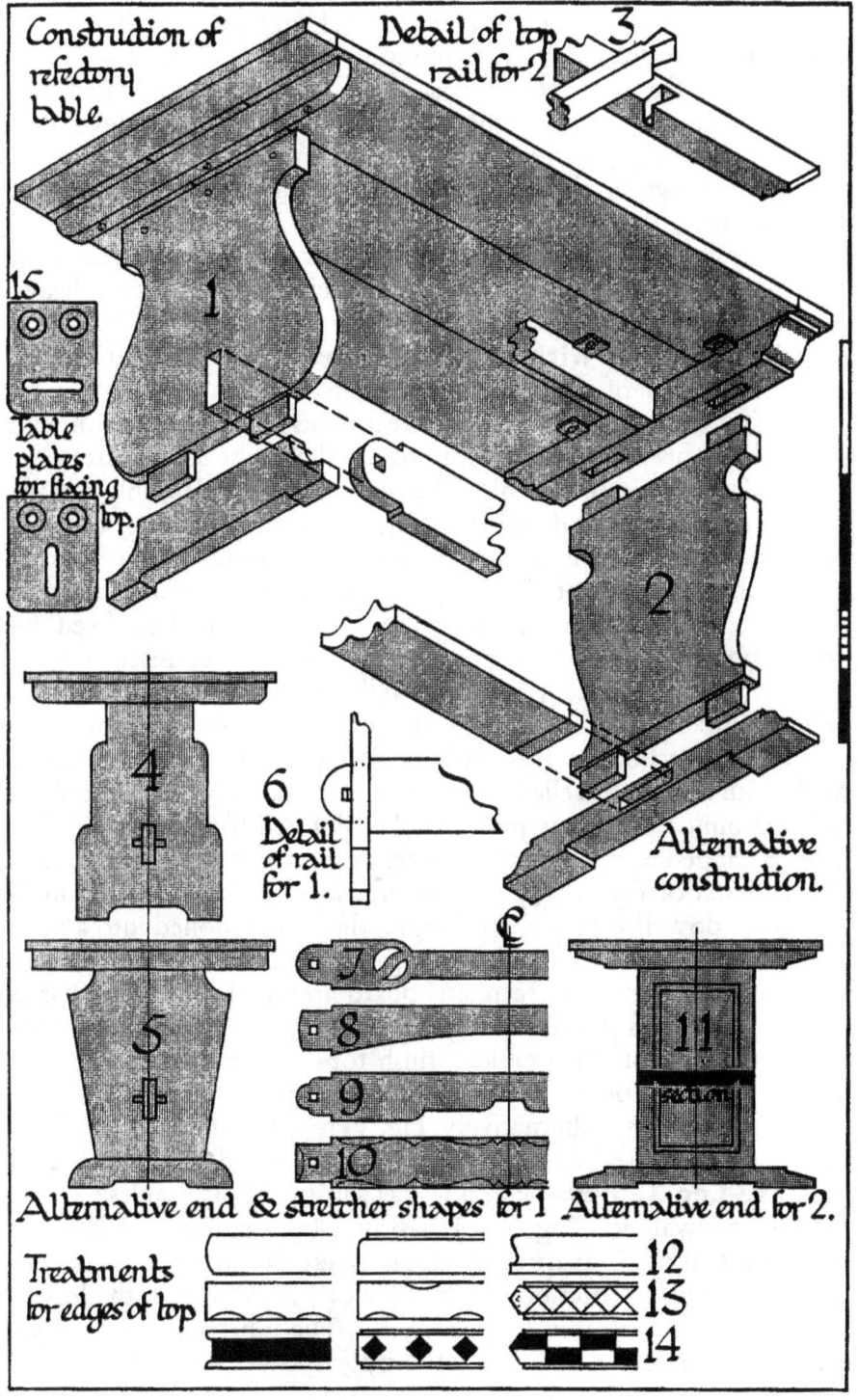

Fig. 4. Refectory Tables with solid ends

could suitably be made in oak, chestnut, or elm. The top is of $1\frac{1}{4}''$ stuff rubbed-jointed, dowelled or tongued together, the ends being clamped. If seating space is required at the ends these must be set in 1′ 3″. In Fig. 4 (1) the ends are $1\frac{1}{2}''$ thick and are tenoned into a foot and joined by a stretcher tenoned through and wedged as in Fig. 4 (6). The top is fixed by screwing through the top stretcher. Fig. 4 (2) shows an alternative construction in which the ends are tenoned into 3″ by 2″ cross stretchers and are joined by a dovetailed top rail as well as by the foot rail. A further treatment for this latter type would be to replace each end by either one or two heavy chamfered or turned legs.

Dining Tables with Pedestal Supports.—Fig. 5 (1) shows the construction of a circular dining table with a centre column. Fig. 5 (5, 9, 13) give alternative treatments for the column and feet, while the plans and elevations to the right show refectory-type tables with similar detail. The rim for the circular table is made as described for the side table in Fig. 2 (4) and the cross rails are slip-dovetailed into it and bridled over the column. This is "boxed up" with four pieces of 2″ stuff, planed to the polygonal section and then fluted. It is tenoned into the base and the feet fixed by dowelling. The X-section pedestal of Fig. 5 (5) consists of three pieces of thick laminated board dowelled together, the outer edges being clamped. It is tenoned to stretchers at top and bottom. The rectangular version of this table, Fig. 5 (7), has rounded corners made with blocks dowelled to the side rails. Fig. 5 (9) has a moulded pedestal built up of four pieces rubbed-jointed together, the joints being arranged to come in the centres of the tenons as in Fig. 6 (10). The pedestal of Fig. 5 (13) consists of a short hexagonal column to which are dowelled four shaped legs; these are tenoned into a plate of laminated board to which the top is screwed. The legs are cut, one "inside" the other from a 2″ board arranged so that there is as little short grain as possible. Fig. 5 (2, 6, 11, 14) give sections for the moulded edges of these tables; flush tops should be of laminated board. Walnut or mahogany would be appropriate for all the examples in Fig. 5; alternatively, Fig. 5 (1, 3) could be ebonized and Fig. 5 (5, 7) veneered with a straight-grained wood such as zebrano.

Gate-Leg Tables.—Fig. 6 (1-14) shows gate-leg tables suitable for oak or walnut. Fig. 6 (2) has an elliptical top and is made with four legs of 2″ square stuff with rails tenoned at top and bottom. The gates, which swing out to an angle of 45° to support the leaves, have each two legs with tenoned rails. The inner leg fits between the rails of the table and is pivoted by $\frac{1}{2}''$ dowels let in at top and

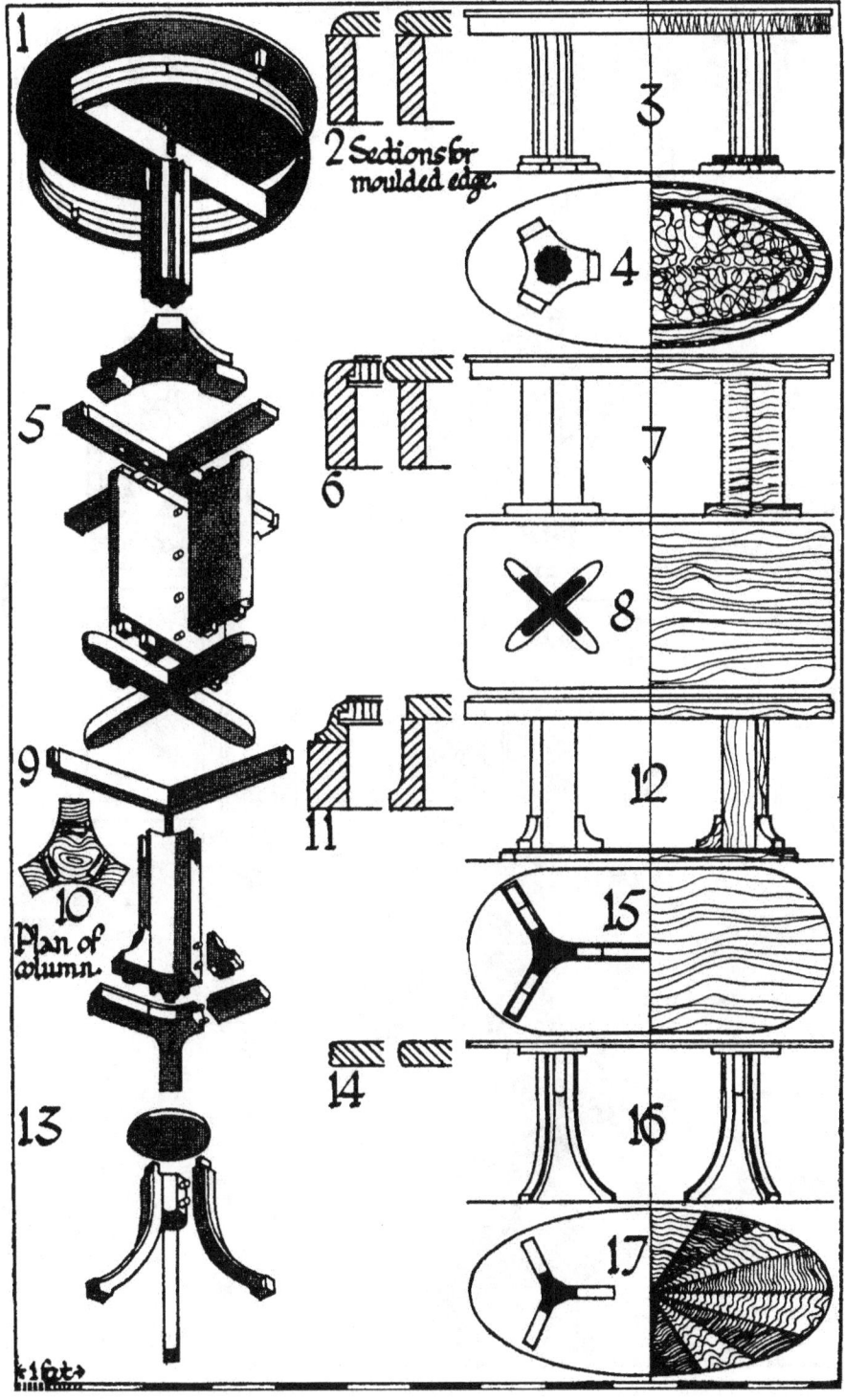

Fig. 5. Circular and other Dining Tables with pedestal supports

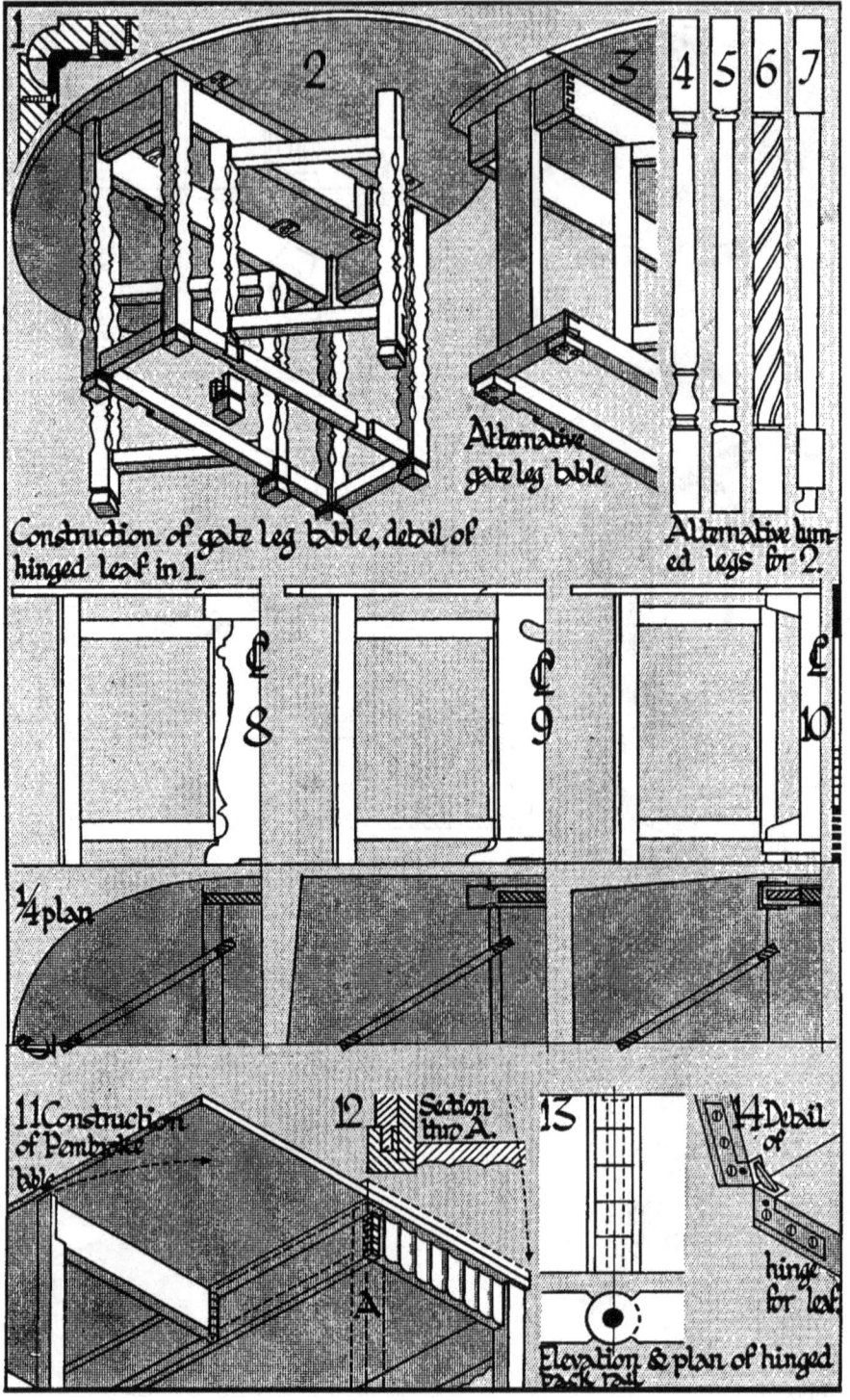

Fig. 6. Gate-Leg Tables

OCCASIONAL TABLES

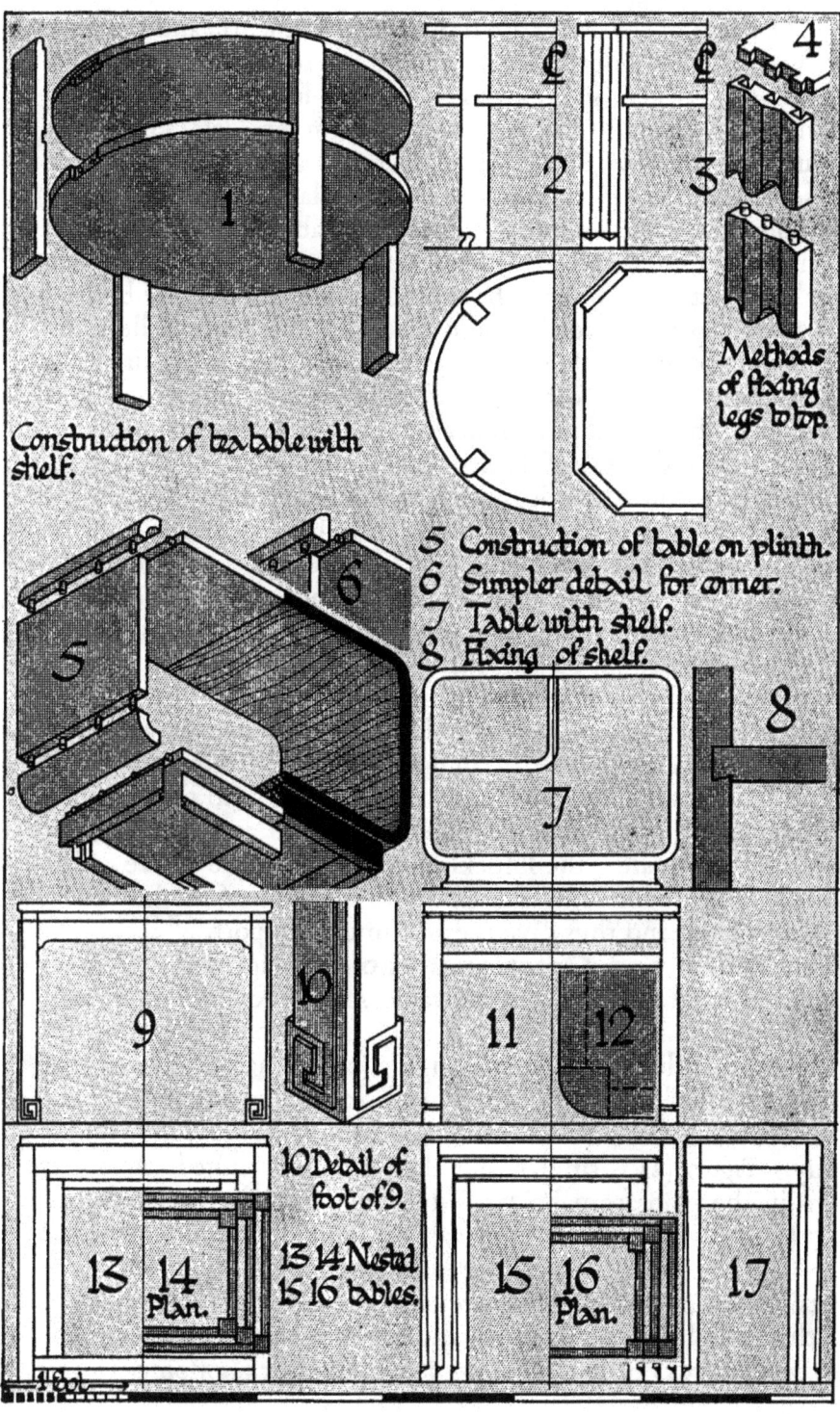

Fig. 7. Tea Tables and Occasional Tables

bottom, a foot being bridled beneath to give the effect of a complete leg. The edges of the leaves are moulded to fit the top and are fixed to it with "rule-joint" hinges, shown in section in Fig. 6 (1). Fig. 6 (4, 5, 6, 7) give suggestions for turned legs alternative to the wagon-bevelled legs; the top and bottom are left square for tenoning to the rails. Fig. 6 (3) is a simpler type of gate-leg table with solid ends of 1½" stuff tenoned into a lap-dovetailed bottom frame and slip-dovetailed into a similar frame above. Fig. 6 (8, 9, 10) are on similar lines and have tops shaped as in the quarter-plan below; the last two examples have tenoned stretchers at the bottom and a wide top rail dovetailed into the ends. Fig. 6 (11) illustrates the construction of a "Pembroke" table; the back leg swings out to a right angle to support a leaf of the same size as the top. It is shown open, the dotted lines indicating the closed position with the leg folded in and the leaf folded back over the top. The table frame is made with three legs with rails tenoned into them in the usual manner; the back rail is double for half its length and the right-hand end dovetailed to the side rail. The second half of the back rail is fixed to the first by a knuckle-joint made by rounding the ends and cutting them into fingers, which are interlaced and pivoted with a steel pin passing through the centre as in Fig. 6 (13); it is tenoned to the fourth leg. When the table is closed the rebate at the top of this leg fits over the dovetails as shown in section in Fig. 6 (12). A special type of hinge is used to connect the leaf and top. This is detailed in Fig. 6 (14); it is cut into the ends and lies flush with the top when opened. The top and leaf together should form a square; the knuckle-joint being in the centre of the back rail, the leg will come practically to the edge of the leaf when the table is open and thus give the maximum support.

Tea Tables and Occasional Tables.—Fig. 7 (1-17) gives examples of small tea and occasional tables suitable for oak and walnut. They should be made about 2' 0" high so as to be conveniently reached from a low easy-chair. Fig. 7 (1) has a top and shelf of $\frac{7}{8}$" stuff to which the legs are dowelled; the grain in both the former should run in the same direction so that the table may shrink equally. Fig. 7 (2) is similar, but the legs are arranged radially as shown in the plan from below, while Fig. 7 (3) has facetted legs. Fig. 7 (4) shows the leg of the latter example dowelled to take the top; above is shown a stronger construction in which the leg is dovetailed to an X-shaped top stretcher and the top slot-screwed to this, the shelf being screwed to another stretcher tenoned below. The corner blocks of Fig. 7 (5) are left square for cramping up and

PLATE XVII

SET OF NESTED TABLES IN ZEBRANO

Serge Chermayeff, F.R.I.B.A.

TABLE AND STOOLS FOR A COCKTAIL BAR; THE WALLS AND FLOOR ARE LINED WITH BIRCH AND SIBERIAN ASH PLYWOOD

Philip Evans Palmer, A.R.I.B.A. *Venesta Ltd.*

PLATE XVIII

WRITING TABLE IN WALNUT AND MACASSAR EBONY

Heal & Son Ltd.

WRITING TABLE IN ENGLISH SYCAMORE WITH SILVERED TOP, PLINTH, AND HANDLES

Crossley & Brown

are afterwards rounded. This table is in laminated board with clamped edges, these and the plinth being cross-banded with a contrasting veneer. Fig. 7 (7) shows a similar table with a hanging shelf slip-dovetailed into the top and ends, Fig. 7 (8) showing the open end of the groove with the shelf in position. The rather Chinese character of Fig. 7 (9) could be further brought out by finishing in red or black lacquer. This example and Fig. 7 (11) are framed up with four legs and tenoned rails, the tops being pocket-screwed.

Nested tables may either lift out from one another as shown in plan in Fig. 7 (14) or pull out from the front as in Fig. 7 (16). In the latter case the two larger tables are made with rather narrow top rails so that the height of the smallest one is not unduly diminished; the tops are of laminated board rebated flush with the top rails and veneered.

Section 13.—Trays

Trays.—Fig. 1 (1-18) (p. 82) give suggestions for trays to be made either in hard wood and polished or to have a painted finish. For a tea tray, 1' 9" long by 1' 2" wide overall is a useful size. They may either be through-dovetailed with a mitre, or mitred and keyed; the latter would be preferable if the tray is to be painted. Fig. 1 (1-9) have handholes and the sides are grooved to take a bottom of solid wood or ply. Fig. 1 (10-13) suggest various treatments for a tray with slip-dovetailed block handles, detailed in Fig. 1 (14). Fig. 2 (9) in the following section ("Wagons") shows the process of shaping these; they are made in one length, the black parts being removed by rebating and chamfering and the curves finished with round and hollow planes. The bottom of the tray is rebated into the frame and is held by mitred fillets as in Fig. 1 (15). The fillets and handles could be in a contrasting wood; mahogany and ebony, maple and mahogany, or sycamore and walnut give attractive combinations of colour. Fig. 1 (16) illustrates the construction of a veneered or painted tray with rounded corners, the laminating of the corner being shown in Fig. 2 (10) of the section on "Wagons." The example detailed in Fig. 1 (17) has moulded sides dowelled into square corner blocks which are afterwards hollowed with bent gouges. Fig. 1 (18) shows nested trays; the sides are rebated to take a flush bottom, which is fixed by gluing and pinning. The handholes are made by boring two holes 1" in diameter and removing the wood between with a chisel.

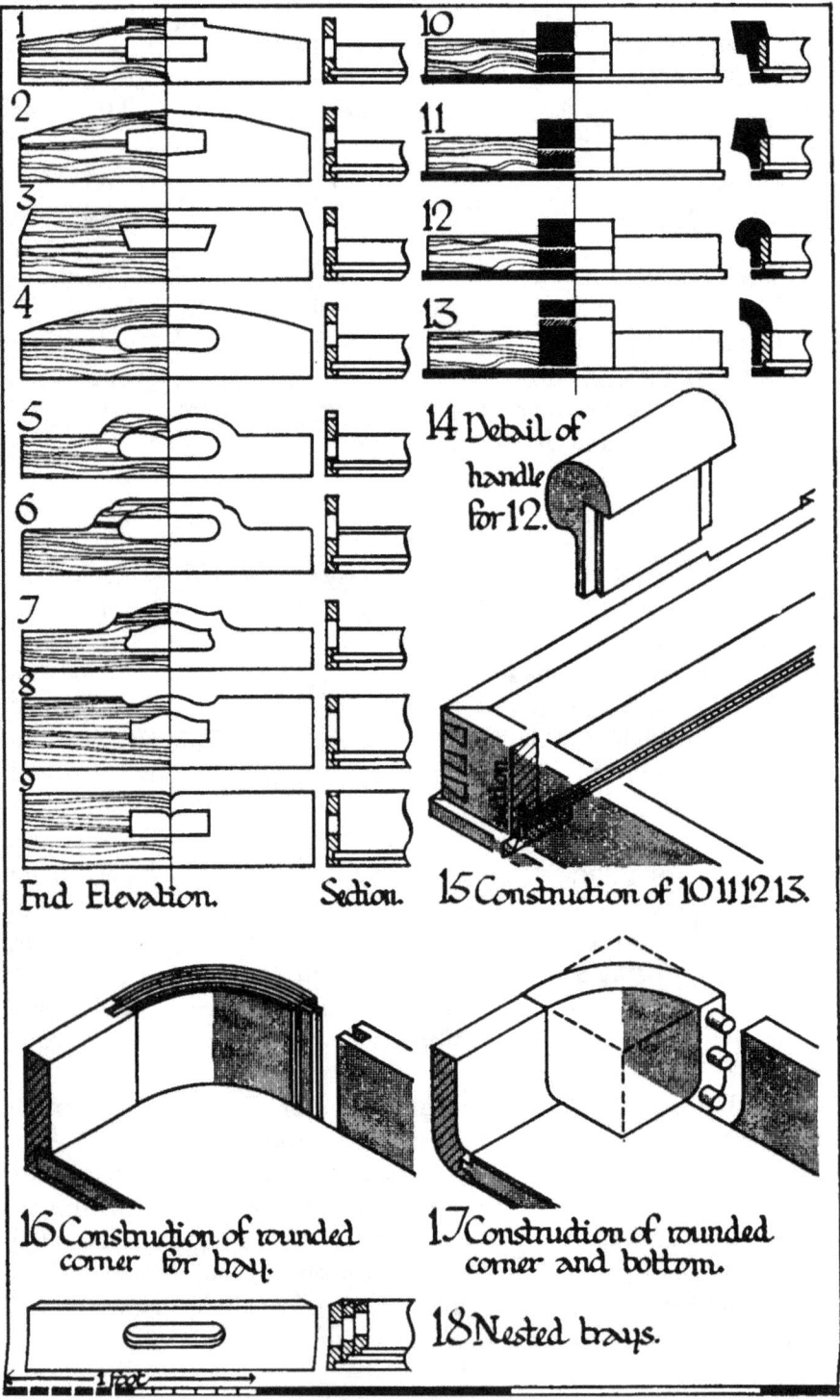

Fig. 1. Trays (*See* p. 81)

Fig. 1. An oak Dinner Wagon with loose tray [Fig. 3 (5)]

Section 14.—Wagons

Dinner Wagons.—Fig. 3 (1-10) shows four simple types of dinner wagon in half-front and end elevation. 2′ 3″ long by 1′ 3″ wide by 2′ 3″ high overall would be a useful size, and they could be made in teak or oak or have a painted finish. Further types of wagon, suitable for garden use, are dealt with in the chapter on " Furniture for the Garden."

The sides are made as complete tenoned frames and are joined by the end rails. In order to ensure correct alignment of top and shelf the legs are " matched " and cramped together as indicated in Fig. 2 (1), which shows the marking-out of Fig 3 (1, 2). The tenoning and rebating of the top rail of this example is shown in Fig. 2 (2); the shelf rails are similar, and both top and shelf are of ply and fixed by screwing from below. Fig. 3 (3, 4) has the shelves stepped $\frac{1}{16}$th back from the rails; if of solid wood they should have either a dowelled or a tongued clamp as in Fig. 2 (3, 4) and Fig. 2 (5) respectively. Fig. 2 (7) shows a mitred clamp for

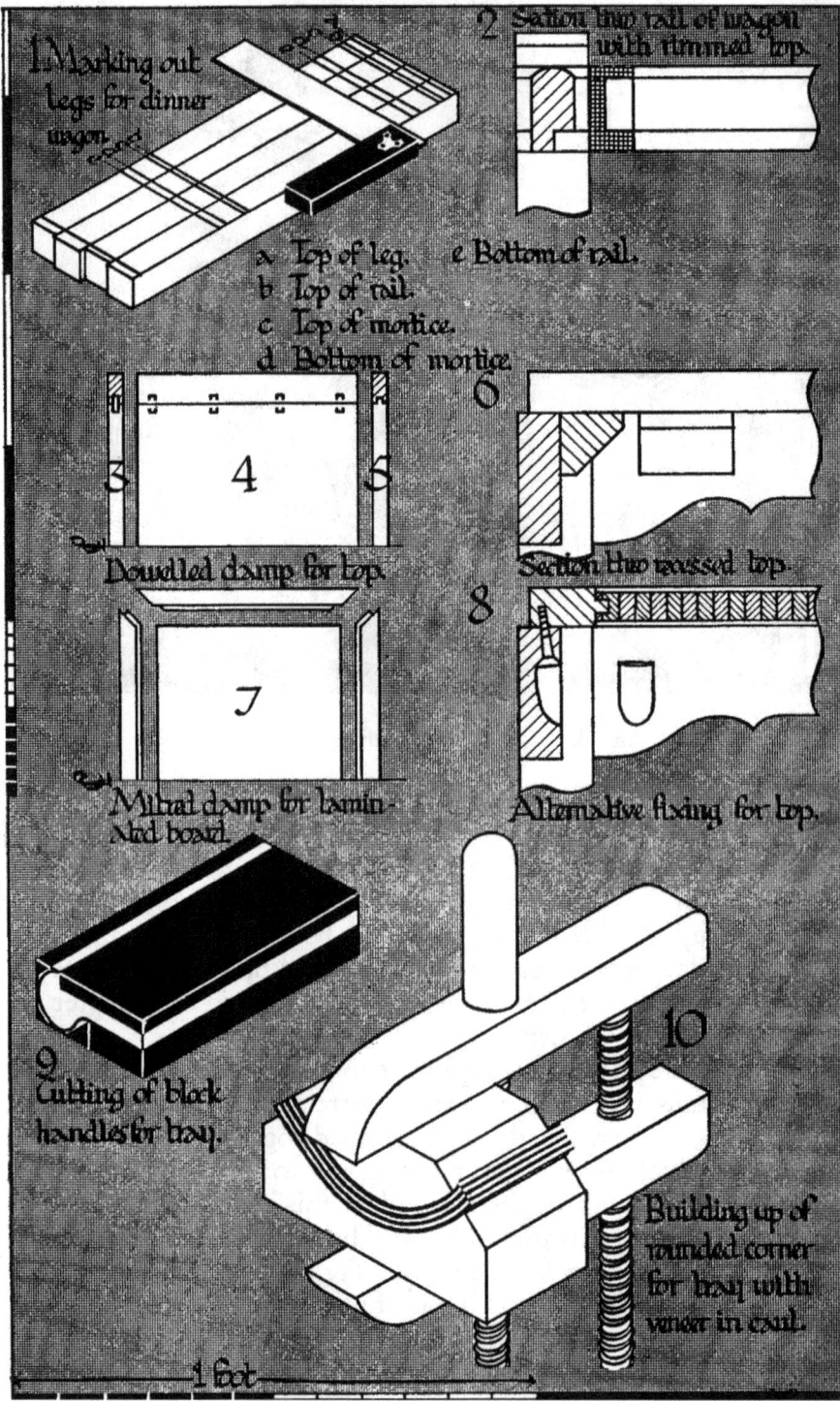

Fig. 2. Constructional details for Trays and Wagons

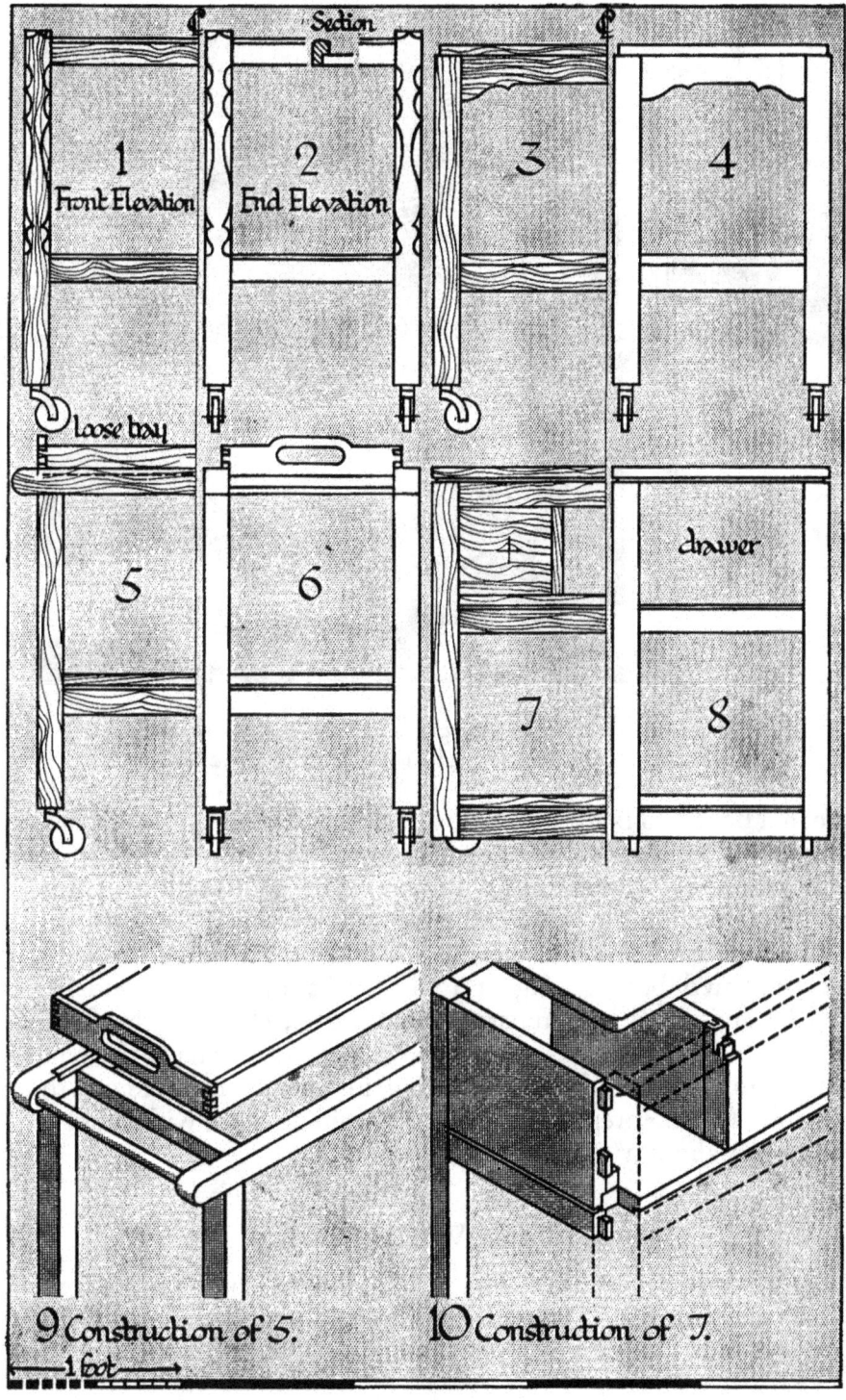

Fig. 3. Dinner Wagons

Fig. 1. A Wall Mirror with carved and gilt head and a Toilet Mirror in maple and ivory [Mirrors, Fig. 2 (7) and Toilet Mirrors, Fig. 2 (2)]

laminated board. Fixing may be by gluing and blocking as detailed in Fig. 2 (6), or by pocket-screwing, Fig. 2 (8). Fig. 3 (5, 6) has a removable tray fitting into a rebate. The construction of this example is given in Fig. 3 (9); the top rails overhang the ends and are bored to take a turned handle ¾" in diameter while the shelf is of laminated board. Fig. 3 (7, 8) has a drawer for cutlery, etc.; the division is of laminated board with a clamp at the front which is stub-tenoned to the rail and bottom. The wide rails below form a plinth, the castors being inside this and screwed to the shelf. All the foregoing examples should be fitted with rubber-tyred castors about 2" in diameter.

SECTION 15.—WALL MIRRORS

Long Wall Mirrors.—Fig. 2 (1-14) gives some suggestions for long wall mirrors. Such mirrors could be placed at the end of a corridor or landing to give light and an illusion of space, or arranged

Fig. 2. Long Wall Mirrors

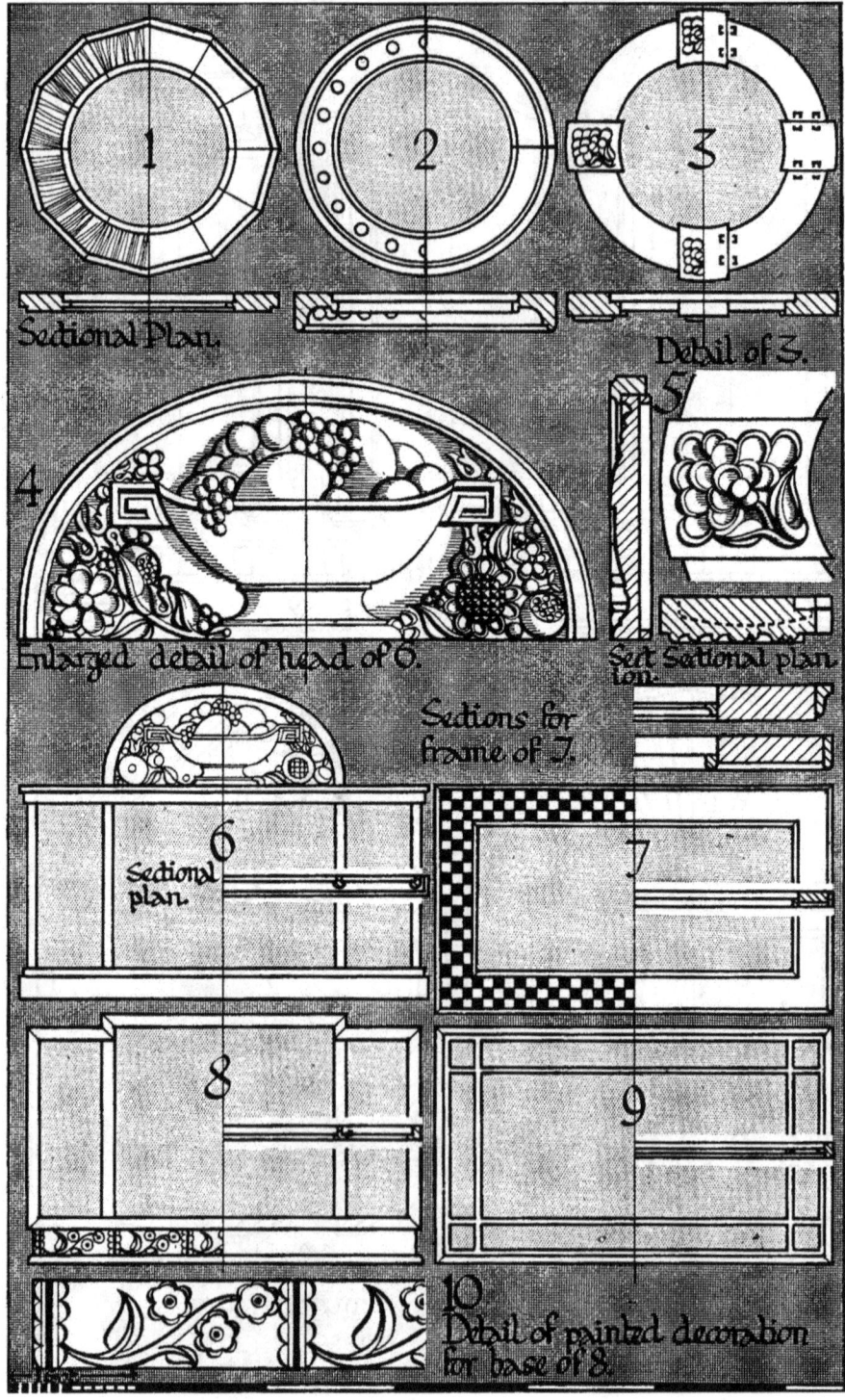

Fig. 3. Circular and Landscape-Shape Wall Mirrors

in a decorative group with, perhaps, a side table and a bowl of flowers. Where the intention is chiefly decorative, coloured mirror-glass has interesting possibilities; this may be obtained in gold, pink, sapphire-blue, etc., to harmonize with the prevailing note in the colour scheme.

Fig. 2 (1, 2, 3) could be veneered in walnut, macassar ebony, or zebrano, or have a painted finish with the mouldings picked out in gold and silver. These are applied to the frame, which may either be tenoned together or cut from ¾" laminated board. The semi-circular moulding in Fig. 2 (1) consists of half a ring built up in segments and turned to the section. If this example is veneered the star motif could be inlaid in a contrasting wood or in mother of pearl. Fig. 2 (4, 5) give sections for the mouldings and detail the fitting of the glass. This is ¼" larger all round than the sight-size of the frame, and is centred by means of chamfered blocks which are glued to the rebate and hold the glass in position. The back, of thin ply, should be fitted so that an air-space is left behind the glass. Fig. 2 (6, 7, 8) show mirrors with a carved head; this may either be in hardwood with a waxed finish or in painted pine. The carving should be drawn out full size and the drawing transferred to the wood by means of carbon paper, the outline being cut with a bowsaw. The figures in Fig. 2 (7) could be treated very simply in two or three flat planes with the edges left square. Fig. 2 (8) gives a suggestion for a monogrammatic design, the letters being raised from a flat ground. This could be painted cream or pale green with the letters in gold. Fig. 2 (9-14) give sections for the frames of these mirrors. They are dovetailed or mitred together and the carving fixed by dowels or by secret screwing.

Circular and Landscape-Shape Wall Mirrors.—Fig. 3 (1-10) shows circular and landscape-shape wall mirrors. The former could be fitted with a convex glass to give a picture of the whole interior. Fig. 3 (6, 8) are overmantel mirrors and are intended to stand on the shelf of the chimney-piece.

Fig 3 (1), if large, should be built up of twelve segments mitred and tongued; small examples may be cut from one piece of laminated board. Fig. 3 (2) is adapted from a Regency mirror, the frame consisting of four segments dowelled together and turned to the section of the moulding. The balls are turned separately and dowelled into position; they could be gilt and the frame ebonized. Solid oak or walnut would be suitable for Fig. 3 (3), the segments being dowelled into square blocks. The semi-elliptical head of Fig 3 (6), built up with three segments, is dovetailed to the top rail.

It is rebated to take the carving which is in 1¼" pine. The vertical bars are half-round in section and rebated for the glass; they are tenoned at top and bottom. The frame of this mirror could be painted in vellum colour picked out with gold, the vase in the carving the same, and the fruit and flowers in pale blue, green, and orange. The frame of Fig. 3 (7) is of hardwood, mitre-halved and with mouldings applied to the edges as shown in the sections above. The chequer pattern could be in ebony contrasted with a lighter wood or with mother of pearl. The " broken " top rail of Fig. 3 (8) is made in one piece with the inner divisions tenoned at top and bottom. The base is separate and is dowelled to the frame. Fig. 3 (9) has a mitred or dovetailed outer frame with the divisions tenoned into it; these are false and come over the face of the glass.

SECTION 16.—WRITING TABLES

This section outlines various treatments for knee-hole and pedestal writing tables and also for secretaires. The pedestal type

Fig. 1. Pedestal Writing Table in walnut [Fig. 3 (7)]

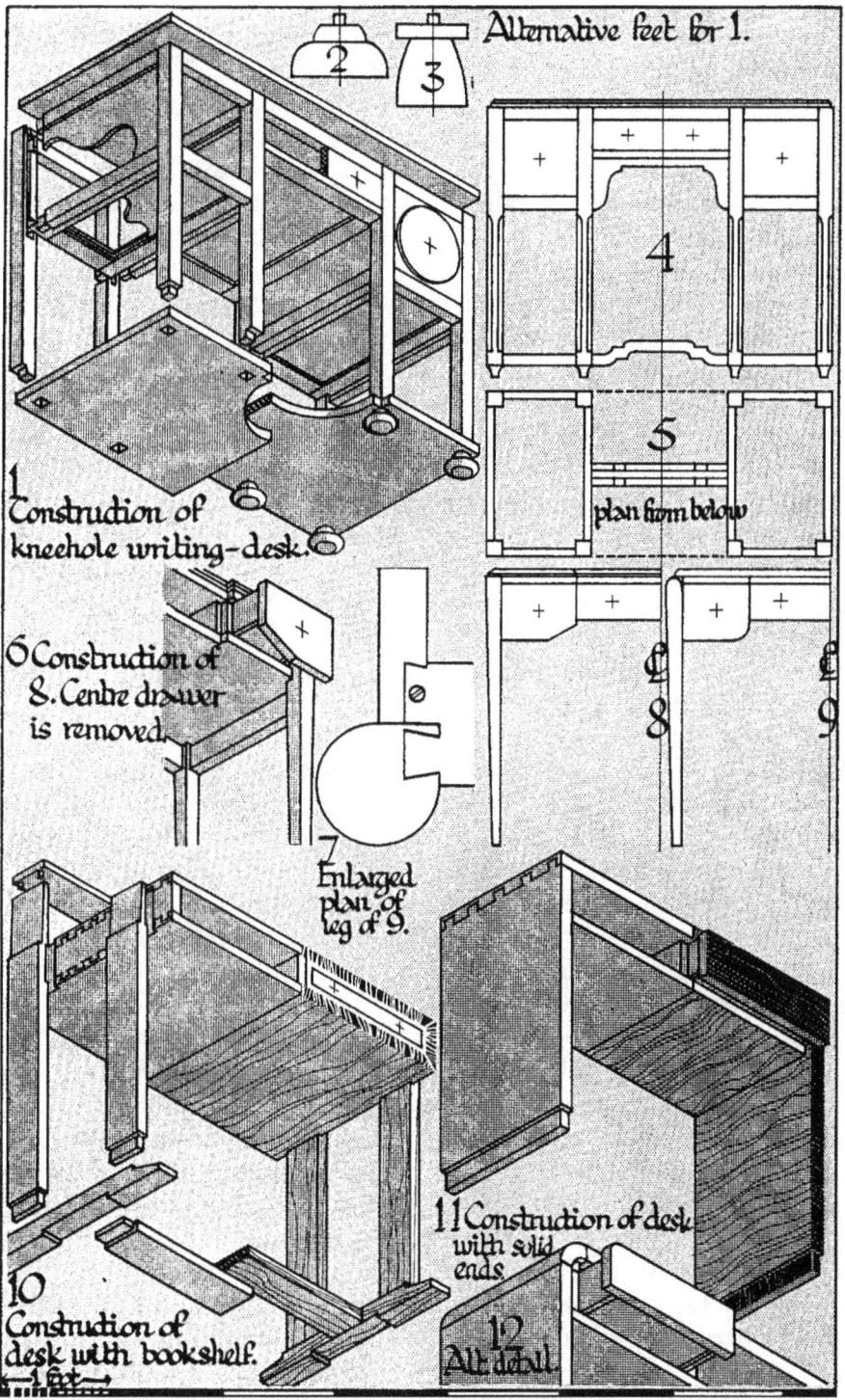

Fig. 2. Knee-Hole Writing Tables

is perhaps the most attractive, but, with a centre space of 1′ 6″ and drawers at either side, must be at least 3′ 6″ wide. If this width is inconvenient a pedestal could be put on one side only and the other fitted with a solid end as in the example in Fig. 3 (8).

Writing tables are usually made slightly below dining table height—about 2′ 5½″ overall. The overall depth should be 1′ 6″, and for types other than the pedestal a width of 3′ 0″ will be found adequate.

Knee-Hole Writing Tables.—Fig. 2 (1-12) shows knee-hole writing tables both with and without drawers at the sides. Fig. 2 (1) is intended to be made in soft wood and painted. The framing consists of eight legs 1½″ square with tenoned rails above and below the drawers; the top rails are continuous at front and back and are bridled over the inner legs. The legs are tenoned through a base of laminated board and the turned feet dowelled up into them. The drawers are made and fitted as described in the section on "Chests of Drawers." Runners for these are tongued to the front rails and are connected by cross rails at the back to form frames for dust-boards of $\frac{3}{16}$″ ply. As a writing table is sometimes seen from behind, the back should be cut from one piece of $\frac{3}{8}$″ ply, rebated into the outer legs and glued across the framing. The top is of solid wood and screwed to table plates cut into the rails. Fig. 2 (4) is of similar construction and is suitable for oak; it has stretchers in place of the shaped base. The apron-piece may either be built up or cut from laminated board and veneered; it is glued to the legs and screwed up into the rail. Fig. 2 (8, 9) show four-legged knee-hole tables for oak and mahogany respectively; the latter example has turned legs left square at the top for tenoning to the rails. The construction is illustrated in Fig. 2 (6), the centre drawer being removed. The frame is made with a bottom of laminated board and the divisions between the drawers tenoned into this and to the top rail. The drawer sides are slip-dovetailed into the fronts so that the shaped part may extend below this bottom, and the centre drawer is set back $\frac{5}{8}$″ to give a "break-front" effect. Fig. 2 (10) is in oak with the edges cross-banded with walnut and has a lap-dovetailed carcase of veneered laminated board. The ends of this are grooved to take the legs, which are screwed from the inside; the back legs extend above the top and are connected by a dowelled rail to form a space for books. Fig. 2 (11) has two ends of solid wood or laminated board which are lap-dovetailed to the top and tenoned to a bottom below the drawers. The latter have the sides slip-dovetailed into the fronts, which close over the division

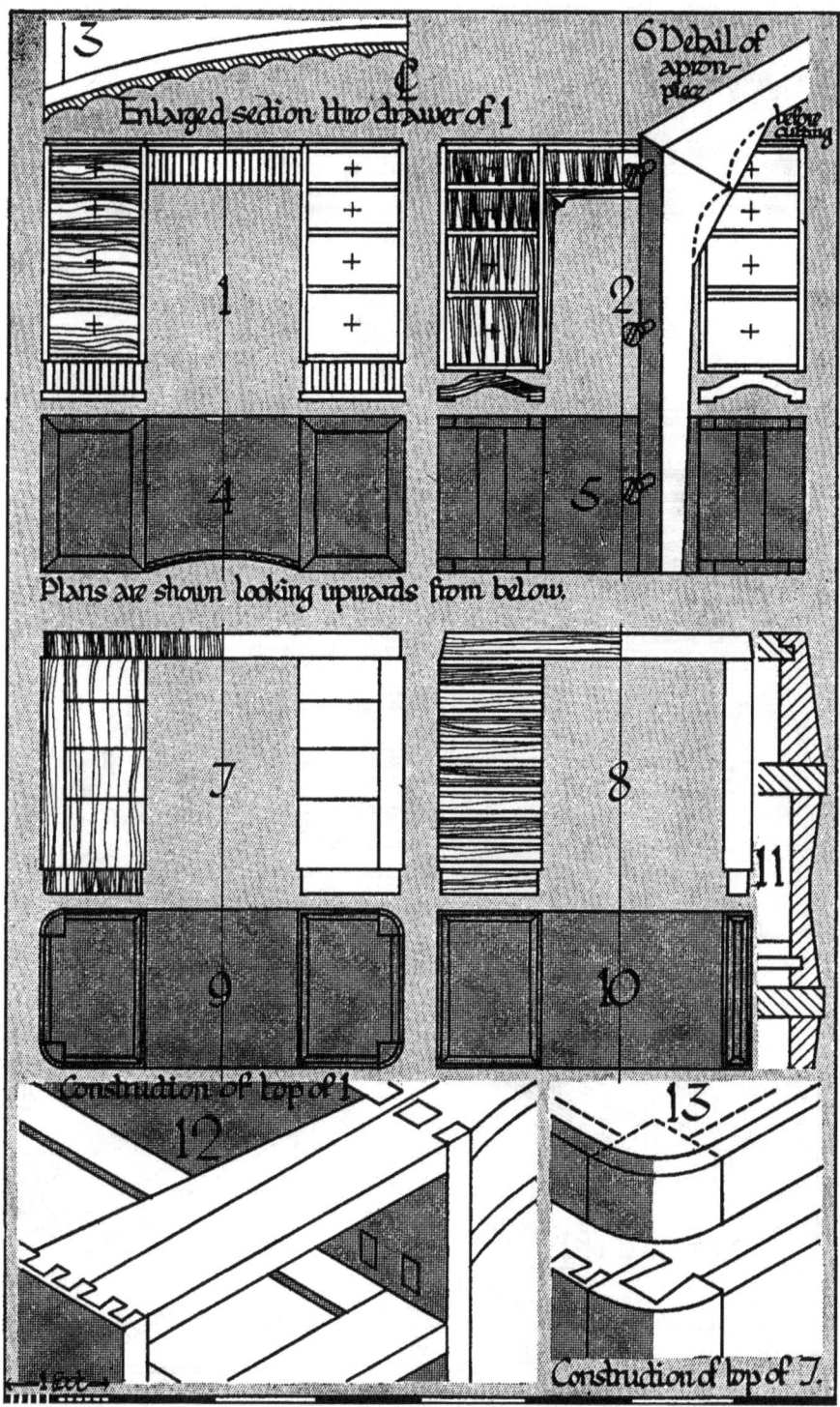

Fig. 3. Pedestal Writing Tables

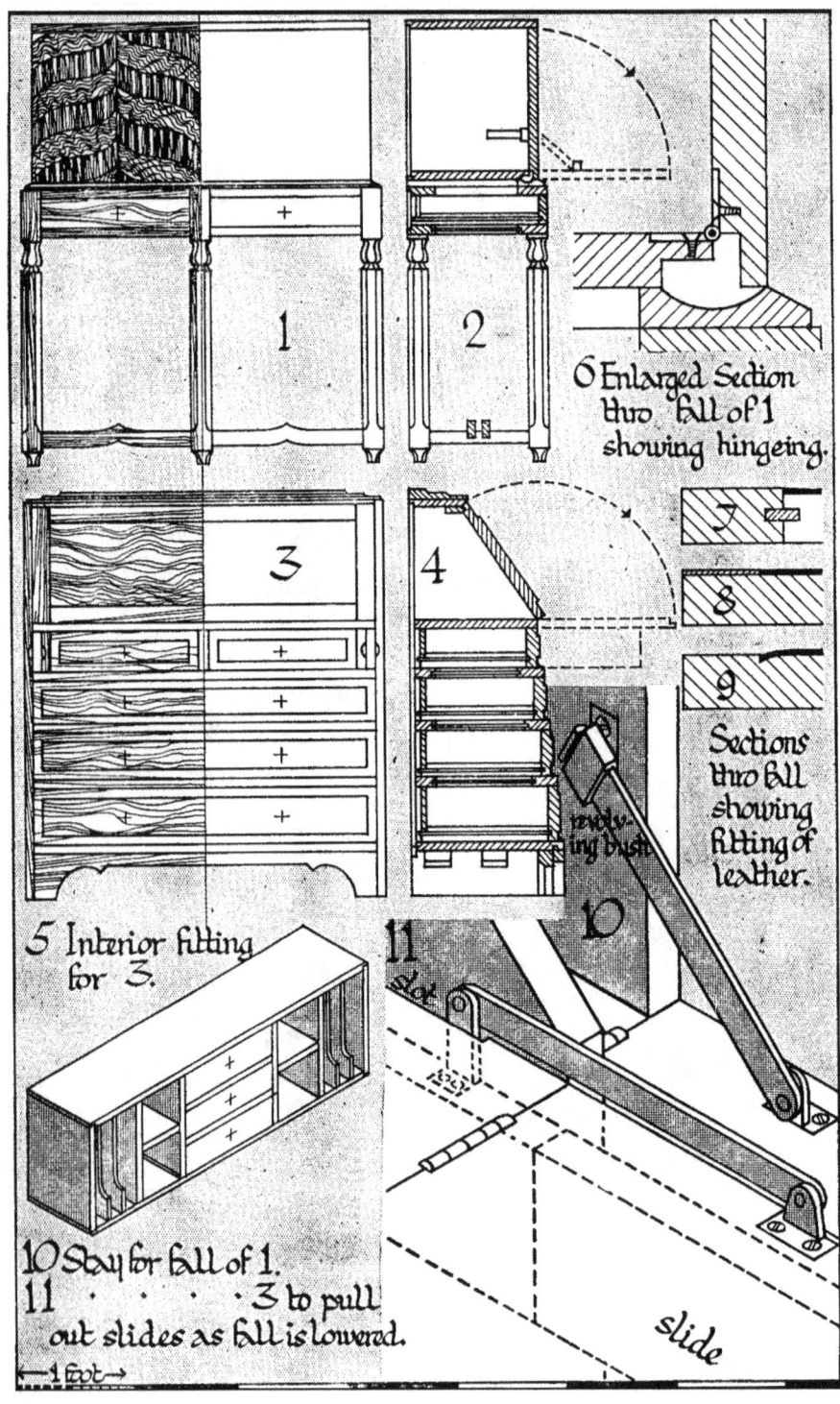

Fig. 4. Secretaires

and also project slightly below the bottom to give a finger-hold for withdrawing them. An alternative detail for this example is given in Fig. 2 (12); the blocks for the corners are rounded on the outside only and have thicknessing pieces glued below the inner face to make a running surface for the drawer sides.

Pedestal Writing Tables.—Fig. 3 (1-13) shows pedestal writing tables suitable for walnut, mahogany, or sycamore. Fig. 3 (1) consists of two lap-dovetailed drawer carcases connected by rails and by the bottom for the centre drawer as detailed in Fig. 3 (12). The concave drawer front is built up in layers and the fluting glued to it in a shaped caul. The top is of veneered laminated board with clamped edges and is screwed from below. The plinths are made as lap-dovetailed boxes and the fluted detail applied as to the drawer front. Fig. 3 (2) is similar in construction, but the pedestals are supported on cradles consisting of two shaped feet joined by a tenoned rail. The mitreing of the apron-piece for the knee-hole is shown in Fig. 3 (6); it is fixed by gluing to the drawer rail and screwing through the sides of the pedestals. The pedestals of Fig. 3 (7) have rounded corner posts into which the ends are tongued, the top and bottom of the carcase being dovetailed as in Fig. 3 (13). This also shows the construction of the frieze, which is butt-glued or tongued to a top of laminated board and cross-banded. It is fixed to the drawer carcases by screwing from below. Fig. 3 (8) has a similar " boxed-up " top but only one pedestal, the right-hand end consisting of a tongued or dowelled box. The drawer fronts of this example employ bevelling as a decorative feature as shown in the section Fig. 3 (11).

Secretaires.—Fig. 4 (1-11) illustrates two types of enclosed writing desk or secretaire. The example in Fig. 4 (1) is intended for a richly figured wood such as English walnut, blackbean, or Indian laurel; the pattern of the front is worked out in two veneers contrasting in colour, texture, or direction of grain. The stand is framed up with five legs of octagonal section and is screwed to the upper part. This consists of a carcase made with lap or secret-mitred dovetails and enclosed by a fall of clamped laminated board. The pieces of veneer for the patterned front of this are first cut roughly to shape and are then fastened, one above the other, between thin boards for cutting and filing to the exact profile. The pattern is then assembled on a flat board and held in place with veneer pins while the joints are being secured with 1" strips of gummed paper. When this has been done the whole sheet may be lifted and veneering proceeded with in the usual manner. The fall is supported by stays as detailed in Fig. 4 (10). The bureau in Fig. 4 (3) is in oak and is made in the same way as a chest of drawers except that there are additional divisions outside the small drawers to enclose the slides. These are withdrawn by means of a finger-grip gouged out on either side. Alternatively, a stay as shown in Fig. 4 (11) could be used; this is connected to the slide and automatically pulls it out as the writing flap is lowered. Fig. 4 (5) shows an interior fitting to take writing paper, envelopes, etc. It is made as a separate carcase with grooved or tenoned divisions and is fitted to the bureau by means of scribing pieces mitred round the outside. The cabinet in Fig. 4 (1) should have a similar interior. Fig. 4 (7, 8, 9) are sections giving three alternative "lippings" for a flap which it is desired to line with leather. Fig. 4 (7) shows a clamped flap with the clamp raised $\frac{1}{16}''$ above the ground, in Fig. 4 (8) the flap is bordered with veneer and in Fig. 4 (9) a groove is formed by gauging and planing.

PLATE XIX

OAK WALL BUREAU DESIGNED FOR NARROW SPACE
The Rowley Gallery Ltd.

BUREAU FINISHED IN WHITE AND BLACK CELLULOSE
Crossley & Brown

PLATE XX

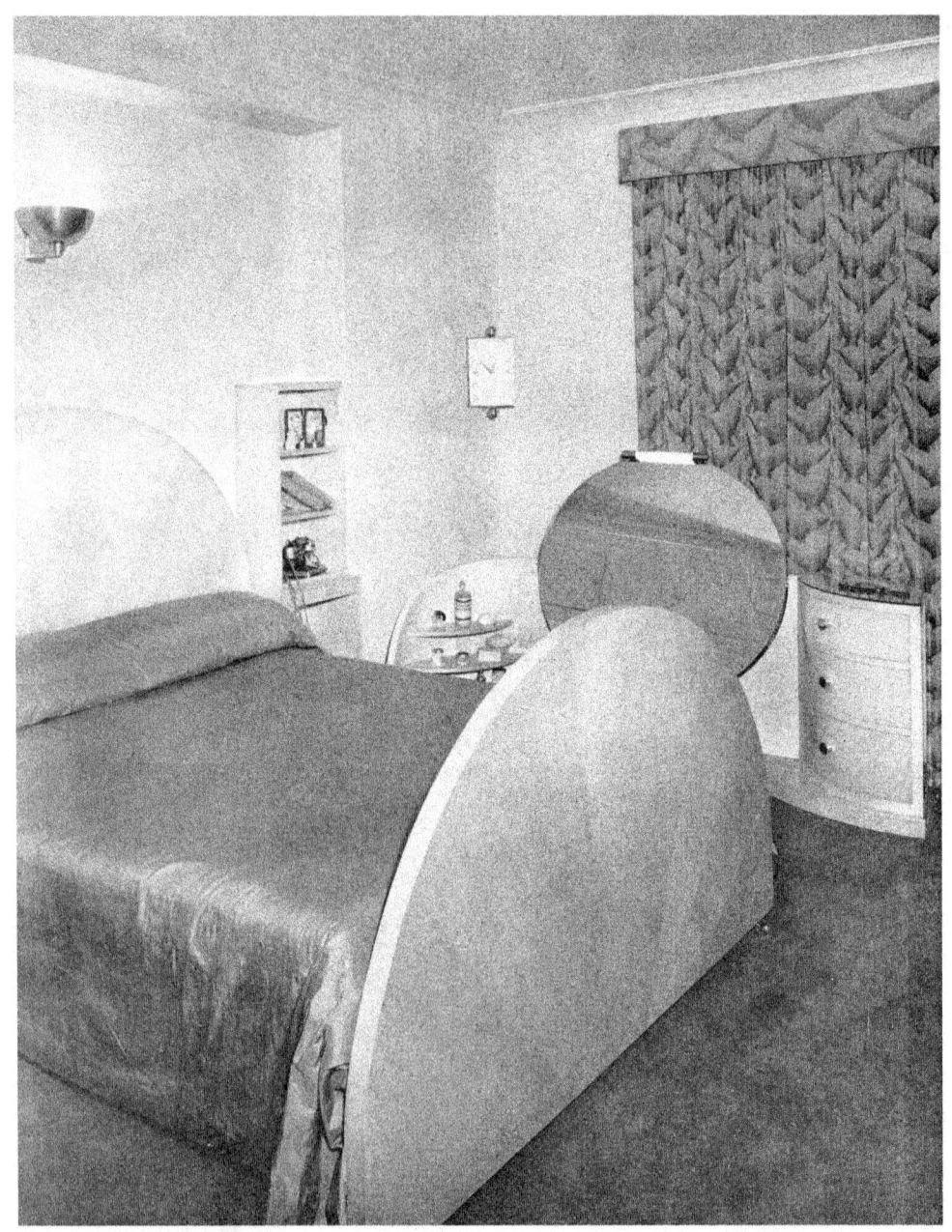

BEDSTEAD IN ENGLISH SYCAMORE

Betty Joel Ltd.

CHAPTER IV

FURNITURE FOR THE BEDROOM

Section 1.—Bedsteads

THE treatments for beds suggested in this section fall into three groups. The simplest treatment is with a divan bedstead, consisting of a spring mattress mounted on legs and obtainable as a complete unit, fitted with a shaped headboard as detailed in Fig. 2. Fig. 4 shows a more elaborate treatment in which a divan is incorporated in a bed-fitment made with a framed backboard and pedestals at either side. The bedsteads proper, Figs. 6 and 7, consist of a head and foot end connected either by side rails to take a mattress or by a combination spring.

Headboards for Divan Bedsteads.—Fig. 2 (1-16) shows a variety of shapes for headboards for fitting to divan bedsteads. They could be made in solid hard wood or veneered laminated board, or, alternatively, in soft wood either painted or covered with material as in Fig. 2 (13-15). A headboard for covering should be padded with wadding and the material fixed by tacking round the edges, the tack heads being concealed by a strip of gimp. The face could have a pattern outlined in braid as in the last two examples. Headboards should have two stiffening battens slot-screwed to the back, fixing being effected by screwing these to the frame of the divan.

Bed-Fitments.—Fig. 4 (1-12) illustrates four types of bed-fitment; they are shown with a double divan, but two single divans could equally well be used. The width should be arranged so that there is about 6″ clearance between the inside ends of the pedestals and the bedding. The divans may either be fixed by screwing through the backboard or left free so that they may be moved out for cleaning. Fig. 4 (1) is suitable for oak or chestnut and has a framed and panelled back with an applied capping as in Fig. 4 (3). The pedestals are made as separate carcases, with a cupboard below and an open space for books above, and are fixed by screwing to the back. Fig. 4 (6) is on similar lines, but the back consists of one piece of laminated board veneered with alternating sectors of light and dark walnut or mahogany; both sides should be veneered to prevent the front " pulling." The pedestals are bow-fronted as in

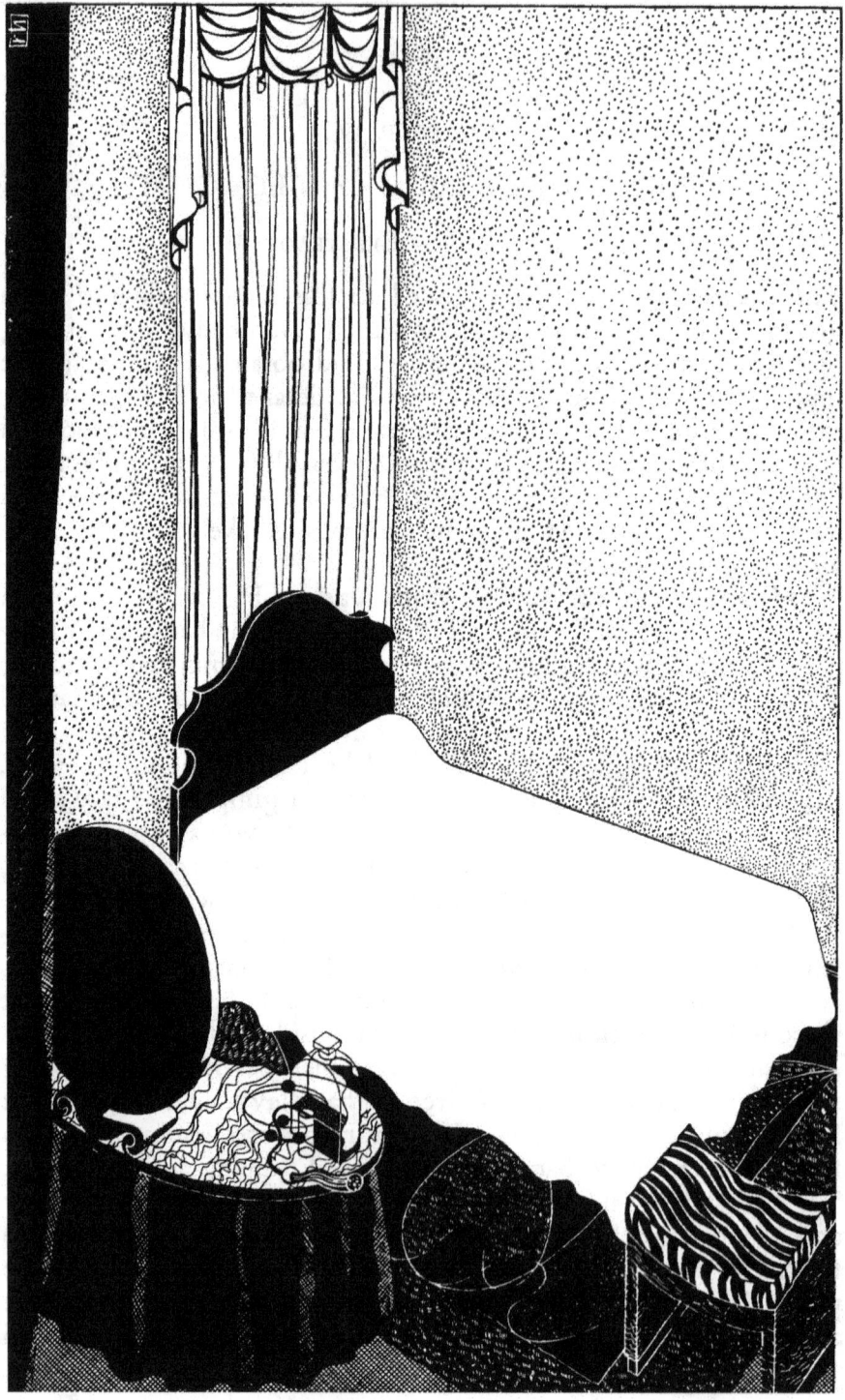

Fig. 1. A Bedroom Scheme with Divan with Shaped Headboard [Fig. 2 (13)]

Fig. 2. Headboards for Divan Bedsteads

Fig. 3. A Bed-Fitment in oak with walnut cross-banding [Fig. 4 (10)]

the plan Fig. 4 (9), the cupboard doors being "coopered-up" and the drawers made with slip-dovetailed sides, as detailed in Fig. 4 (8). The pedestals of Fig. 4 (10) are screwed to backs of veneered laminated board which extend to under the cornice and are connected by tenoned cross rails. The outer ends are made the same height for half their depth and are tongued to a front to form a space for shelves, as seen in the section Fig. 4 (11). The cornice is "boxed-up" separately and is dowelled to the tops of the pedestals. It is fitted with a rail for the curtain behind the bed; a strip light could be arranged in the front so that it is concealed from view.

Bedstead Fittings.—The bedsteads in Figs. 6 and 7 consist of a separate head and foot end which are connected by side rails of wood or metal. These are fixed to the posts by a fitting of which Fig. 5 (1, 2) show two of the many types. These have to a great extent superseded the French bolts shown in Fig. 5 (3), although the latter are still used for large and heavy work. The rails are slotted on the inner side to receive the bolts, which have a ball head so that they may be turned with a tommy-bar to engage with nuts

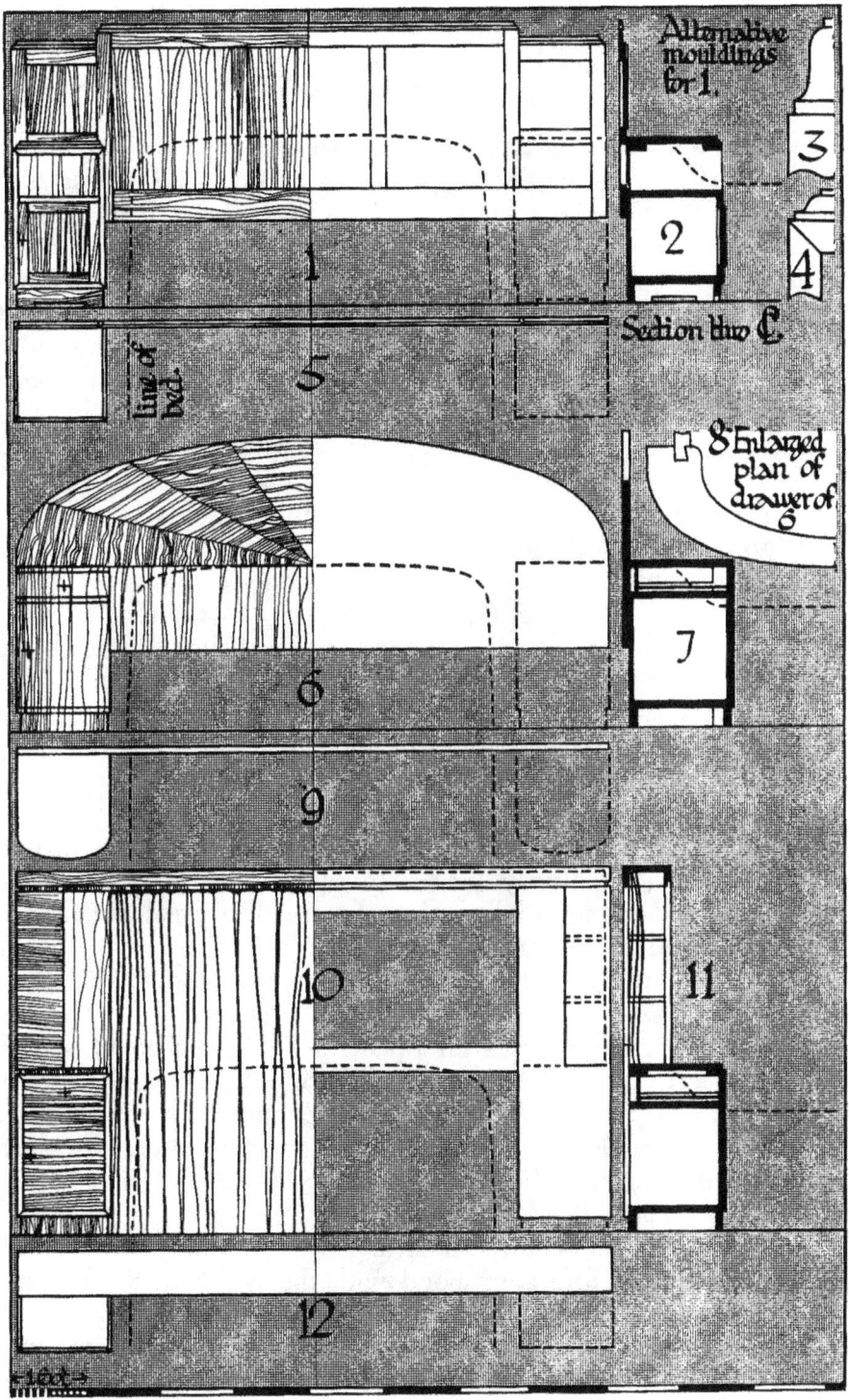

Fig. 4. Bed-Fitments

let into the posts. Above the side rails comes the mattress, which is positioned by blocks or turn buttons; the width over the rails should be equal to that of the mattress to give a flush side to the bed. The Somnus "Inta" fitting, detailed in Fig. 5 (1), may also be obtained with the angle reversed so that the open face of the rail is on top and the mattress fits between the sides and is thus automatically positioned. In this case either a Somnus base mattress, made $\frac{1}{2}$″ narrower to fit between the rails, must be used or $\frac{1}{2}$″ added to the width of the ends. With a combination spring, side rails are unnecessary as the spring is contained in a rigid steel frame which is made complete with the fittings for locking to the posts of the bedstead.

The width of bedsteads is governed by the width of mattresses available. For single beds these range from 2′ 6″ to 3′ 6″ and for double beds up to 5′ 0″. The fittings are usually arranged to give a height of about 1′ 6″ to the top of the mattress; deep side rails may be rebated so that the mattress fits between them. In deciding the position of the fitting the height of the castors should also be taken into consideration. These may be either of the socket or the screw pattern as in Fig. 5 (4, 6) respectively. In the former type a hole is bored in the bottom of the leg to take the socket and the pin of the castor pushed in so that it clips over the spring top. For a square leg a castor ring, as shown in Fig. 5 (5), to fit over the plate of the castor will give a neat finish; circular patterns for turned legs may also be obtained.

Bedsteads with Stump Foot Ends.—Fig. 6 (1-9) illustrates bedsteads with stump foot ends. Oak or walnut would be appropriate; alternatively, the first two examples could be painted. The head end of Fig. 6 (2) consists of a bevelled panel, stiffened by a slot-screwed batten, and screwed or dowelled to two 3″ by 1$\frac{1}{2}$″ posts which are recessed to give a flush face in front. The foot is made with two short posts connected by a tenoned rail. The head of Fig. 6 (3) is framed up with a panel of laminated board, slightly raised as in the section Fig. 6 (1). Fig. 6 (4, 6) are similar in construction, the panel at the head being tenoned into square posts; the latter example has a scrolled top and is veneered with two "matched" leaves of burr walnut. The rounded corners at head and foot of Fig. 6 (8) are made as in Fig. 6 (9) and are tongued to panels of laminated board. The fittings are screwed to the flat panel, which must therefore correspond with the width of the mattress, the overall width of the bed being about 6″ beyond this.

Bedsteads with Panelled or "Slatted" Head and Foot Ends.—The examples in Fig. 7 (1-12) show various panelled

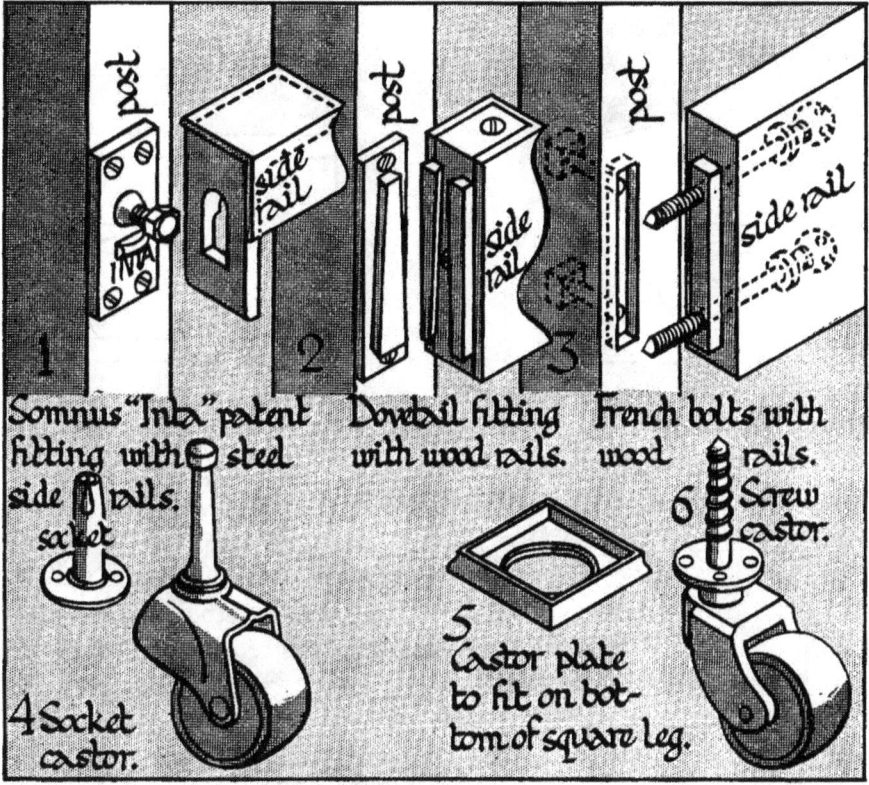

Fig. 5. Bedstead Fittings

and "slatted" treatments for beds made with a high foot end. The first two examples could appropriately be made in oak and the remainder in walnut or mahogany. The ends of Fig. 7 (3, 4) are framed up to take panels of solid wood, the latter having moulding mitred round the inside of the framing as in the section Fig. 7 (2). The posts at the foot of this example extend to the ground and have an applied plinth moulding. The rails of the "ladder-back" bedstead, Fig. 7 (5), are tenoned to a central upright, which is itself tenoned to the bottom rail. The construction of Fig. 7 (7) is given in Fig. 7 (6); the moulded capping is applied and fixed by dowels. The foot of Fig. 7 (8) is made of one piece of laminated board dowelled to a thinner rail to form the recessed plinth, while the head end consists of a similar panel screwed to two posts connected by a cross rail. Fig. 7 (12) is similar in construction and may be made with panels either of solid wood or of laminated board with clamped edges.

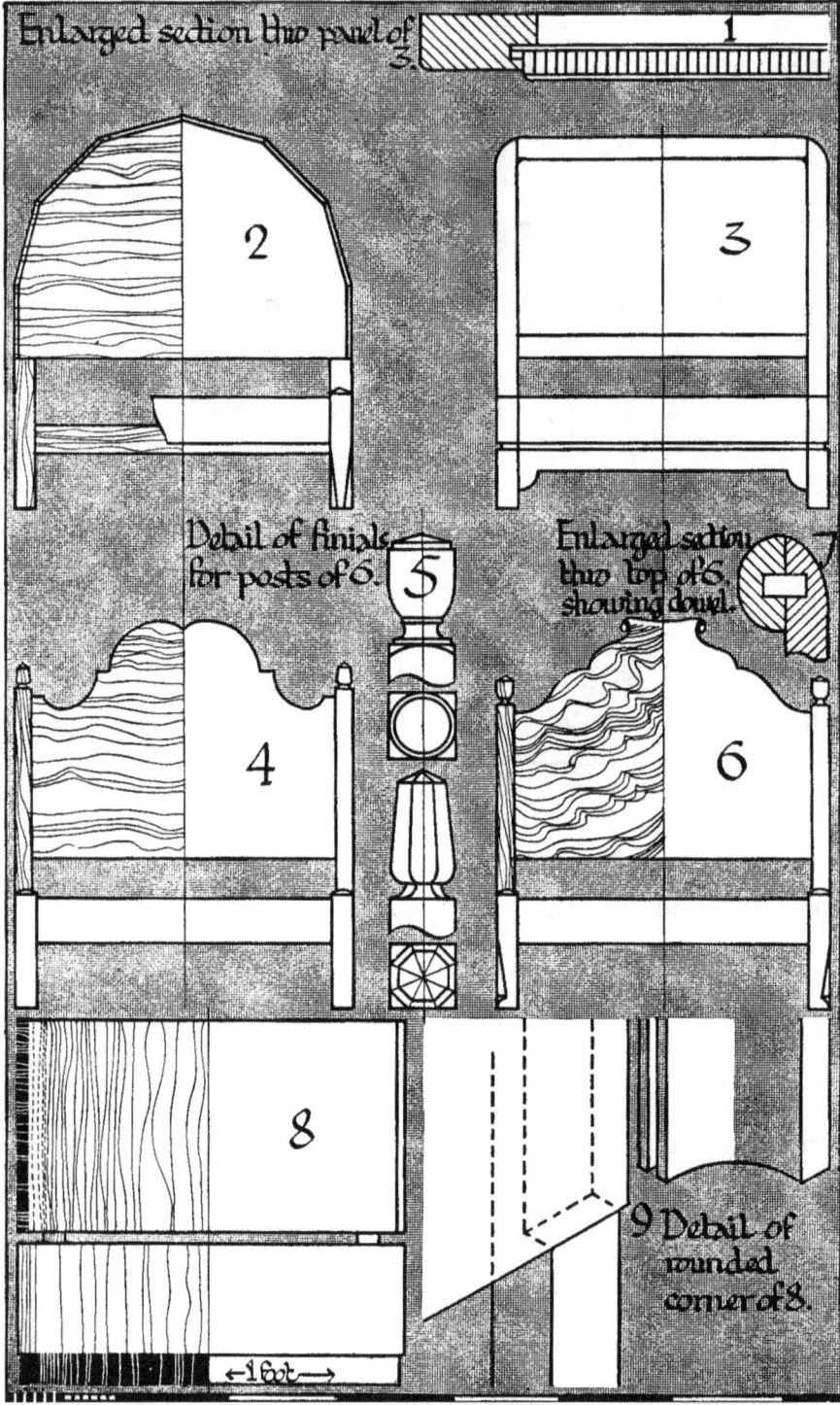

Fig. 6. Bedsteads with stump foot ends

PLATE XXI

BEDROOM FURNITURE IN WALNUT

Heal & Son Ltd.

BED-FITMENT IN ENGLISH SYCAMORE WITH EBONY FACINGS

Betty Joel Ltd.

PLATE XXII

ENGLISH OAK CHEST OF DRAWERS WITH STAND

Gordon Russell Ltd.

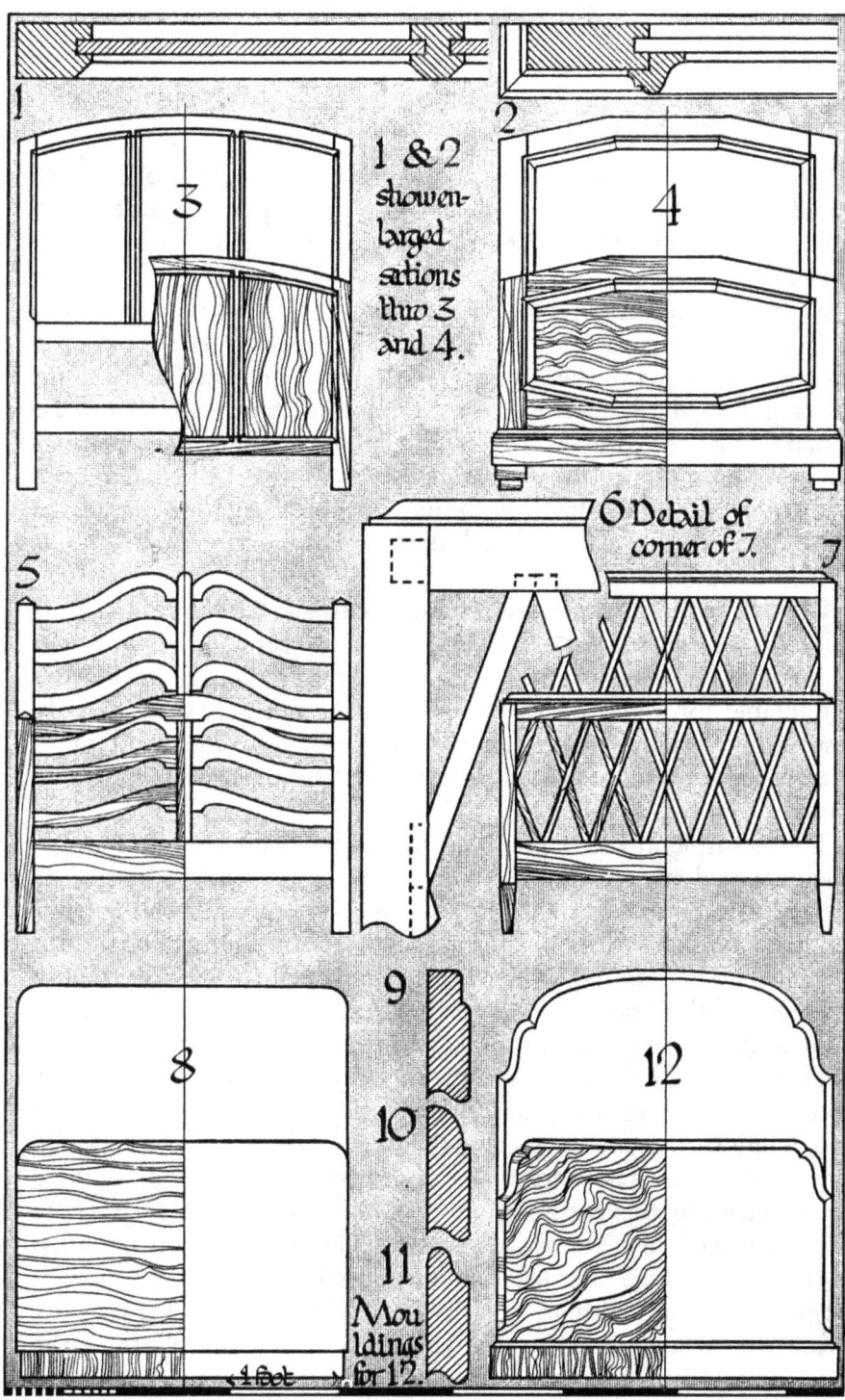

Fig. 7. Bedsteads with panelled or "slatted" head and foot ends

SECTION 2.—CHESTS OF DRAWERS

The average overall sizes for chests of drawers are 3′ 0″ to 3′ 6″ in width and height by 1′ 6″ deep; for the larger size a depth of 1′ 8″ is often preferable. The drawers should range from 5½″ to 9″ deep.

There are two methods of construction. The first, frequently used abroad, consists of making the drawers to the exact size and then gluing up the carcase with them in position. With the second method, which is the more usual practice, the carcase is made first, the drawer fronts fitted tightly into the openings and the backs of the drawers marked from the fronts. In both cases the carcase and drawers should be about $\frac{1}{32}$″ longer at the back; this enables a well-fitted drawer to tighten slightly as it is withdrawn.

Chests of Drawers with Dovetailed Carcase.—Fig. 1 (1-9) shows chests of drawers with a carcase made with simple lap, concealed lap, or secret-mitred dovetails. The last is preferable for veneered work as all end grain is covered. Oak, chestnut, or walnut would be suitable, either in the solid or as veneers. For a painted finish pine or American whitewood could be used.

The example in Fig. 1 (1-4) has the drawer rails and the bottom slip-dovetailed or tenoned between the carcase ends. These are grooved to take the drawer runners, which are tenoned to the front and back rails to form a frame as shown in the sectional plan Fig. 1 (2). The dust-board is ¼″ thick and fits into a groove round the inside of this frame. The division between the top drawers is tenoned at top and bottom and clamped to a rail screwed to the centre runner. Fig. 1 (5) shows the construction of a drawer. Slips, detailed in Fig. 1 (6), are glued to the drawer sides to increase the running surface and to receive the bottom, which is slot-screwed to the back rail. The bottoms of long drawers should be divided by a munting to prevent sagging. Fig. 1 (8) is made as a complete carcase screwed to a framed-up stand. Fig. 1 (9) is similar and is a 3′ 0″ square drawer unit for building up with other unit furniture. The plinth is faced with $\frac{3}{16}$″ black-stained hornbeam; it is set back ¼″ from the front, but is flush at the ends so that the plinth of the next unit may be butted against it to give the effect of a continuous base.

CONSTRUCTIONAL DETAILS

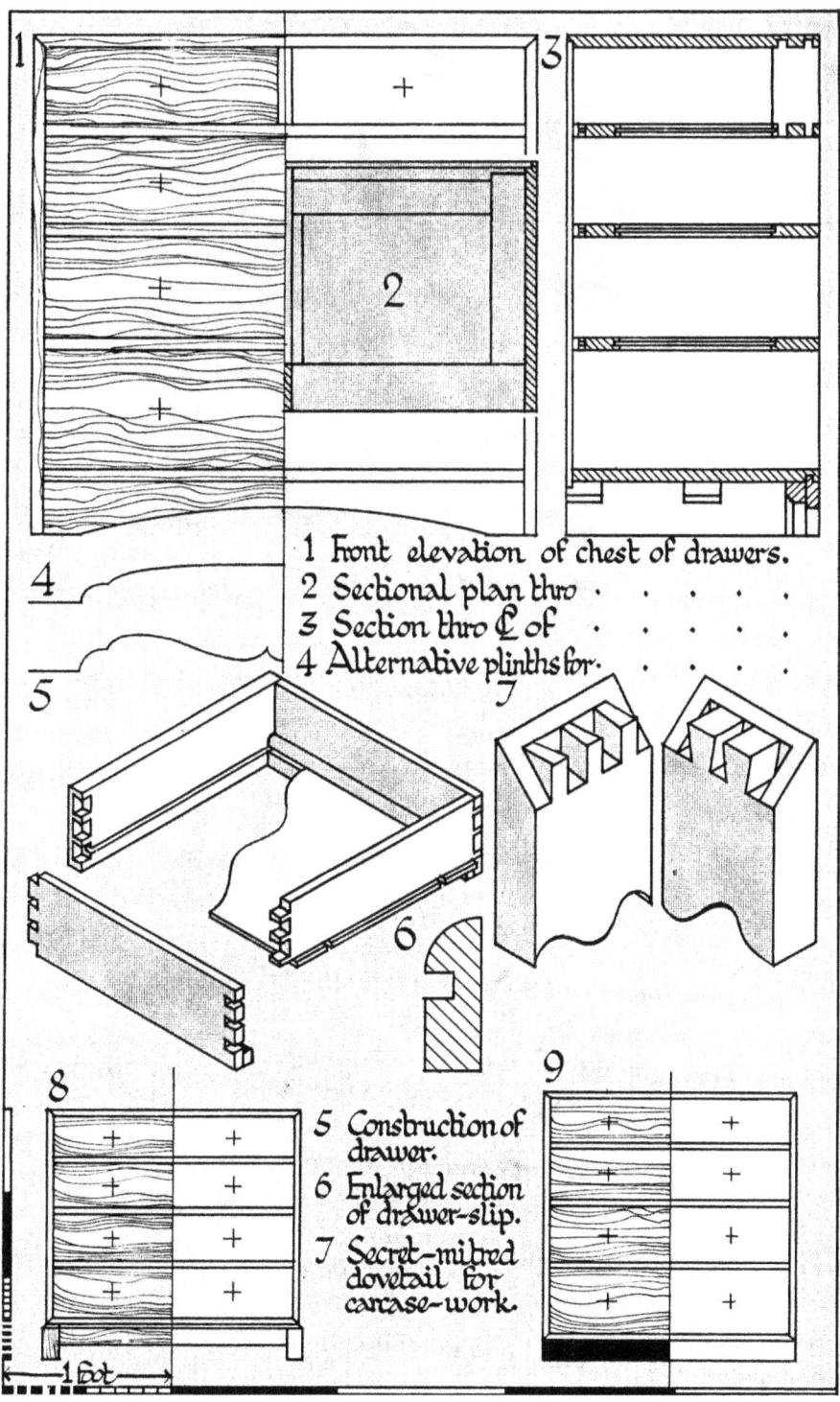

1 Front elevation of chest of drawers.
2 Sectional plan thro · · · · · ·
3 Section thro ℄ of · · · · · ·
4 Alternative plinths for · · · · ·
5 Construction of drawer.
6 Enlarged section of drawer-slip.
7 Secret-mitred dovetail for carcase-work.

Fig. 1. Chests of Drawers with dovetailed carcase construction

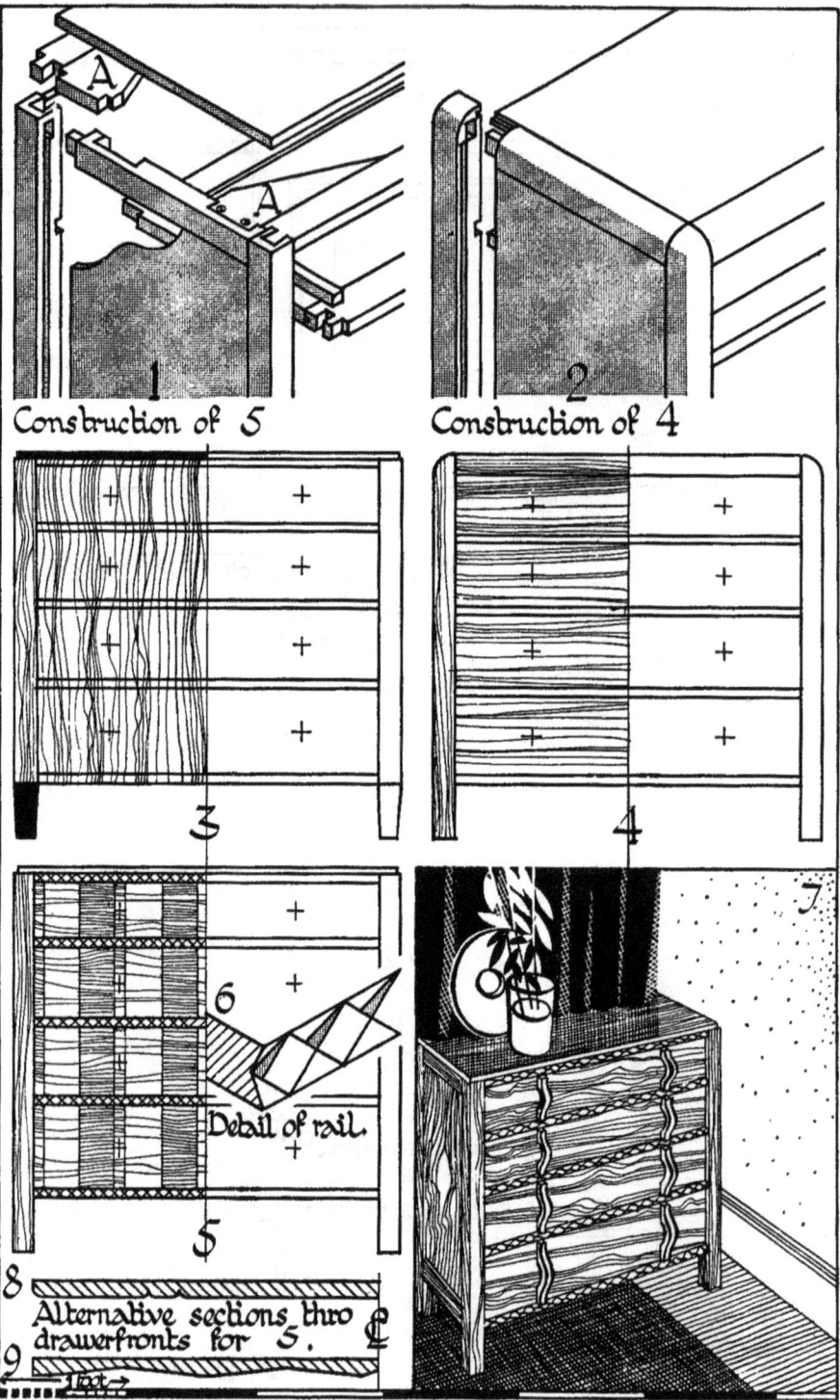

Fig. 2. Chests of Drawers with post and rail construction

Chests of Drawers with Post and Rail Construction.—

Fig. 2 (1) shows the construction of Fig. 2 (5); the ends are framed up to take a $\frac{3}{8}''$ panel and are joined by dovetailed rails, brackets (A, A) being glued to these to make a longer joint. The drawer rails are tenoned into the front posts and notched at the back. The drawers run between strips flush with the inner faces of the posts. The false top is slot-screwed from below. Fig. 2 (8, 9) give sections for the moulded drawer fronts; alternatively, they could be kept plain and the handles patterned as in Fig. 2 (7). Fig. 2 (2) gives the construction of Fig. 2 (4). The ends and top are $\frac{3}{4}''$ thick and are rebated into grooved posts and rails; if solid wood is used for these panels there should be a bead or shallow sinking round the edge to break the joint. The rounding of the corners is done after the carcase has been assembled. Fig. 2 (3) is similar in construction to Fig. 2 (5), but the ends are of 1" stuff rebated flush into the posts without cross rails. The front and ends are veneered with a wood with a rather definite stripe such as stripy walnut, sapele mahogany, or macassar ebony.

SECTION 3.—DRESSING MIRRORS

Adjustable Cheval and Toilet Mirrors.—Fig. 1 (1-11) shows examples of cheval mirrors and also of toilet mirrors of the " swing " and " triptych " types. The frames could appropriately be made in oak or walnut. The glass for the cheval mirrors should be about 5' 3" high by 1' 3" to 1' 6" wide; it is attached to a panelled backboard mounted on swing-movements as detailed in Fig. 1 (11). The framing of Fig. 1 (1) consists of two posts tenoned into shaped feet, which are connected by a halved rail, the brackets at the base being dowelled to the posts and tenoned to the feet. In Fig. 1 (2, 3) the uprights are joined above the mirror by a dovetailed rail and a second cross rail is tenoned below. The swing mirrors in Fig. 1 (5, 6) are similar in construction to the foregoing, but are without the top rail; in the case of small mirrors such as these the backboard may be of $\frac{1}{2}''$ ply. Fig. 1 (7, 8) shows " triptych " mirrors consisting of two wings hinged to a wide centre section. The moulded frames are mitred and keyed and the turned feet, detailed in Fig. 1 (10), screwed from below.

Frameless mirrors are attached to the backboard by means of metal clips, which are screwed to the edge of the wood and lap over the glass. Fig. 2 (1) shows three types of these.

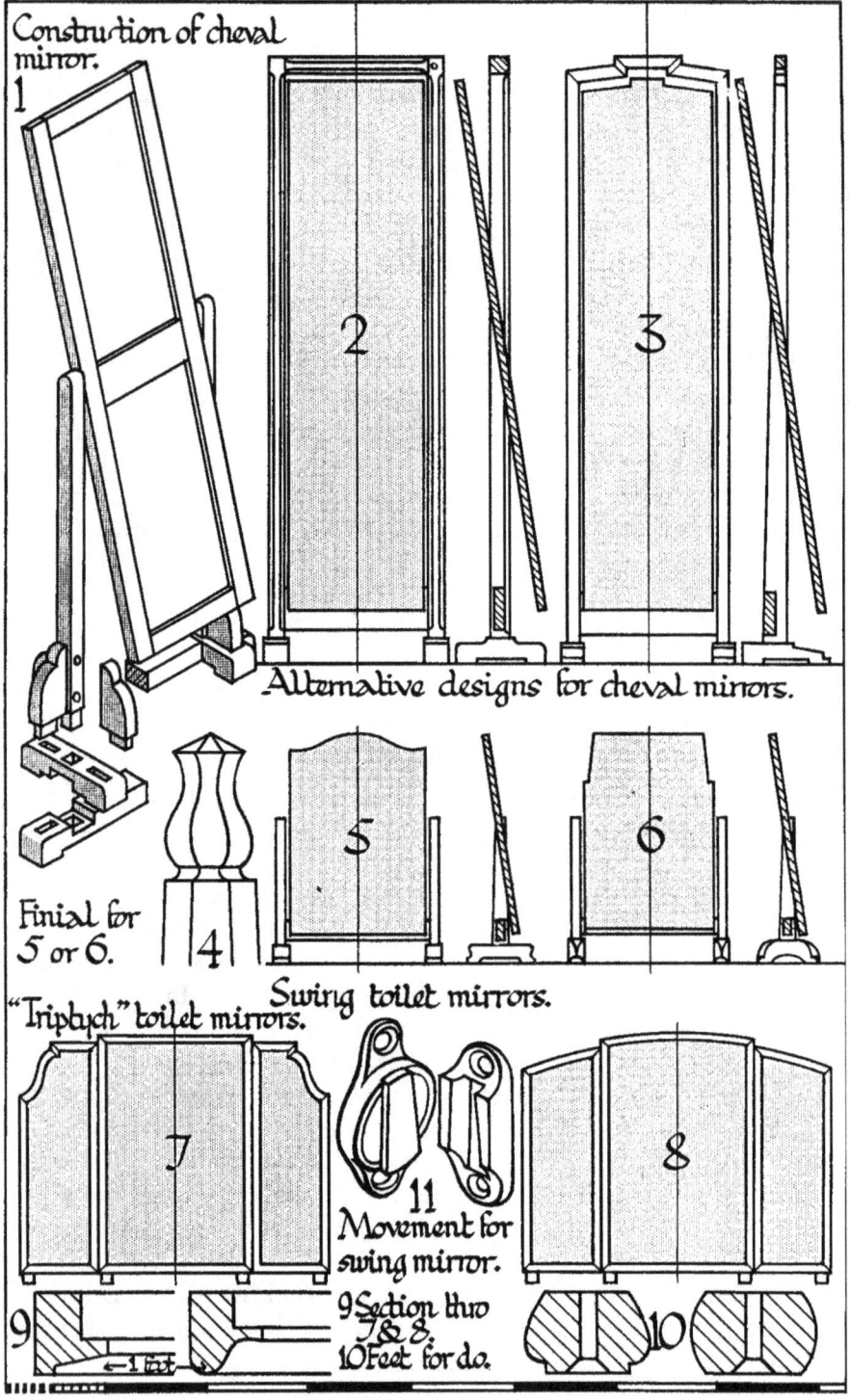

Fig. 1. Adjustable Cheval and Toilet Mirrors

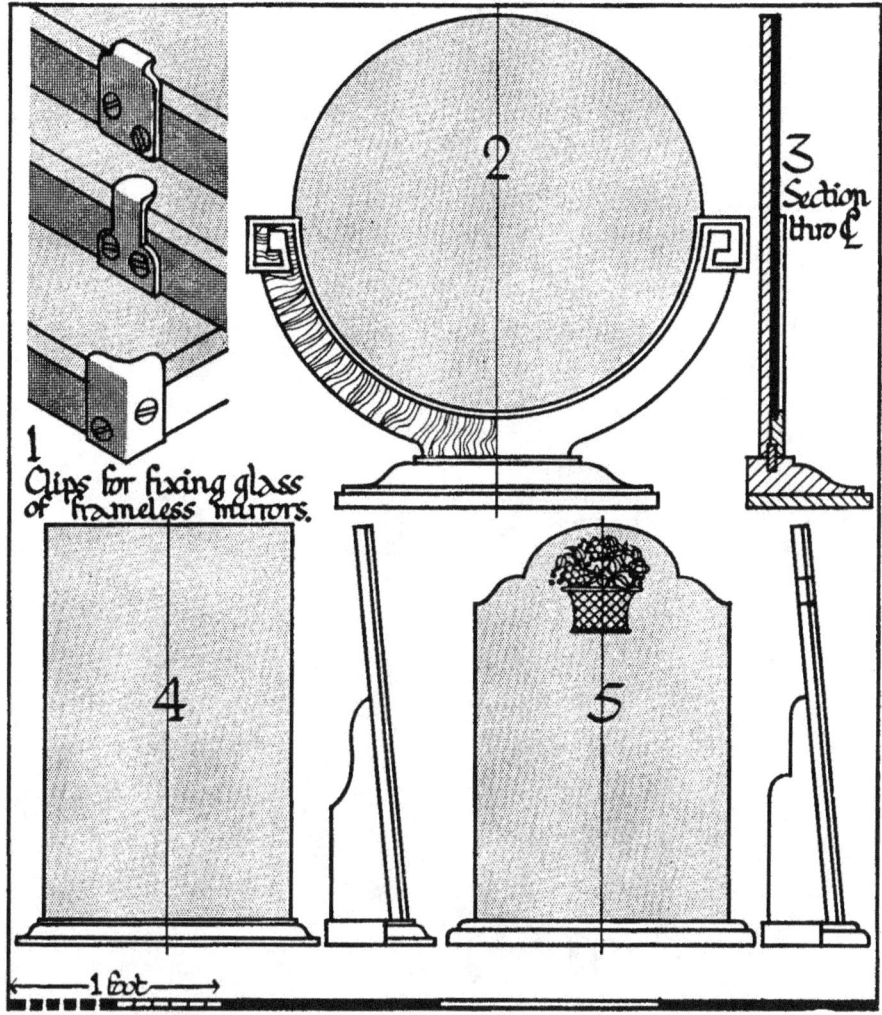

Fig. 2. Fixed Toilet Mirrors

Fixed Toilet Mirrors.—Further types of toilet mirror are illustrated in Fig. 2 (1-5). Fig. 2 (2) could be in mahogany and ebony, or a light wood such as amboyna or maple could be used and the line and scroll inlaid in ivory or holly. The backboard is of laminated board with the semicircular frame applied as a facing and dowelled to the moulded base. The bases of Fig. 2 (4, 5) are T-shaped in plan, the backboard being screwed to these and to shaped brackets. The decoration on the latter example is painted on the back of the glass before this is silvered.

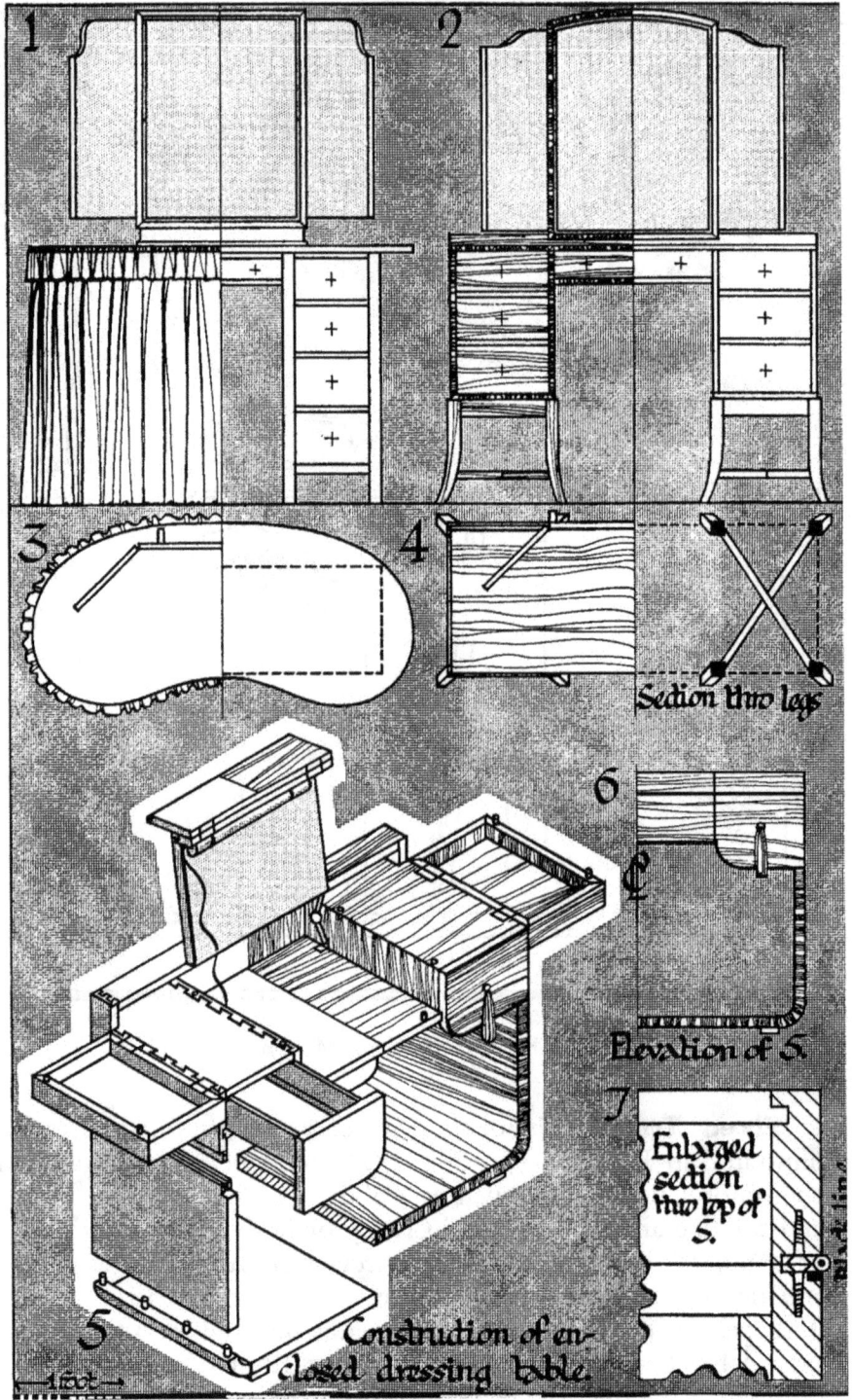

Fig. 1. Knee-hole Dressing Tables

PLATE XXIII

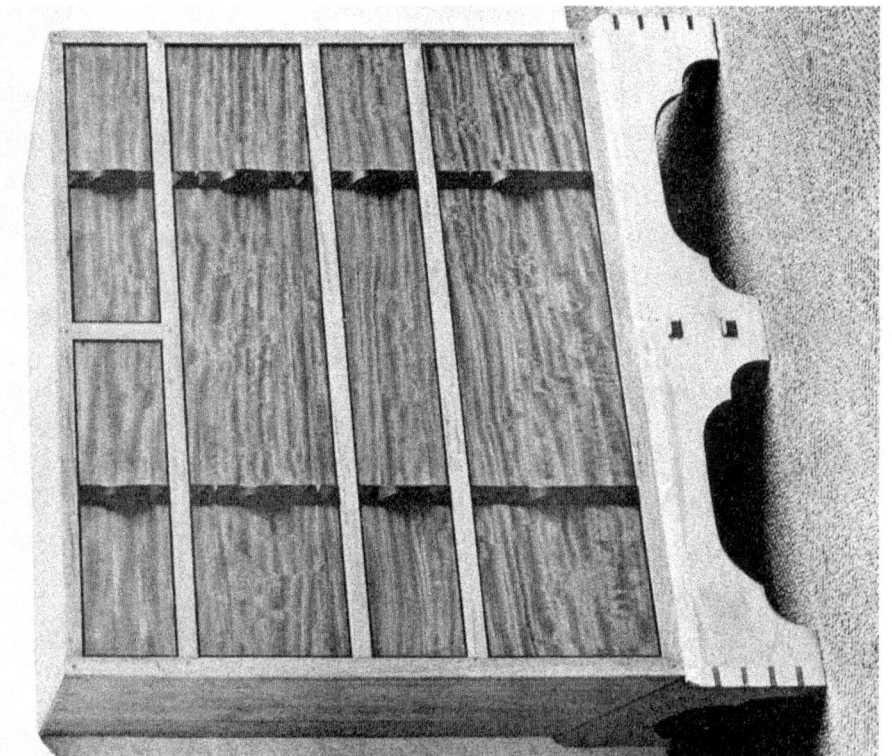

MAHOGANY CHEST OF DRAWERS WITH EBONY HANDLES

Gordon Russell Ltd.

CHEST OF DRAWERS IN WALNUT

Crossley & Brown

PLATE XXIV

Maurice Adams
Maurice Adams Ltd.

CUPBOARD CHEST AND DRESSING TABLE IN AUSTRALIAN WALNUT

Section 4.—Dressing Tables

Dressing tables of the knee-hole and pedestal types are dealt with in this section, together with some examples of dressing chests. The latter are useful where space must be saved, as they may be made with long drawers to take the place of a chest of drawers. The cheval and wing mirrors of the pedestal type of dressing table will give side and back as well as front views when dressing and also obviate the need for a separate full-length mirror.

The knee-hole and pedestal types must be at least 3' 6" wide with an overall depth of 1' 6". The former should be about 2' 5" high and the pedestals of the latter 6" to 9" lower.

Knee-hole Dressing Tables.—Fig. 1 (1-7) illustrates three dressing tables of the knee-hole type. The top of Fig. 1 (1) is kidney-shaped in plan and has a rod on the under side to take a curtain which meets in the centre. The edge is fitted with a 6" valance with a "gimp" finish. The drawer carcases are each framed up with four legs and are connected by dovetailed rails at front and back and also by a solid bottom below the centre drawer. This is slip-dovetailed between the side rails of the pedestals, which are made sufficiently deep for the purpose. The centre mirror swings in a dovetailed frame to which the wings are hinged, the mirror backs being of laminated board. The mirror is fixed by two long brackets screwed to the top of the dressing table and to the back of the frame. Fig. 1 (2) is in solid walnut or Indian laurel with cross-banded edges. It is made with a solid top to which the inside ends of the drawer carcases are tenoned and the outer ends lap-dovetailed. The stands are framed up separately, the legs being bevelled on the inside for tenoning to the stretchers. The triple mirror is made as in the previous example and the brackets screwed to the back of the carcase. Fig. 1 (5) shows the construction of an enclosed dressing table; it is veneered with a straight-grained wood such as stripy walnut or zebrano with inlaid lines of ebony. It may also be used as a writing table, the lid above the well being lowered and the trays folded in to form a level top as in Fig. 1 (6). The upper part has a continuous bottom to which are tenoned the ends and the sides of the well. The drawer sides are housed into the fronts so that the latter may hang below the bottom and conceal the edges of the carcase; they close flush with the front rail, which is hinged to the lifting top and is shown folded back. This top has a frameless mirror on the under side, with strip light above, and is

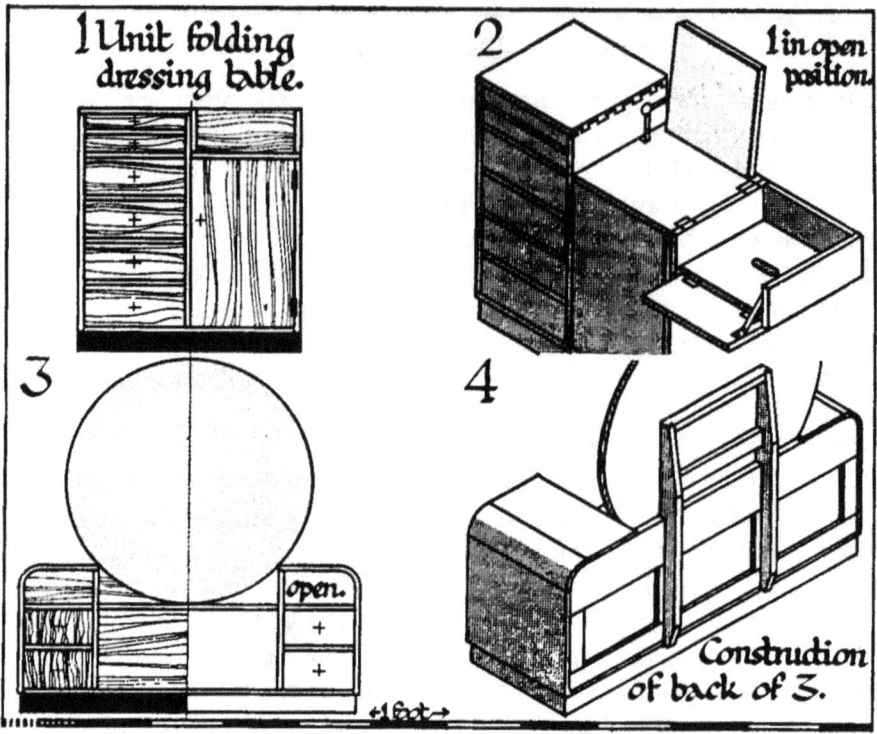

Fig. 2. Unit and Pedestal Dressing Tables

fitted with a friction-joint or stay to keep it at the desired angle. The trays are mitred or lap-dovetailed and are grooved for a flush top, as shown in section in Fig. 1 (7). The stand is made with rounded corners, detailed in Fig. 5 (1, 2), and is tongued to the upper carcase.

Unit and Pedestal Dressing Tables.—Fig. 2 (1) shows an enclosed dressing table made as a 3′ 0″ square unit; Fig. 2 (2) shows it in the open position. The carcase is lap-dovetailed with a tenoned division, the top of the right-hand section being "boxed-up" separately and hinged to the end; it has a fall-front supported by a stay. The back of the frameless mirror is hinged so that it may lie flat when the top is closed. Below is a cupboard with a flush door of veneered laminated board. The plinth is lap-dovetailed and is faced with black-stained hornbeam. Fig. 2 (3) has two pedestals connected by the base and by a framed back; between them is an adjustable shelf of wood or plate-glass. The construction of the back is shown in Fig. 2 (4), the mirror being hinged to the framed support and fitted with a stay at the bottom. Fig. 5 (3, 4)

PLATE XXV

DRESSING TABLE IN WALNUT

P. E. Gane Ltd.

PLATE XXVI

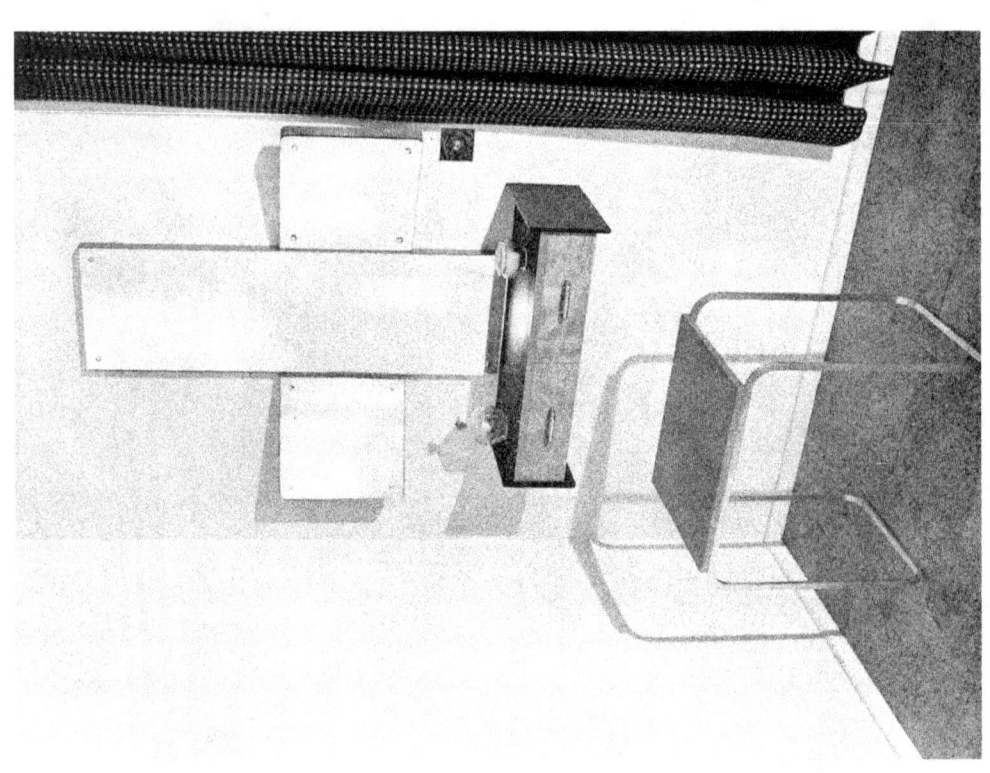

DRESSING FITMENT WITH TRIPLE MIRROR
P. E. Gane Ltd.

DRESSING TABLE IN WALNUT
Crossley & Brown

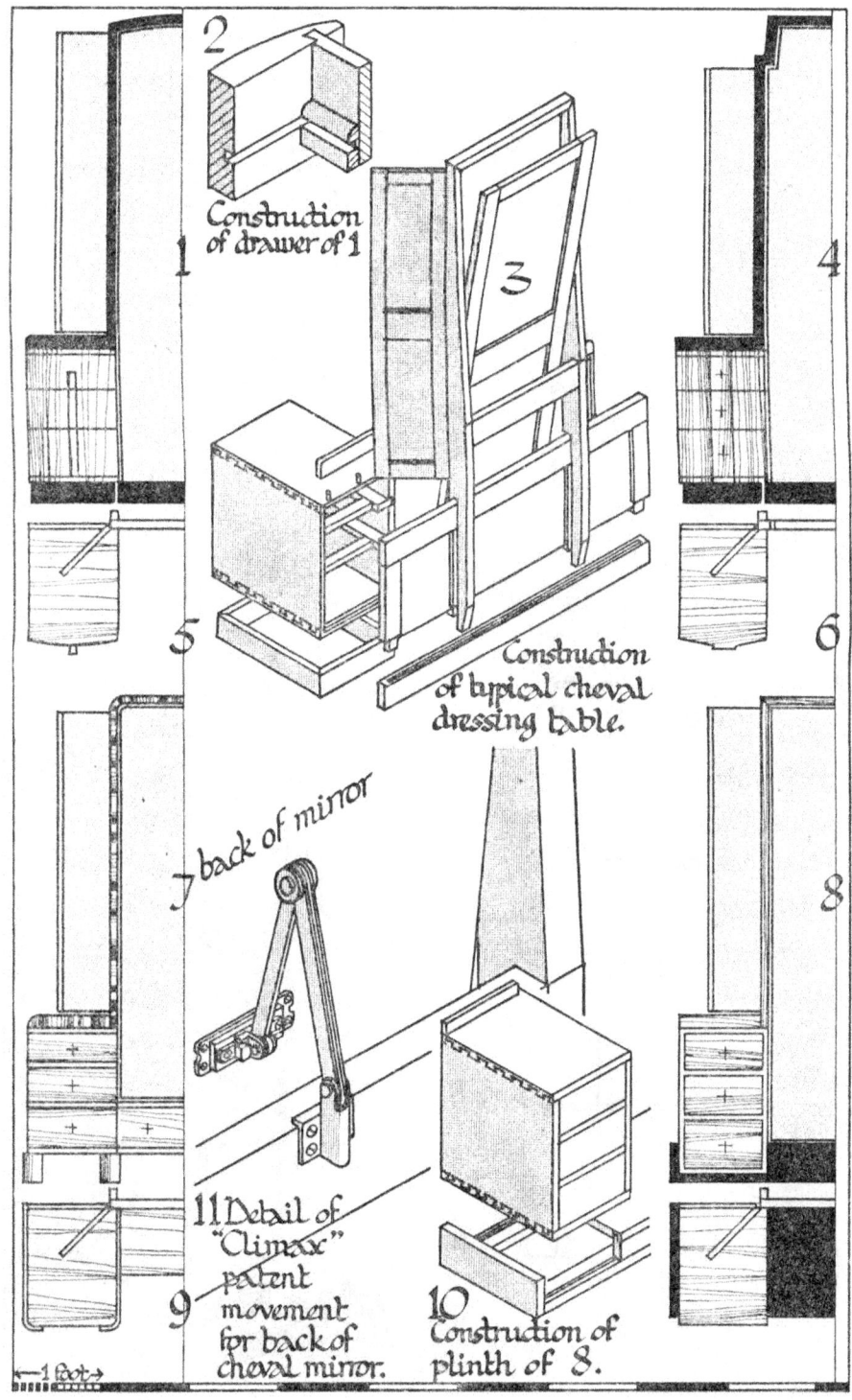

Fig. 3. Pedestal Dressing Tables with Cheval Mirror

116 DRESSING TABLES

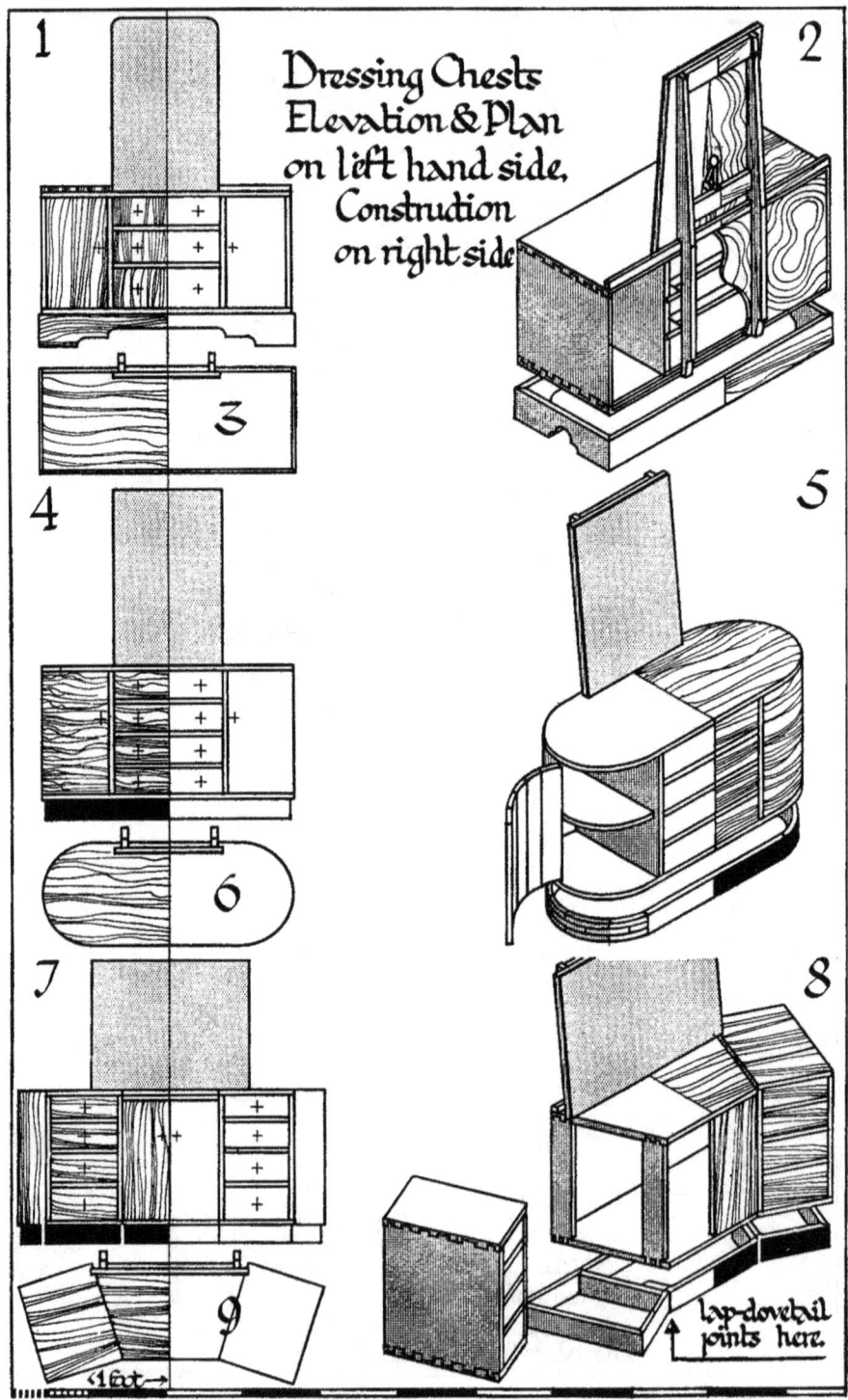

Fig. 4. Dressing Chests

CONSTRUCTIONAL DETAILS

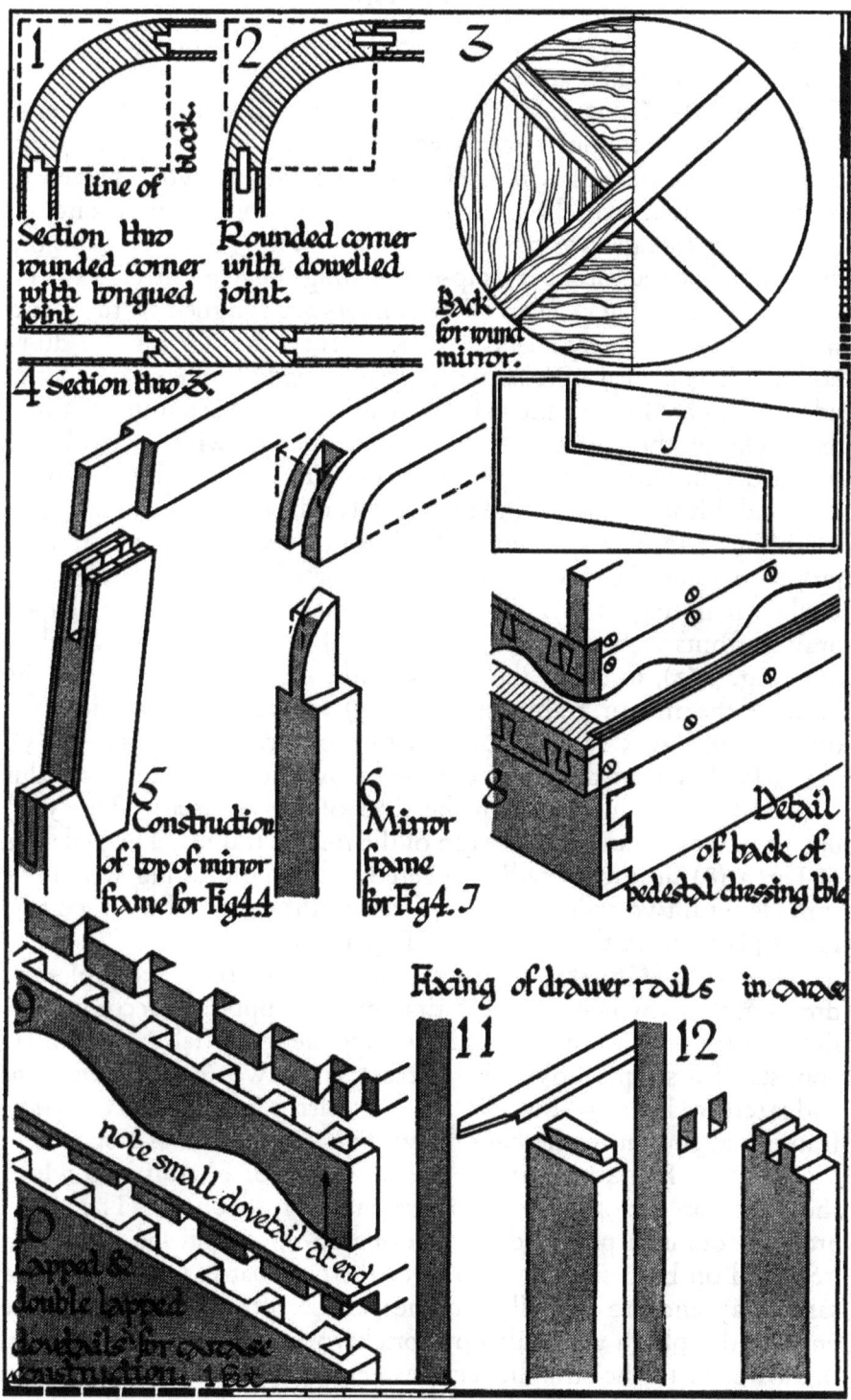

Fig. 5. Constructional details for Dressing Tables

detail the mirror back; it is made with two 3" rails halved together and grooved to take panels of ¾" stuff.

Pedestal Dressing Tables with Cheval Mirror.— Fig. 3 (1–11) gives four alternative treatments for pedestal dressing tables with cheval and wing mirrors. They are shown veneered in walnut with macassar ebony or a similar dark wood used as contrast. The drawer carcases are lap-dovetailed as in Fig. 5 (9 or 10), and the drawer rails fixed either by slip-dovetailing, detailed in Fig. 5 (11), or by tenoning, Fig. 5 (12). The runners are tongued to these and are connected by a rail at the back to form frames for the dust-boards. The cheval mirror swings in a tenoned frame to which the side mirrors are hinged and is fitted with a stay to keep it in position; the backs of the mirrors should be framed up with ¾" stuff and panelled. In Fig. 3 (1, 4) the pedestals are "tied" by the back only and this should therefore be framed and panelled as in Fig. 3 (3). With Fig. 3 (7, 8) a continuous back is not necessary as no strain is put upon it and the carcases are simply rebated for a filling of ⅜" ply, as shown in Fig. 5 (8). The two former examples have shaped drawer fronts worked from the solid with the sides slip-dovetailed, as in Fig. 3 (2), to cover the carcase ends. The canted sides for the head of the mirror frame in Fig. 3 (4) are cut one "inside" the other, as in Fig. 5 (7), and bridled to the uprights as in Fig. 5 (5). Fig. 3 (7) has a third drawer carcase below the cheval mirror; this is fixed by screwing through the sides of the pedestals. Fig. 5 (6) details the construction of the top of the mirror frame. The pedestals of Fig. 3 (8) fit into a cradle veneered with a contrasting wood. It is made with two rails lap-dovetailed into the ends and tongued to a raised platform in the centre as in Fig. 3 (10).

Dressing Chests.—Fig. 4 (1–9) shows some examples of dressing chests which combine drawer and cupboard accommodation. Oak or walnut would be suitable materials. Fig. 4 (1) consists of a simple dovetailed carcase with two tenoned divisions and is screwed to a cut-out plinth. The mirror is hinged to a vertical framing as shown in the back view, Fig. 4 (2), and has a stay as in Fig. 3 (11). Fig. 4 (4) has a top and bottom of ⅞" stuff into which the divisions enclosing the drawers are stub-tenoned. The doors are a quadrant in plan and are "coopered-up" as in Fig. 4 (5) and veneered on both sides; the ends of the cupboards are made in the same way and are dowelled to the carcase top and bottom. The ends of the plinth are built up "brickwork fashion" and tongued or dowelled to the straight section. Fig. 4 (7) is made up of three dovetailed carcases screwed together as shown in the plan, Fig. 4 (9).

PLATE XXVII

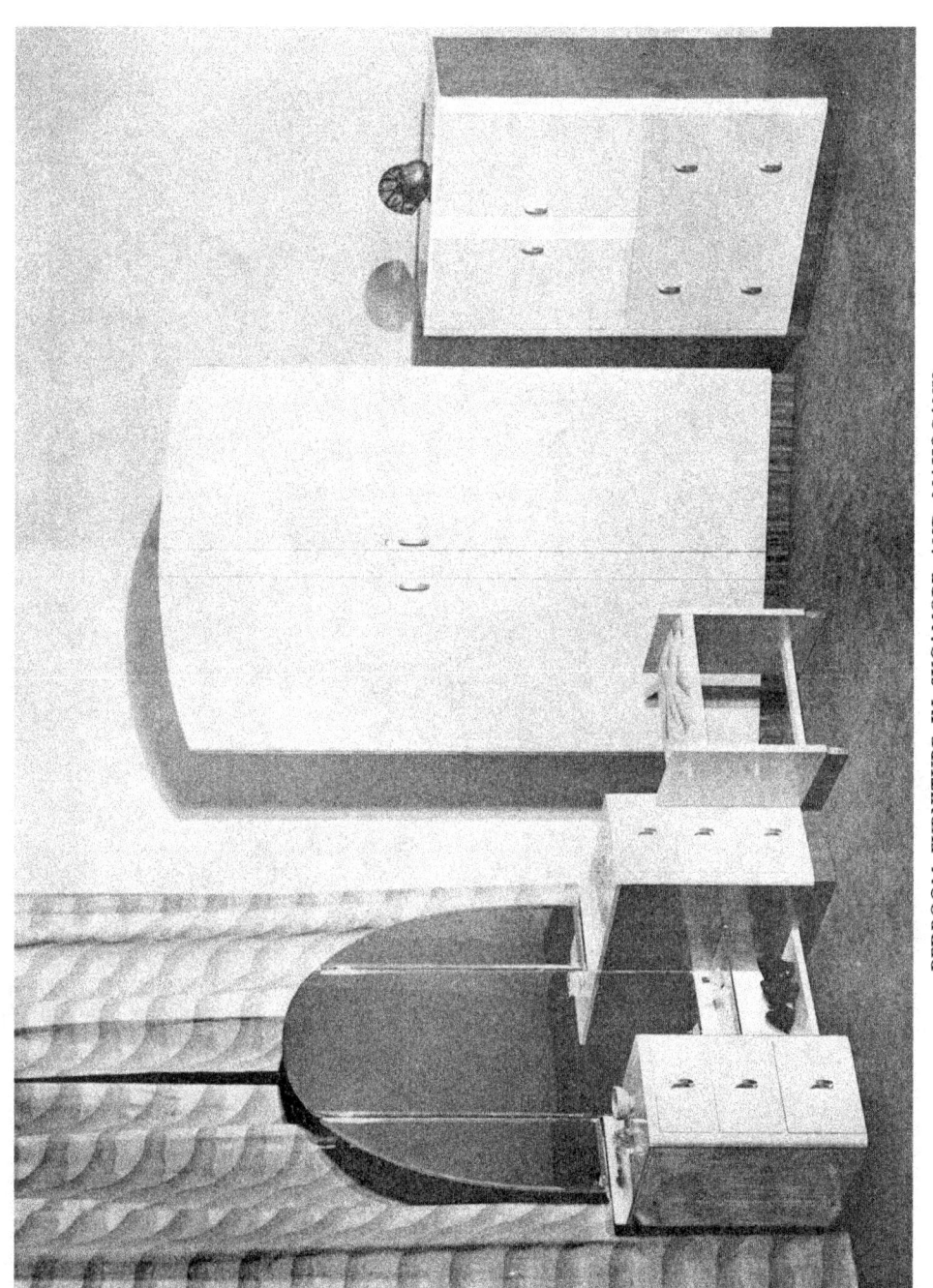

BEDROOM FURNITURE IN SYCAMORE AND MAHOGANY

The Bath Cabinet Makers Co. Ltd.

PLATE XXVIII

DRESSING CHEST AND WARDROBE IN OAK

P. E. Gane Ltd.

Fig. 1. A Wardrobe in sycamore with walnut plinth [Fig. 3 (6)]

The plinth of this example has a straight rail at the back, and the section under the cupboard in front is made with a lap-dovetailed angle and is screwed to the cross rails.

Section 5.—Wardrobes

Wardrobes are usually made 3' 0" to 3' 6" wide by 1' 6" deep overall. For the accommodation of ladies' dresses the height inside should be not less than 5' 6". If the whole interior is used for hanging space the latter width would enable two rows of coat or dress hangers to be used side by side. Alternatively, the wardrobe could be made deeper and the rod for hangers fitted parallel with the front. A useful arrangement for a 3' 6" wardrobe is to use one half for hanging and to fit the other with trays, shelves, etc. Some suggestions for an interior of this type are given in Fig. 4.

Wardrobes with Post and Rail Construction.—Fig. 2 (1-8) shows wardrobes for oak or chestnut. They are framed

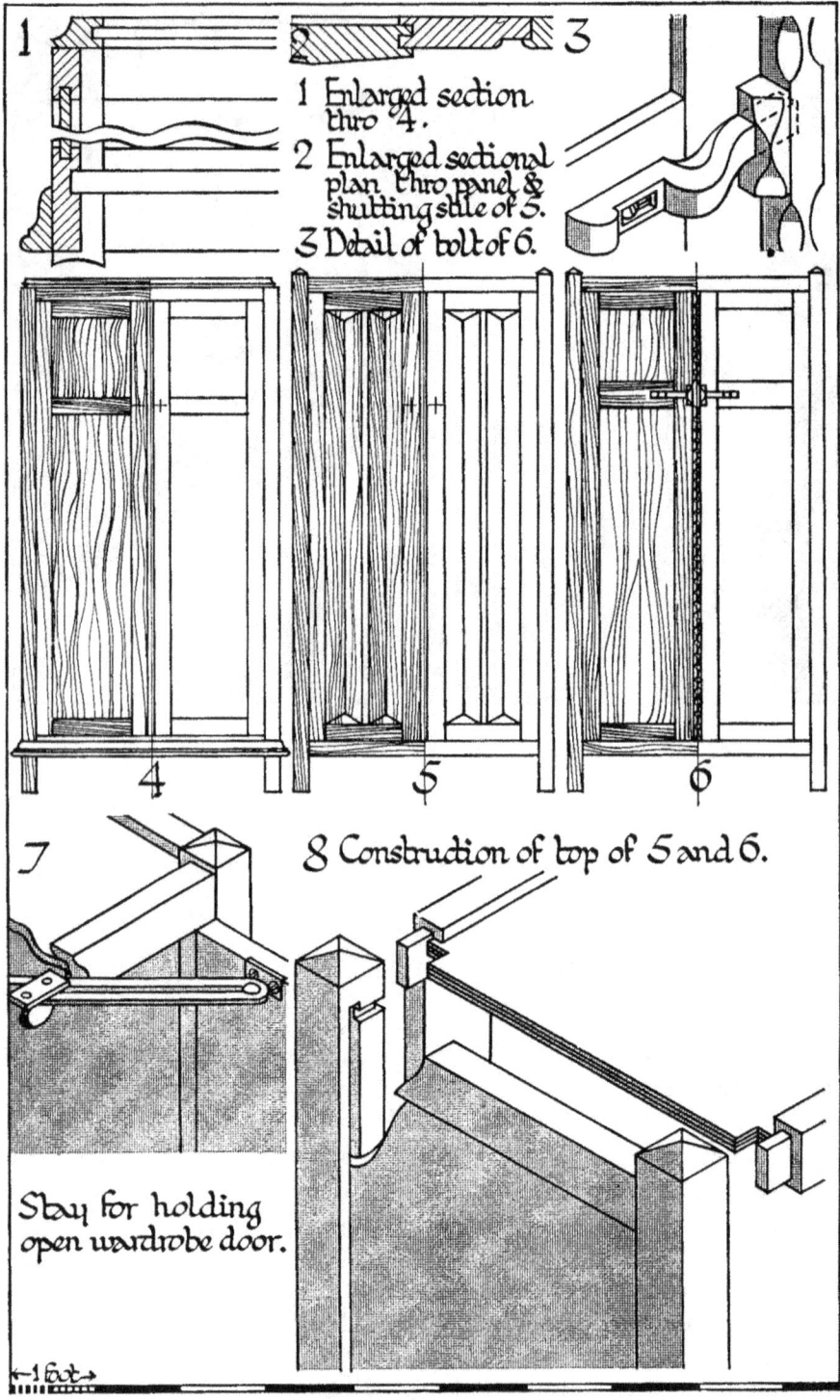

Fig. 2. Wardrobes with post and rail construction

PLATE XXIX

WARDROBE IN MAHOGANY

J. Henry Sellers

PLATE XXX

WARDROBE IN CHERRY WITH WALNUT HANDLES AND BOX AND WALNUT INLAY
Gordon Russell Ltd.

up with posts and rails and panelled, the ends having a third rail dividing them into two panels. The construction of Fig. 2 (4) is shown in the section Fig. 2 (1); the top consists of a moulded frame grooved to take a ply panel. The door panels of Fig. 2 (5) are planed into facets to give a contrast of light and shade as detailed in the section Fig. 2 (2), which also shows the shutting joint. The construction of the top of this example is given in Fig. 2 (8), the rails being grooved for a panel which is notched into the posts. Fig. 2 (6) has a framed centre division which is tenoned at top and bottom and projects $\frac{7}{8}''$ beyond the doors to receive the wooden bolts, detailed in Fig. 2 (3). These are slotted at the outer end for a round-headed screw, the other end passing through a block on the edge of the door. This and the edge of the division could have a simple gouge-cut pattern. The backs of these wardrobes should be panelled or "munted" and screwed into a rebate on the posts and rails.

Wardrobes with Dovetailed Carcase Construction.— Fig. 3 (2, 3, 4) each consist of three lap- or secret-mitred dovetailed carcases screwed together and to a plinth with a break-front. The centre carcase is intended for hanging while the wings are fitted with fillets for adjustable shelves. Fig. 3 (2) is for painting or ebonizing and has doors of solid wood clamped at top and bottom and fluted as shown in section in Fig. 3 (1). Fig. 3 (3, 4) are in walnut or Indian silver-grey wood, the doors being of laminated board with mitred clamps and veneered in a simple pattern. The splayed centre door of the latter example consists of two pieces of laminated board tongued to an upright. The carcases of Fig. 3 (5, 7) are also dovetailed and the doors are veneered in oak or walnut with inlaid lines of ebony. Fig. 3 (8, 9) show alternative treatments for mahogany. Fig. 3 (6) has the ends tongued into rounded corner posts and a dovetailed top and bottom.

Fitted Wardrobes.—Any of the foregoing examples could be adapted for interior fittings as shown in Fig. 4 (1-6), a width of 3' 6" being necessary. The left-hand section has a rod for clothes hangers at the top and shoe rails below. The right-hand section has a shelf at the top for hats, etc., and four trays and four small and two large drawers underneath. The construction of a tray is shown in Fig. 4 (3), the fillet being removed to show the dovetailing. Fig. 4 (4) gives alternative detail, and Fig. 4 (5) shows a simpler type of tray with a $\frac{1}{2}''$ ply bottom and three sides screwed from below and dovetailed at the back. Fig. 4 (2) illustrates three methods of fitting trays; the bottom three have the sides grooved to fit fillets

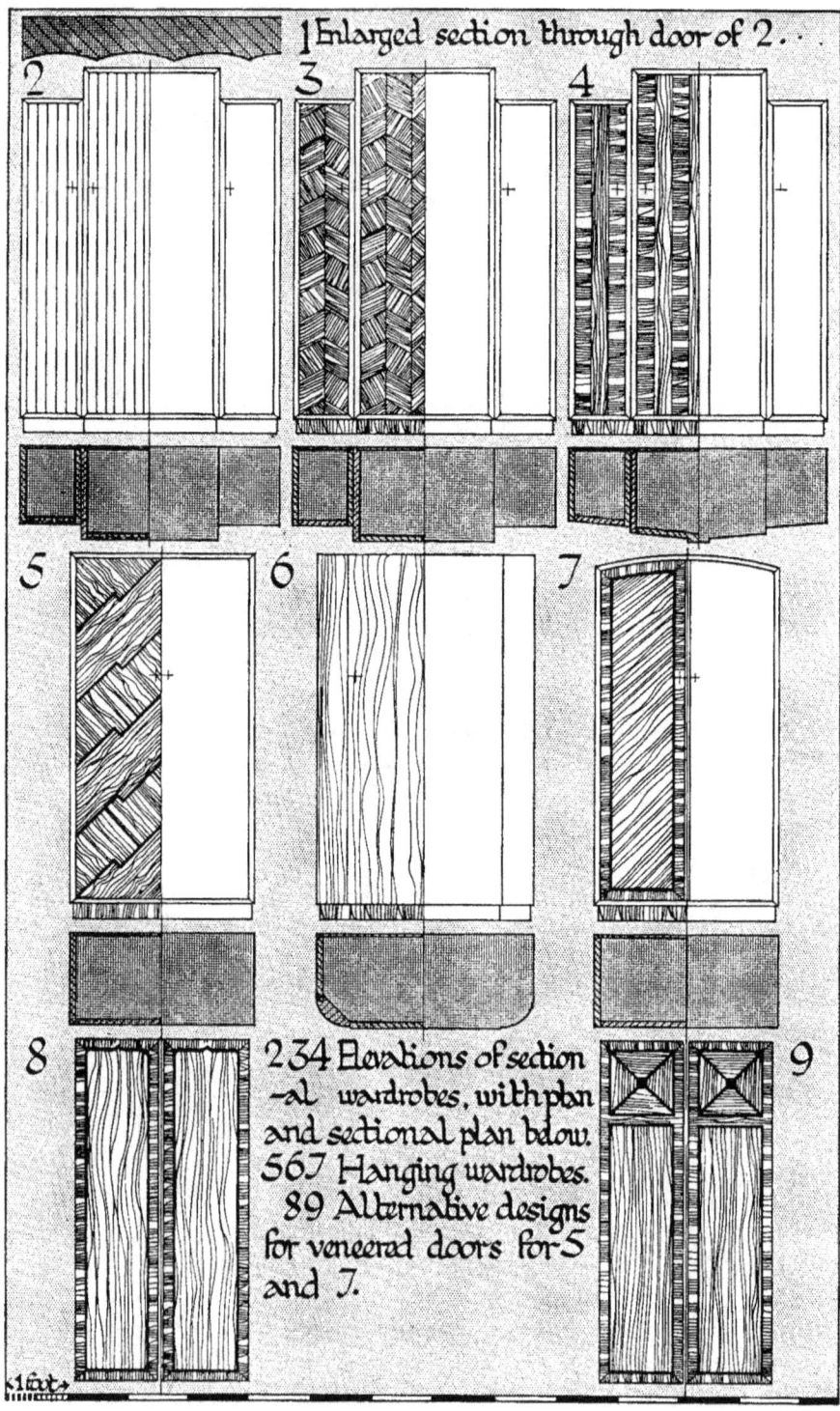

Fig. 3. Wardrobes with dovetailed carcase construction

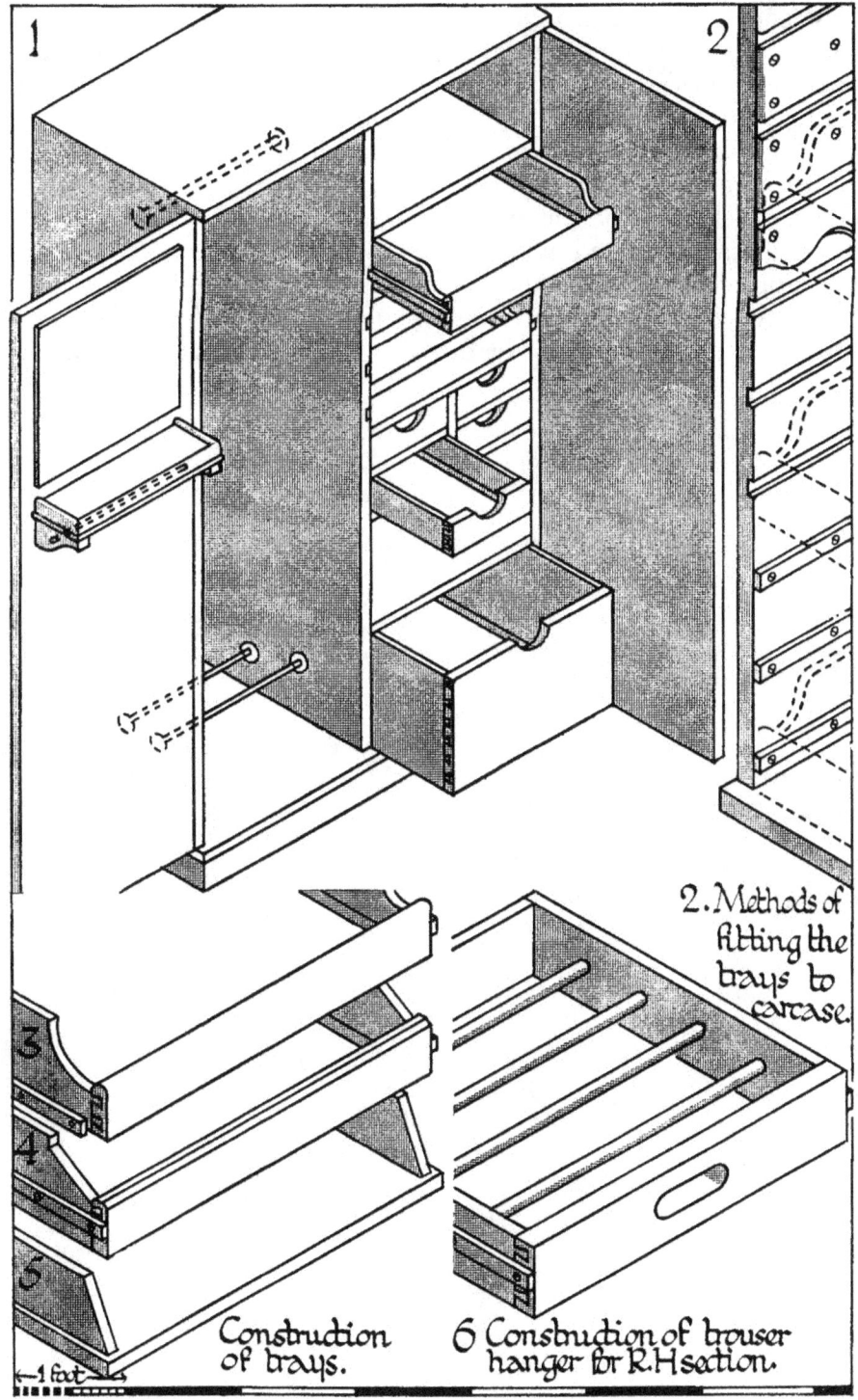

Fig. 4. Interior Fittings for Man's Wardrobe

screwed to the carcase, in the next three the fillets are screwed to the trays and the carcase grooved, while in the top three the grooves are formed by screwing strips of wood to the carcase. The drawers could be replaced by a trouser hanger as shown in Fig. 4 (6); this is fitted like a tray and consists of a dovetailed frame with $\frac{3}{4}''$ dowels glued into holes in the sides. The left-hand door of the wardrobe is fitted with a small frameless mirror with a tie-rail below. Alternatively one of the doors could have a full-length mirror. Both should be fitted with a stay as detailed in Fig. 2 (7). In wardrobes with drawers or trays it is essential that the doors should be hinged over the carcase ends to enable them to be withdrawn. Otherwise a false end must be fitted to give the necessary clearance.

Fig. 1. A Group of Garden Furniture [Seat, Fig. 2 (7), Chair, Fig. 5 (10), Table, Fig. 7 (4)]

CHAPTER V

FURNITURE FOR THE GARDEN

THIS chapter suggests a variety of treatments for seats, chairs, and tables for use in the garden. They are of simple and robust construction, decorative interest being obtained chiefly by shaping and by the " latticing " of rails and slats. All the examples illustrated are suitable either for hard wood or for soft wood with a painted finish.

The best hard woods for garden furniture are teak and English oak. There is a good range of the former available from Indian and African sources; it contains a preservative oil which renders it particularly suitable for outside work, " Moulmein " teak being rather richer in oil and darker in colour than the African varieties. Oak will eventually weather to a silver-grey colour; this may be

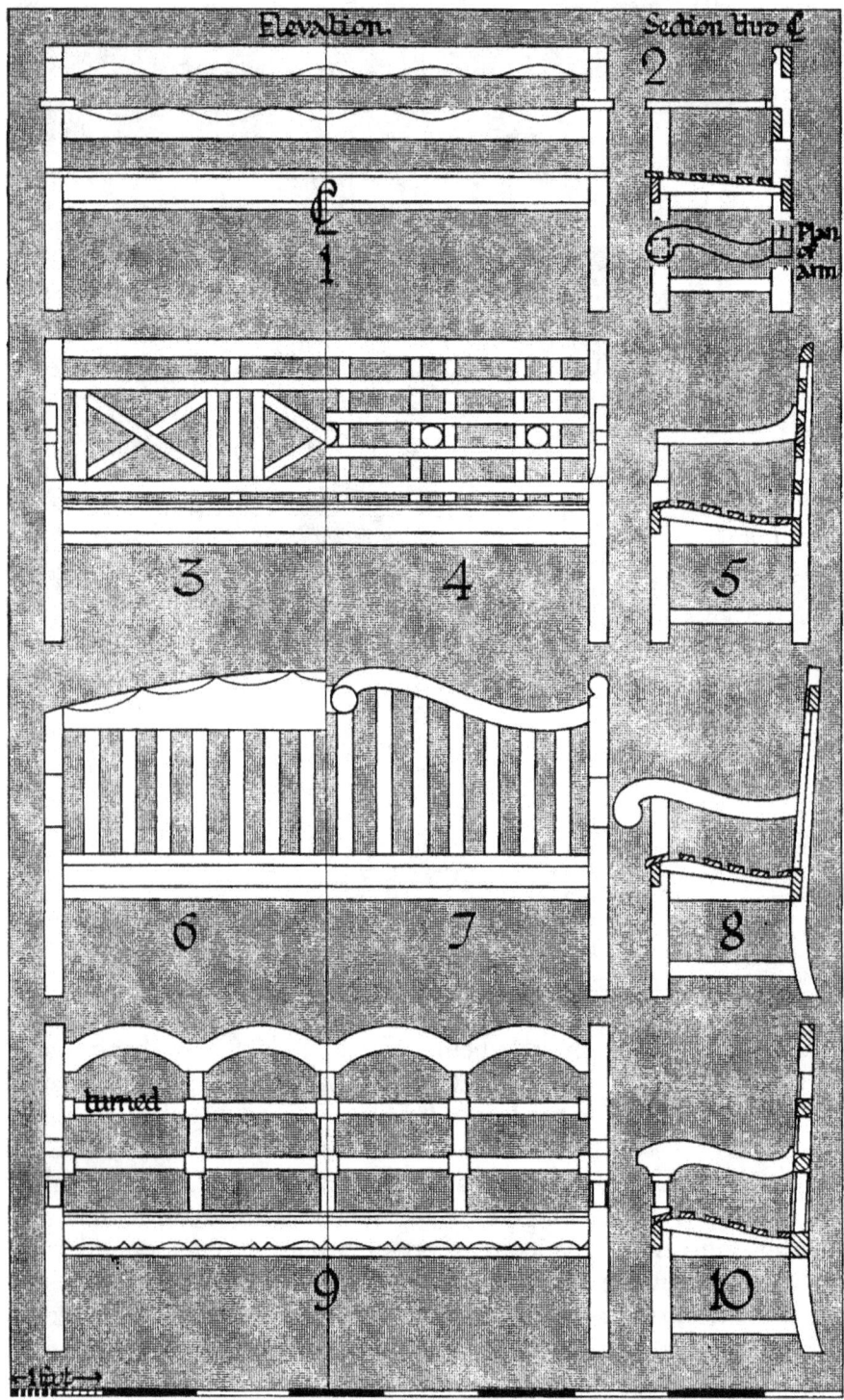

Fig. 2. Garden Seats

hastened by painting it with quicklime mixed with water, which will assist the bleaching process and will also cut into the soft parts of the grain and give an attractive ribbed texture. Alternatively, oak may be polished with raw linseed oil, which produces a good dull polish but darkens the wood considerably.

In the garden a gay and colourful effect is not out of place, and painted garden furniture has many interesting possibilities beyond the usual treatment in white or green. Pinks, reds, and vivid blues could be used and harmonized or contrasted with brightly coloured fabrics in garden umbrellas, deck-chairs, etc. The most suitable material for painted work is yellow deal, as free from knots as possible. It should have a priming coat of red-lead paint and at least three undercoats before the finishing colour.

Ordinary glue should never be used for garden furniture. Joints may be secured and made waterproof either with very thick white-lead paint or with a mixture of red lead and gold size. The wedging or pegging of tenons will give added strength and, for work in hard wood, may be employed as a decorative feature.

Garden Seats.—Fig. 2 (1-10) shows four types of garden seat in front elevation and section, Fig. 2 (4, 7) giving alternative backs for Fig. 2 (3, 6) respectively. The long rails are stub- or through-tenoned to the end framing and the arms tenoned to the back and to the top of the front leg. A centre rail should be tenoned from front to back to prevent the seat sagging. This consists of $2\frac{1}{2}"$ by $\frac{3}{4}"$ battens fixed either by pocket-screwing from below or by sinking the screw head in a hole on the upper side and filling this with a pellet; a length of pelleting is shown in Fig. 3 (6). The waved bevelling on the back of Fig. 2 (1) is done with a spokeshave, the construction of this example being detailed in Fig. 3 (1, 5). The backs of Fig. 2 (3, 4) are built up by halving and tenoning to the outer rails and the corners of the arm and back made with a pegged dovetail as in Fig. 3 (2, 3) respectively. Fig. 2 (9) has a plain turned detail, the long rails being continuous and tenoned to the ends. They are connected by short turned sections made with a 1" "pin" at either end for dowelling to the square blocks.

Garden Chairs.—Fig. 4 (1-10) shows various small chairs for garden use. Fig. 4 (1) follows normal practice in chair construction and has a back shaped from the solid and a slatted seat. The back and seat of Fig. 4 (2) are of canvas and may be removed in wet weather. The material for the back has the ends doubled over and sewn to form a tube which slips over the turned uprights, while the

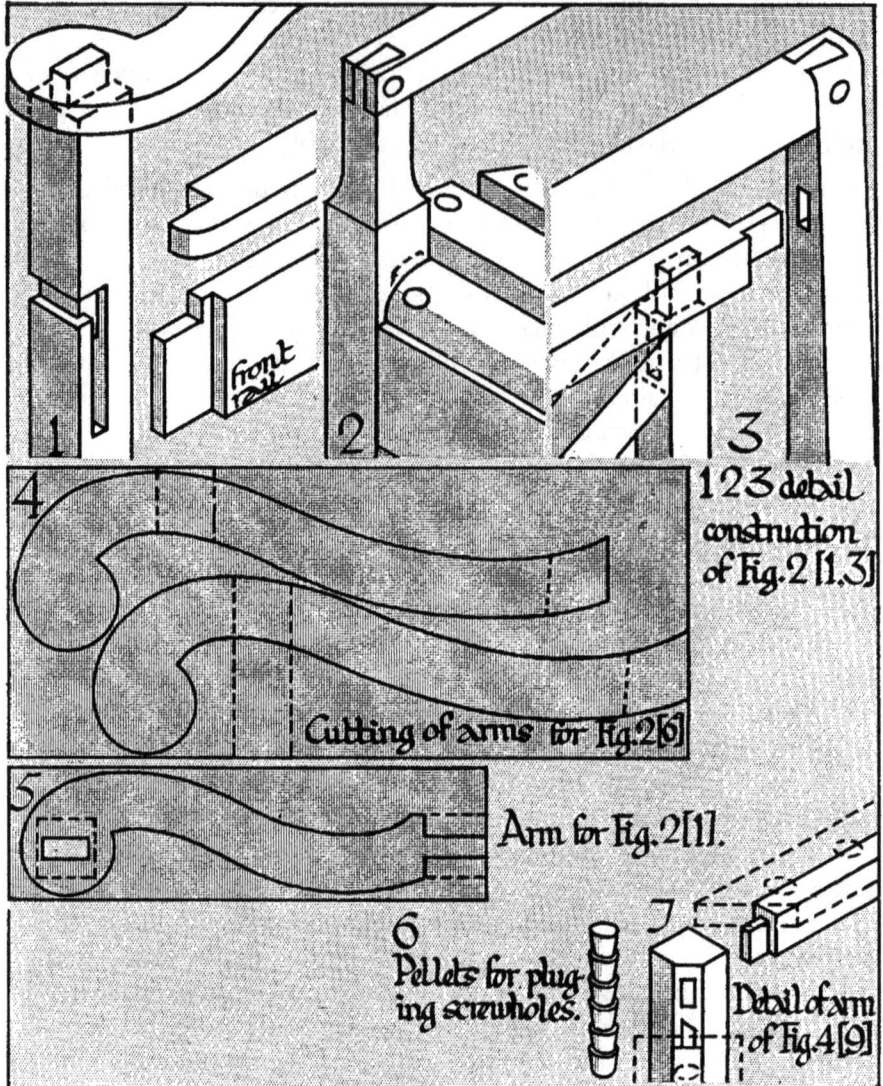

Fig. 3. Constructional details for Figs. 2 and 4

seat has rods at either end fitting into slots in the legs. Fig. 4 (3, 4) show the construction of two types of folding chair. The seat of the former is pivoted at the front and slotted to fit over a ¾″ dowel fixed between the uprights of the back. Fig. 4 (4) folds like a deck-chair and is opened by hooking the arms over projecting bolts. The arm-chairs in Fig. 4 (7, 8) are made 2′ 4″ high overall so that they will fit under a table of the type shown in Fig. 7 (12). Fig. 4 (7)

PLATE XXXI

GARDEN SEATS IN TEAK

Heal & Son Ltd.

PLATE XXXII

GARDEN TABLE IN TEAK

Wrinch & Sons Ltd.

TEAK TABLE DESIGNED FOR THE TERRACE OF THE HOUSE OF COMMONS

H.M. Office of Works

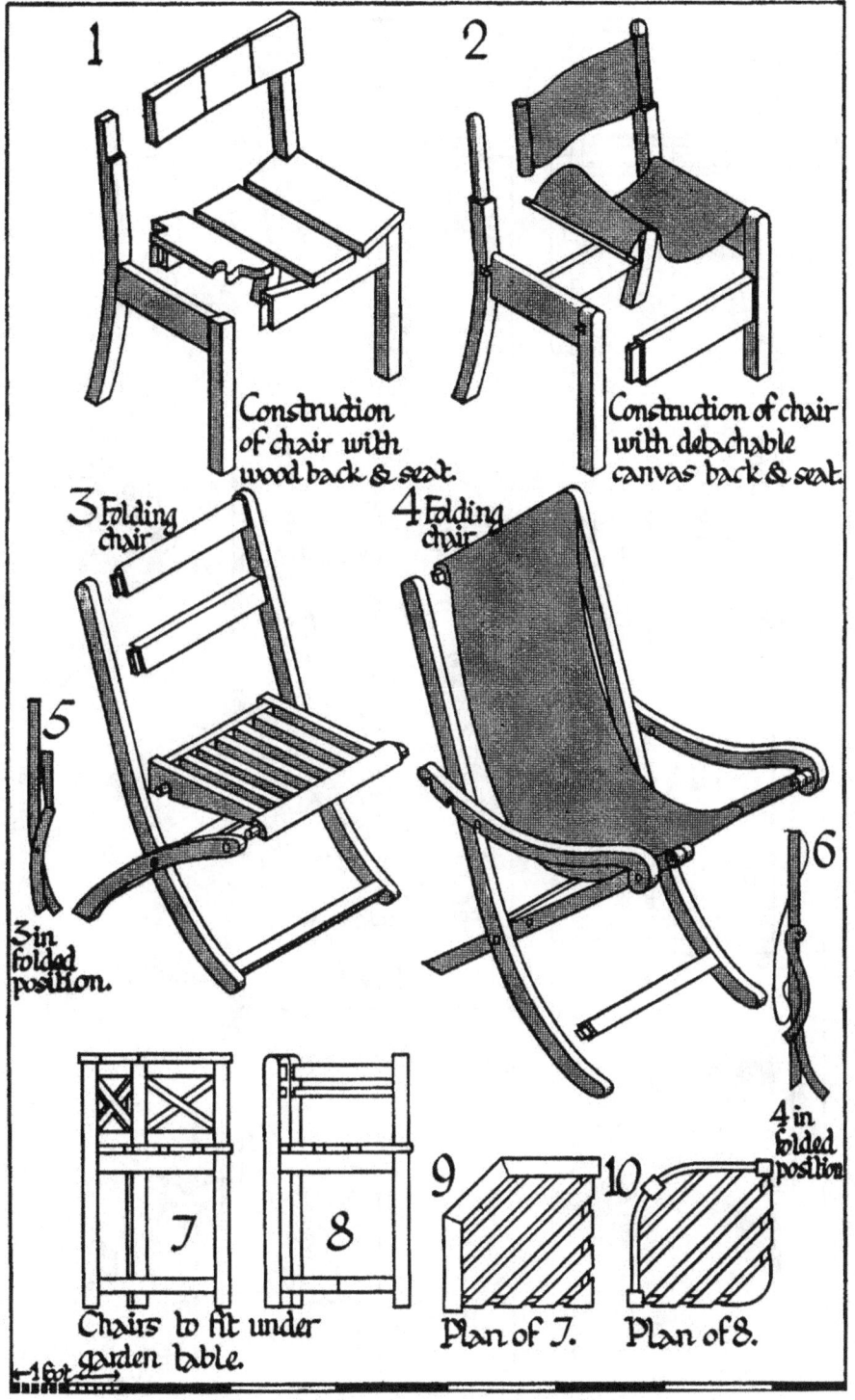

Fig. 4. Garden Chairs

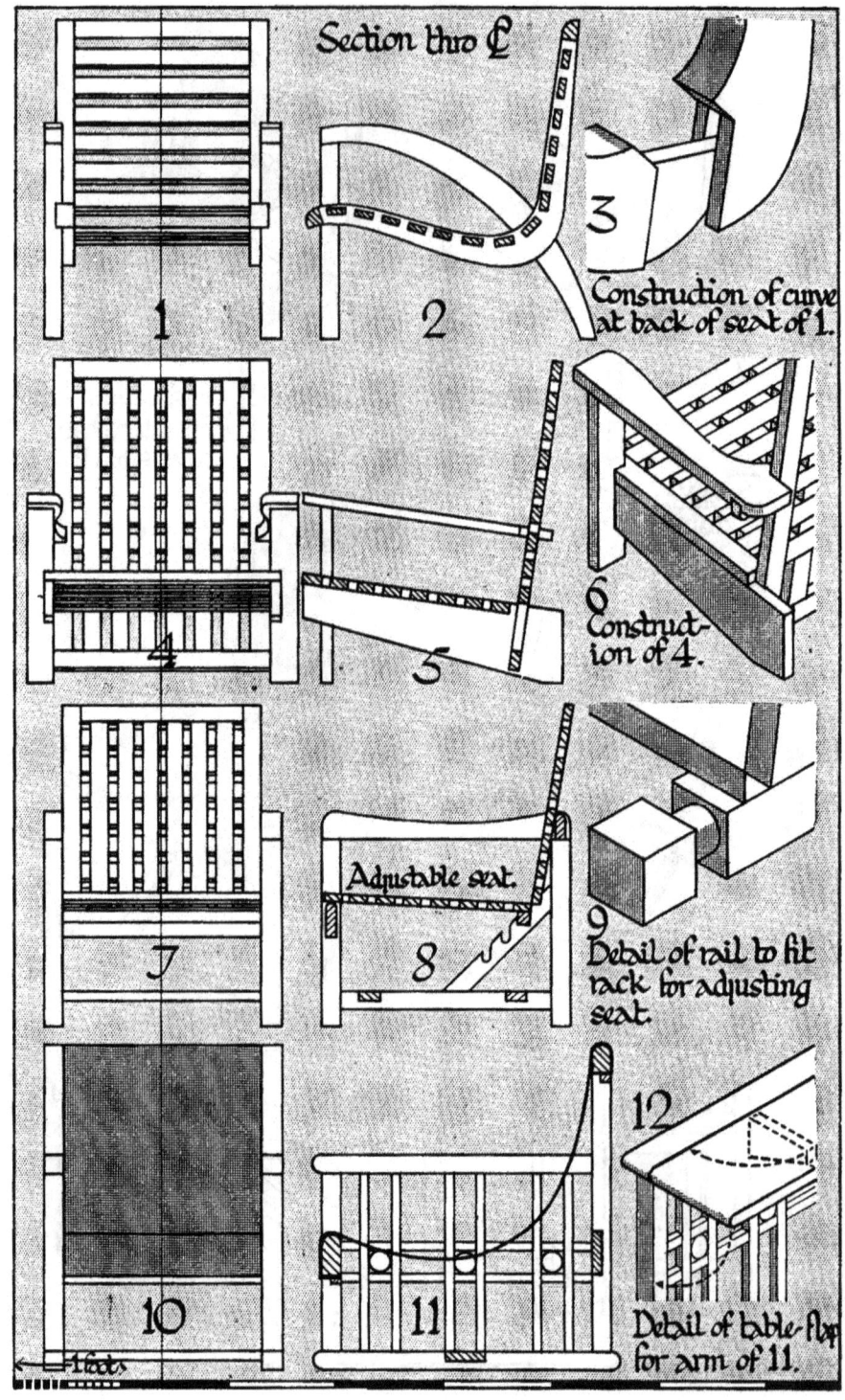

Fig. 5. Garden Arm-Chairs

GARDEN ARM-CHAIRS AND TABLES

has five legs with rails tenoned as detailed in Fig. 3 (7), the flat top of the arm being mitred and fixed by screwing and pelleting.

Garden Arm-Chairs.—Further garden chairs are illustrated in Fig. 5 (1-12). The seat and back of Fig. 5 (1) are made in one piece with slats tenoned between shaped ends; these are notched to take the arm and front leg, which are dovetailed together and fixed by screwing or pegging. Fig. 5 (7, 10) consist of framed ends connected by cross rails. The former has the back and seat hinged together and adjusted by a rail which fits into a rack tenoned across the angle of the end. This rail, detailed in Fig. 5 (9), is screwed to the under side of the seat, which, with the back, is free to move within the framing. Fig. 5 (10) has a canvas seat as in a deck-chair; a folding shelf to take a book or glass may be attached to the arm with hinged brackets as in Fig. 5 (12).

Adjustable Garden Arm-Chairs.—Alternative types of adjustable arm-chair are shown in Fig. 6 (1-16); although intended primarily for the garden they would also be suitable for use indoors. They are shown with flat cushions which are attached by means of tapes and, for outdoor use, should preferably be covered with waterproof material. In Fig. 6 (3, 5) the back only is adjustable, being pivoted with a dowel at the bottom and resting on a rod which fits into slots cut in the arms as detailed in Fig. 6 (1). In the case of Fig. 6 (10, 12) adjustment is effected by slots on the under side of the seat frame which slip over the front rail and lock seat and back in the desired position. Both frames are made $2\frac{1}{2}''$ deep; the back frame is hinged inside the seat with $\frac{1}{4}''$ bolts and nuts and hangs from a $\frac{3}{4}''$ rod fitted between the ends of the chair. Fig. 6 (12) has ends $1''$ thick, blocks being screwed to the top to make up sufficient thickness for the arm.

Garden Tables.—Fig. 7 (1-17) gives some suggestions for garden tables with slatted tops of various types. Fig. 7 (1) is constructed as in Fig. 7 (7), the stretchers being bolted together and one of the rails made with dry joints so that the table may be dismantled for storage during the winter. Alternative shapings for the legs are given in Fig. 7 (2, 3). The top consists of a tongued or mitre-halved outer frame rebated to take the slats which are $\frac{1}{2}''$ thick and halved together in a chequer pattern. The circular top for Fig. 7 (4) is made with four tenoned segments grooved to fit tongued slats spaced $\frac{1}{4}''$ apart, an alternative treatment being shown in Fig. 7 (17). Each stretcher rail in this example is tenoned into the adjacent rail as seen in the plan Fig. 7 (8). Fig. 7 (10) is a low tea-table for use with deck-chairs, etc. The legs are hinged to the

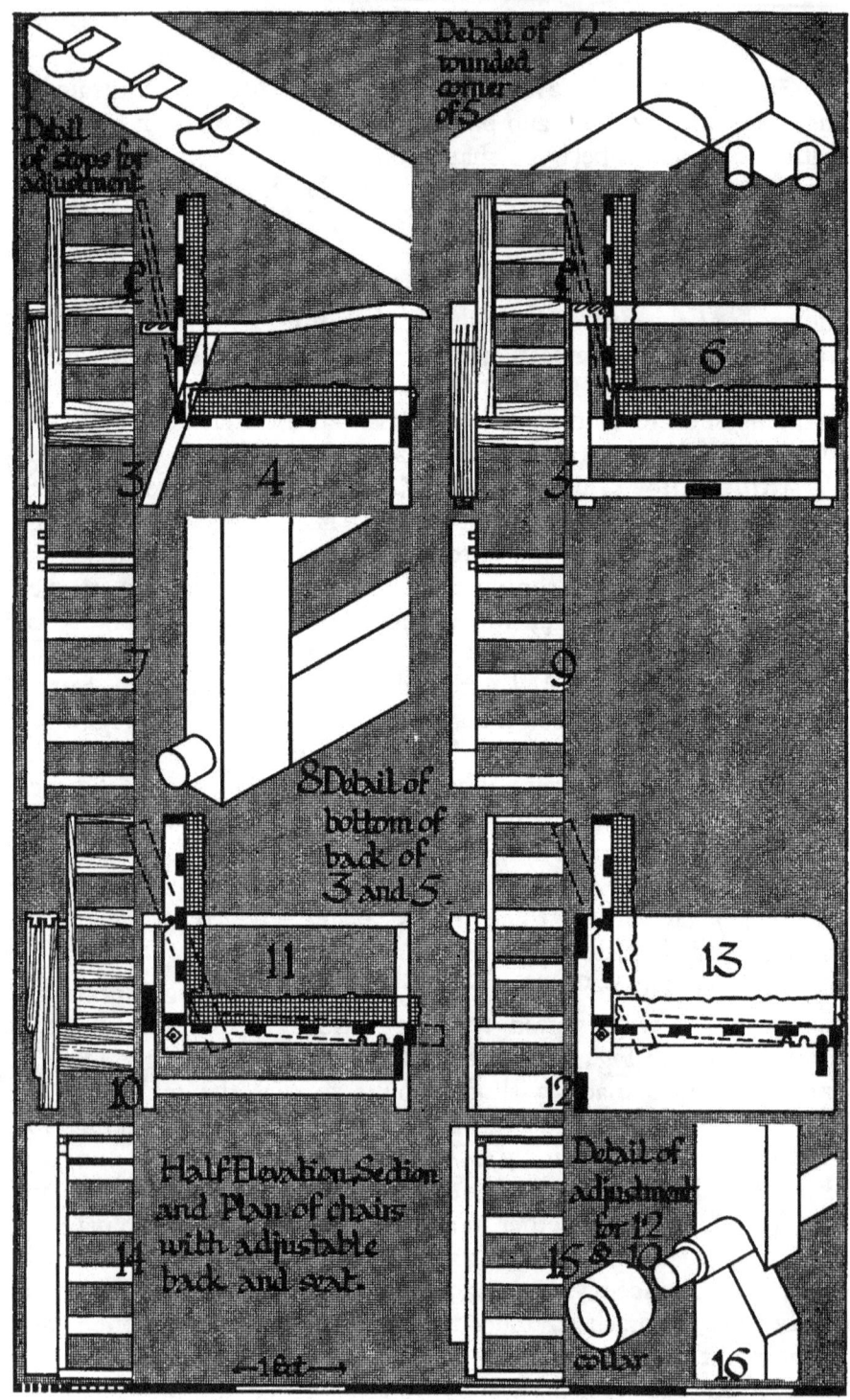

Fig. 6. Adjustable Garden Arm-Chairs

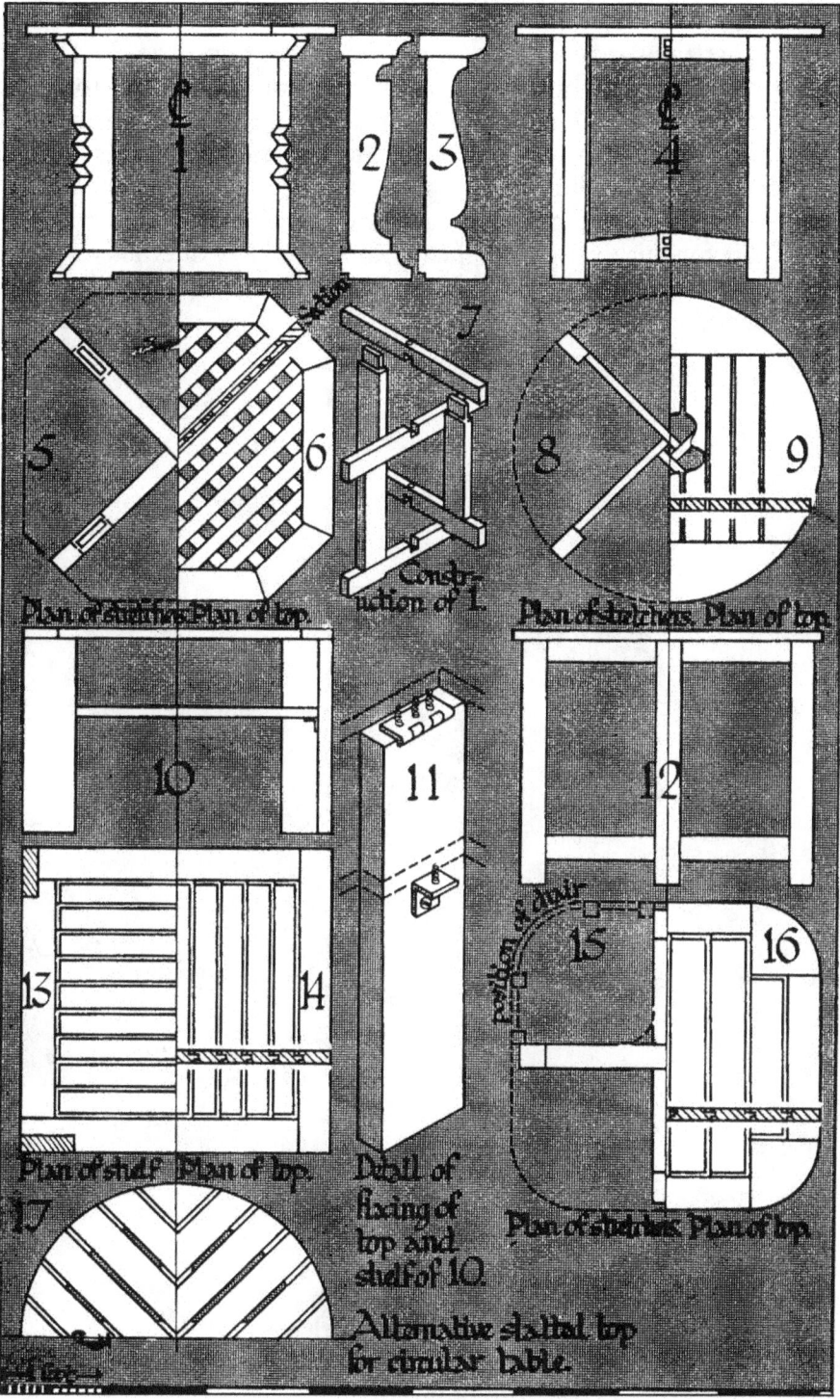

Fig. 7. Garden Tables

top so that they may be folded flat for storing and the shelf fixed by screwing to angle brackets. The slats in top and shelf are tongued and grooved, the rebates on the top faces being wider to form sinkings and conceal the joints when the top is assembled. Fig. 7 (12) is intended to take four chairs which fit in between the stretchers, as shown in the plan, Fig. 7 (15), and are thus kept dry during rain. The chair for this example is shown in Fig. 4 (8); alternatively, the other type of chair, Fig. 4 (7), could be used and the table made with canted corners to match.

Fig. 1. Garden Seat and Tubs in cast concrete [Fig. 2 (5) and Fig. 5 (10)]

CHAPTER VI

GARDEN ITEMS IN CAST CONCRETE

This chapter gives some suggestions for the construction of moulds or "formes" for casting garden seats, tubs, bird-baths, etc., in concrete. As normal woodworking practice is involved the process is thought to be of interest here. Concrete is essentially suitable for such a purpose in that it is absolutely permanent and unaffected by weather, whilst in appearance it combines well with brick or natural stone; also any number of items may be produced from the same mould with little additional labour or expense. The coloured cements now obtainable open up further interesting possibilities.

The moulds consist of rectangular boxes with shaped blocks or mouldings nailed to the inside to give variations in detail. Hollow items such as tubs are made by using another box as a core and packing the concrete in the space between this and the outer box.

135

The best material for the moulds is well-seasoned deal, the parts being screwed together so that they may be separated to remove the finished cast. Brass screws should be used, or iron screws greased to prevent them rusting in. The inside of the mould is waterproofed to prevent it absorbing moisture from the wet concrete and thus swelling and becoming distorted. This may be done by brushing over with paraffin, but if the mould has small detail or will be used several times, it should preferably be painted or varnished.

The concrete mixture is made up with Portland cement 1 part, washed sand 2 parts, and aggregate 4 parts. The latter should be up to $\frac{1}{4}''$ diameter and may consist of broken brick, broken stone, gravel, or coke breeze. To give a finer texture for small work the proportion of aggregate should be reduced. The mixture is thoroughly tamped down into the mould in order to break up air bubbles and give sharp, clean edges. Iron bars, pipes, thick wire or strip are used as reinforcement and are worked in with the concrete during the filling process; care should be taken to ensure that these are at least $\frac{1}{2}''$ below the surface.

Concrete Garden Seats.—Fig. 2 (1-12) illustrates moulds for garden seats with solid ends. In Fig. 2 (1-4, 11) the seat consists of a flat concrete slab resting on the ends. These may be kept steady either by making them sufficiently thick to stand firmly on the ground, or by making them longer than seat height so that about 9" may be buried. Fig. 2 (9) shows the mould for Fig. 2 (1); the blocks at the sides are bandsawn to shape, and the top of the concrete levelled with a "float" or by dragging a straight-edge across it. Fig. 2 (5, 6, 7) are made in the same way, but have a seat of $1\frac{1}{2}''$ oak or elm which is housed into the concrete ends. The housing is formed by a strip of wood nailed to the bottom of the mould as in Fig. 2 (10). Two $\frac{3}{8}''$ bolts are fixed in this so that they are embedded in the concrete when the mould is filled. The wood seat is bored and slotted so that nuts may be tightened on these bolts to fix it to the ends as shown in section in Fig. 2 (8). The mould for the ends of Fig. 2 (11) is shown in plan in Fig. 2 (12); the matrix for the flutes is made by planing a deal fillet to a rounded section and nailing lengths of this to the sides. The slab seat is cast in a box with an open top and should be reinforced lengthwise with two $\frac{3}{8}''$ bars.

Concrete Bird-Baths.—Fig. 3 (1-8) shows the construction of moulds for two types of bird-baths. The first type is cast without a bottom, as in Fig. 3 (1), and is afterwards cemented to a flat slab. Fig. 3 (5-8) give sections and half-elevations of alternative detail

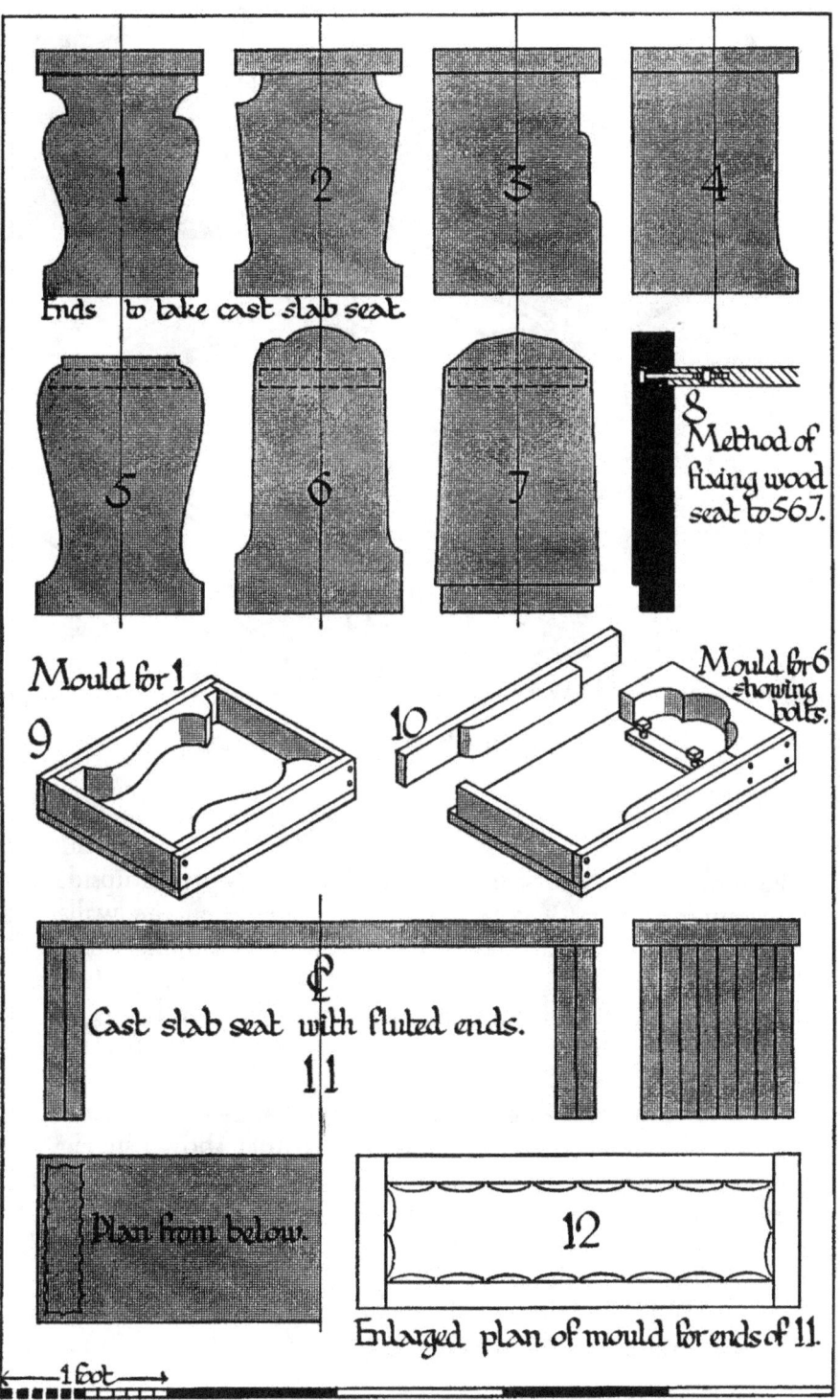

Fig. 2. Moulds for Concrete Garden Seats

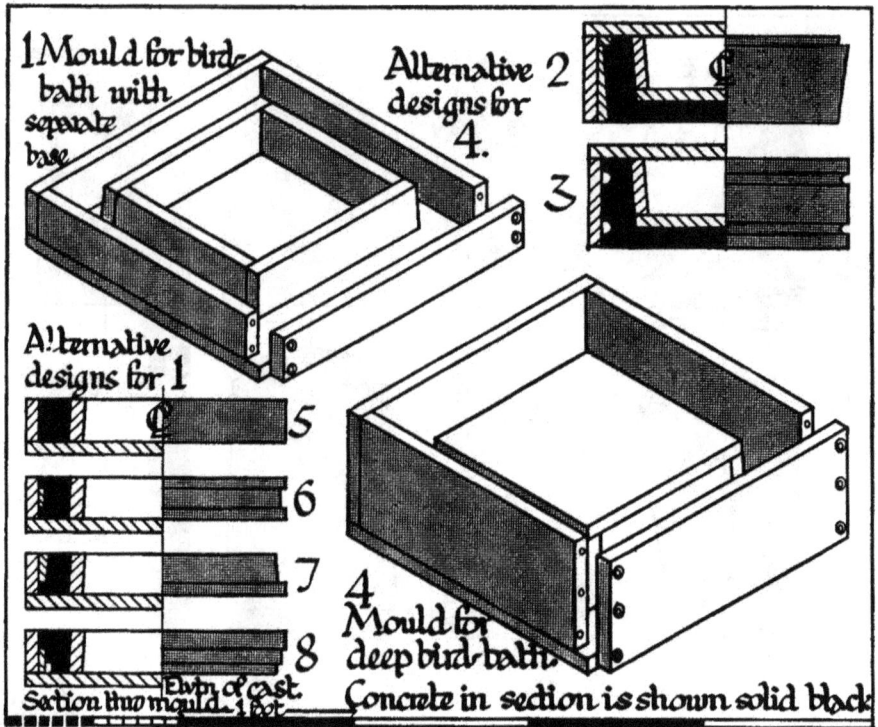

Fig. 3. Moulds for Concrete Bird-Baths

produced by mitreing and nailing fillets round the inside of the mould. The mould shown in Fig. 3 (4) is for a rather more advanced type with a bottom cast in with the sides. It is placed upside down for casting and has a core about $1\frac{1}{2}''$ lower than the walls. It is important to note that these cores should have sloping sides and be thoroughly waterproofed, otherwise they may swell and be difficult to remove. The walls may be reinforced with two lengths of thick wire or strip bent into squares and placed about $1''$ from top and bottom respectively.

Concrete Bird-Baths and Pedestals.—The bird-baths in Fig. 4 (1-9) are cast in moulds similar to that shown in Fig. 3 (4), but have rather more elaborate detail; pedestals, suitable either for these or for sundials, are also shown. The scalloped step in Fig. 4 (5) is cut out in $\frac{3}{8}''$ ply and mitred round the sides of the box; the pattern for the sinking in Fig. 4 (6) is also fretted out in ply. Fig. 4 (7) has fluted sides made as described for the seat in Fig. 2 (11). The construction of the mould for Fig. 4 (8) is detailed in Fig. 4 (9).

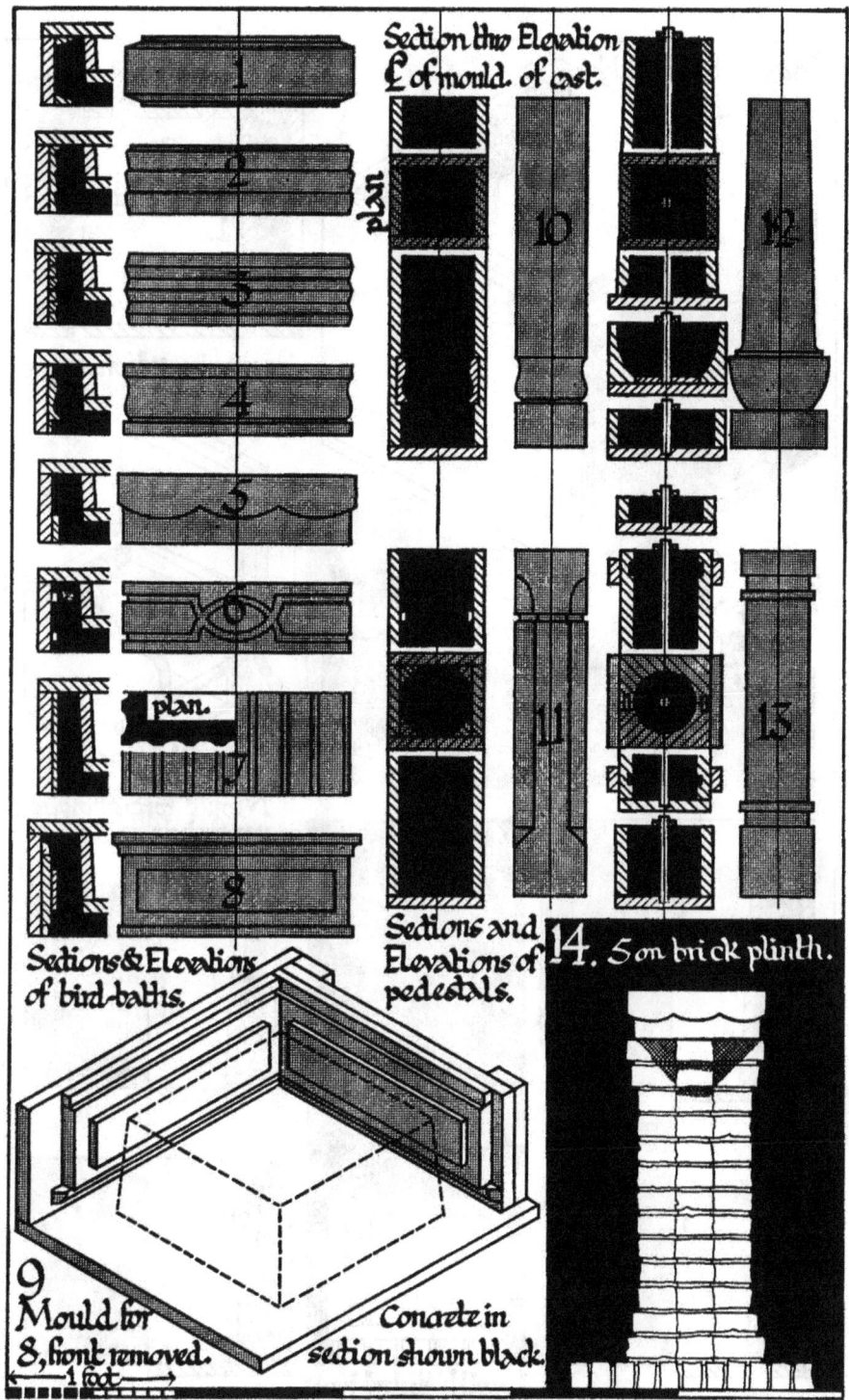

Fig. 4. Moulds for Concrete Bird-Baths and Pedestals

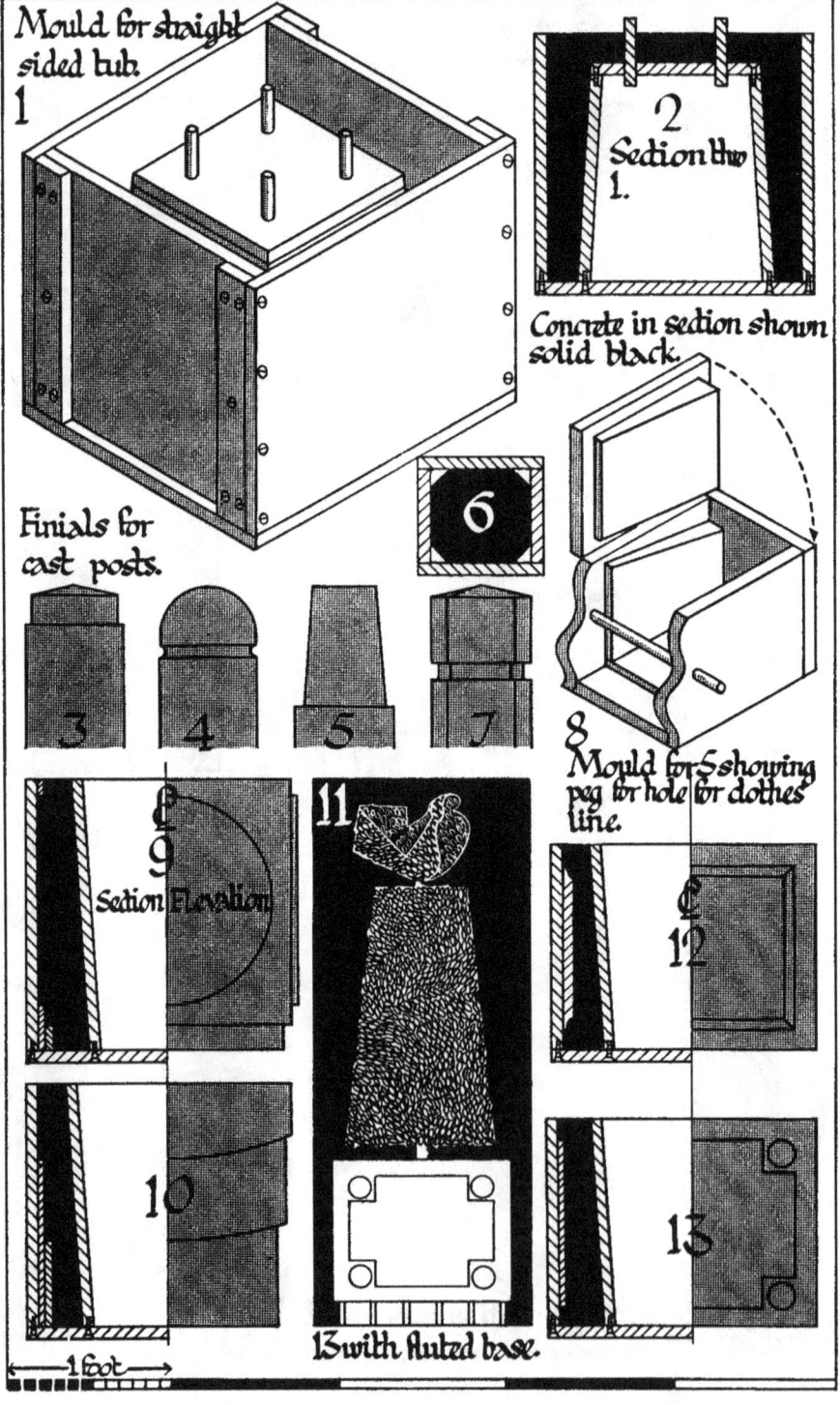

Fig. 5. Moulds for Concrete Posts and Plant Tubs

The edges of the tablets to form the sinkings in the sides should be slightly chamfered towards the centre of the mould so that they may be more easily withdrawn from the concrete; this also applies to the sinkings on Fig. 4 (5, 6). If the interior of the mould is painted this should be done before the tablets, mouldings, etc., are fixed in order to keep the angles sharp.

The pedestals in Fig. 4 (10, 11) are cast in four-sided boxes with an open top as shown in the section and interpolated plan; the octagonal part of the latter example is formed by fillets of triangular section nailed to the corners of the mould. Fig. 4 (12) could most conveniently be made in three separate moulds and the parts cemented together and registered by a rod passing through the centre. The hole for this is made by fixing a length of slightly thicker rod in each mould; this should be greased and is centred by a batten nailed across the top of the mould and removed before the concrete is hard. Fig. 4 (13) is also made in three sections and consists of a round column with a square capital and base. The mould for the middle section is made with two pieces of $3\frac{1}{2}''$ deal hollowed with round planes and connected by cross battens. For short and thick columns such as the foregoing, reinforcement is unnecessary, but if they are made appreciably thinner two or three $\frac{3}{8}''$ rods should be used.

Concrete Posts and Plant-Tubs.—Fig. 5 (1-13) shows moulds for the casting of posts and also of tubs for plants or trees. The latter may be made either with or without bottoms, the moulds used being similar to those used for bird-baths in Fig. 3 (1) and Fig. 3 (4) respectively. A tub without a bottom has the advantage that it may be placed over a hole in the paving so that the roots of the plants in it can extend down into the earth and are thus prevented from becoming "pot-bound." Fig. 5 (1) shows a mould for a straight-sided tub with a bottom; it is turned upside down for casting, and pegs are fixed in the top of the core to provide holes for drainage. The ends of the mould are battened to receive the screws from the sides; this is a stronger construction suitable for larger work and also gives a better hold for the screws so that they do not become unduly loose if the mould is used several times. The tubs shown in section and half-elevation in Fig. 5 (9-13) are made open at the bottom; the raised panels in the first example are obtained by cutting circular holes in four pieces of $\frac{3}{8}''$ ply and nailing them to the sides of the box. The plinth is formed by fillets at the bottom of the mould; alternatively a separate plinth may be made as in Fig. 5 (11). Fig. 5 (3-7) shows finials for concrete posts suitable for gate or fencing posts or to take a clothes-line. The body of the post is made in a long trough with one side open for the straight part, but closed in at the end to form the finial as in Fig. 5 (8). Fig. 5 (7) is an exception in that the mould is made with four sides and the concrete poured in at the end. These posts should be reinforced with two $\frac{3}{8}''$ rods or pipes running the full length, while the sides of the tubs should have two pieces of the same material bent into a square and spaced about 9″ apart.

CHAPTER VII

WOODWORK FOR SCHOOLS

THE purpose of this chapter is not to define a rigid woodwork course, but rather to offer suggestions for exercises which teachers may adapt to their own particular aims and to the capacities of their pupils. The exercises are grouped into three progressive stages to correspond roughly with the first, second, and third years of a woodwork course for boys of eleven onwards. For the fourth year and after, some of the simpler designs in the sections on "Boxes and Caskets," "Clocks," "Stools," "Trays," etc., may be of use.

All the objects suggested as exercises serve a useful purpose and thus provide a link with everyday life to prevent the woodwork period becoming a series of abstract manipulations. Also, under the test of use, any defects in their work are convincingly demonstrated to the pupils and the problem of design put on a rational basis instead of being only regarded as a matter of "taste."

The earlier exercises are easily and quickly made, interest being aroused by doing instead of by learning how to do. The fact that results may be obtained with few and simple tools will also encourage boys to attempt such things at home on their own initiative. The essential joints are introduced gradually as the need for them is felt; a pupil may find that the nailed box that he has made does not stand up to daily wear and tear, and so will have a direct incentive to learn how to make a dovetailed joint to improve his future efforts. Such an occurrence will give the teacher an opportunity to touch on the history of the craft. He could, for instance, draw a parallel between this and the evolution of the dovetailed or panelled chest from the "hutch," and thence back to the laborious and wasteful method of digging out the inside of a tree trunk.

The pupils should always prepare a full-size working drawing of the projected exercise, all necessary dimensions being clearly marked. The success of the earlier exercises depends on little more than accurate marking-out on the wood and thus, from the beginning, the importance of the drawing and its relation to the finished job is implanted in the mind. This first stage will be more

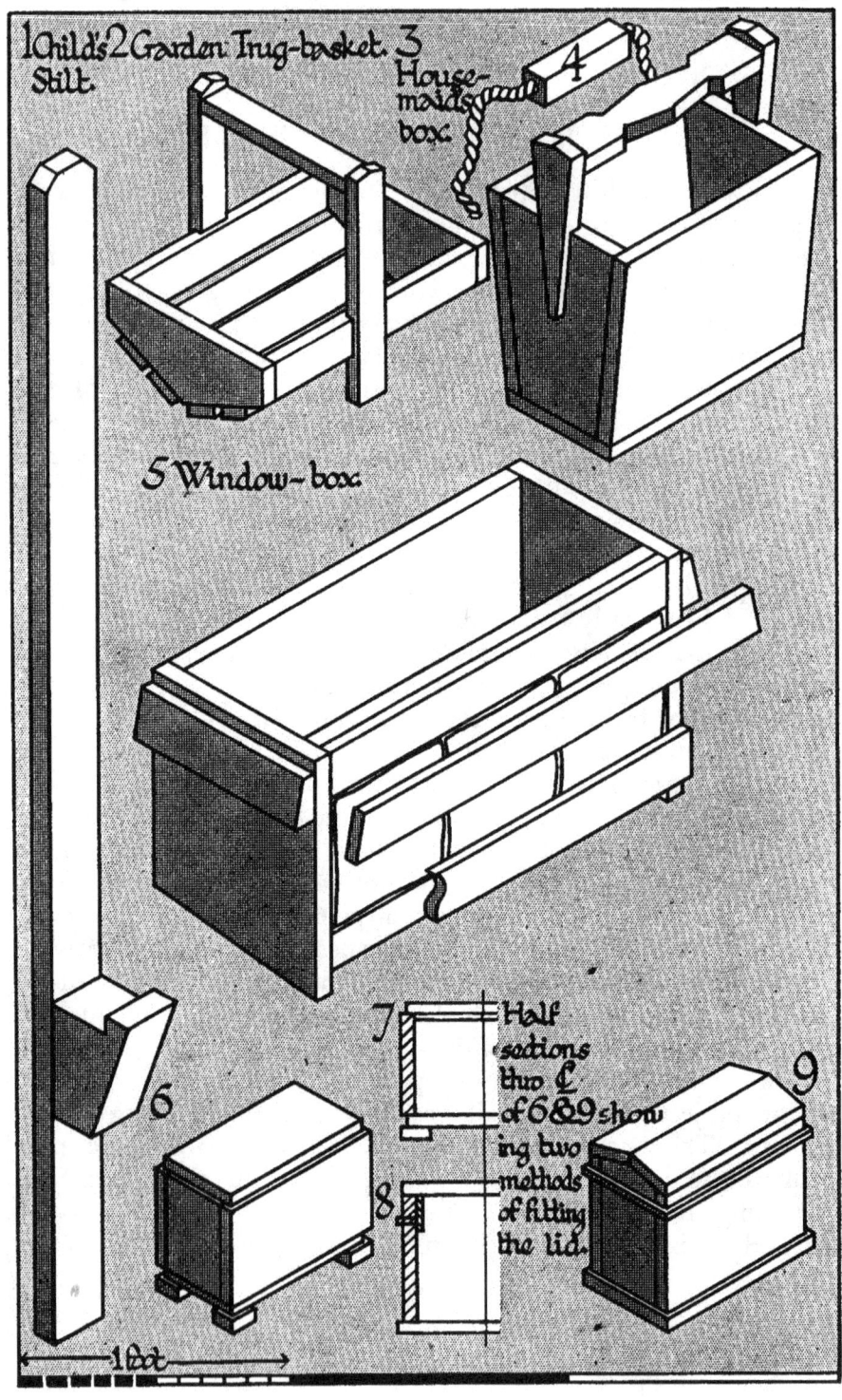

Fig. 1, Group 1. Stilts, Trug-Basket, Housemaid's Box, Window-Box, Caskets

valuable and interesting to the pupils if they are allowed to design their own work, the designs illustrated indicating the line of approach. Even in the simplest exercises many variations in shaping, etc., are possible, and by choosing or originating for himself a boy can acquire a greater personal interest in his work and also some insight into the dependence of design on the limitations of tools and materials.

Further value as "expression" would be given to the exercises by allowing the pupils to paint and decorate the simpler examples. In order to rule out the idea that the purpose of paint is to conceal defects, the workmanship should reach a reasonable standard before this is attempted. Painted decoration should be drawn as directly as possible with the brush, as there is little educational value in laboriously drawing out a repeating pattern in pencil and then filling it with colour. At the best this can only inculcate neatness which, by itself, is rather a doubtful virtue. If a direct treatment proves impracticable, stencils of varnished paper might be used. Figs. 9 and 10 give some suggestions for patterns for the decoration of caskets, cabinets, etc. They are adapted chiefly from archaic Greek and Persian pottery which abounds in inspiration for patterns built up of two or three geometrical units. With advanced pupils simple carving might also be attempted. A possible approach would be to start with gouge-cut border patterns and to proceed to relief work with raised silhouettes.

It is now recognized as desirable that there should be a great degree of correlation between the teaching of art and handcraft. Both subjects would benefit by this in that art in the school sometimes tends to become too abstract and unrelated to real things, and woodwork to call for little more than mechanical skill of hand. The problems of design and pattern will enable both teachers to co-operate so that this part of their work may have a definite objective and be applied to practical construction in wood.

Group I.—The first group, Figs. 1 and 2, consists of exercises in sawing and nailing, the wood being supplied to the class planed to thickness.

Fig. 1 (1) is one of a pair of stilts and consists of a shaped block nailed to a 2" by 1" upright. The trug-basket and housemaid's box are self-explanatory; Fig. 1 (4) shows an alternative handle for the latter made of a block threaded on a length of rope. The window-box in Fig. 1 (5) has three tiles in the front which are fixed by battens lapping over at top and bottom. Fig. 1 (6-9) show simple caskets suitable for painted decoration.

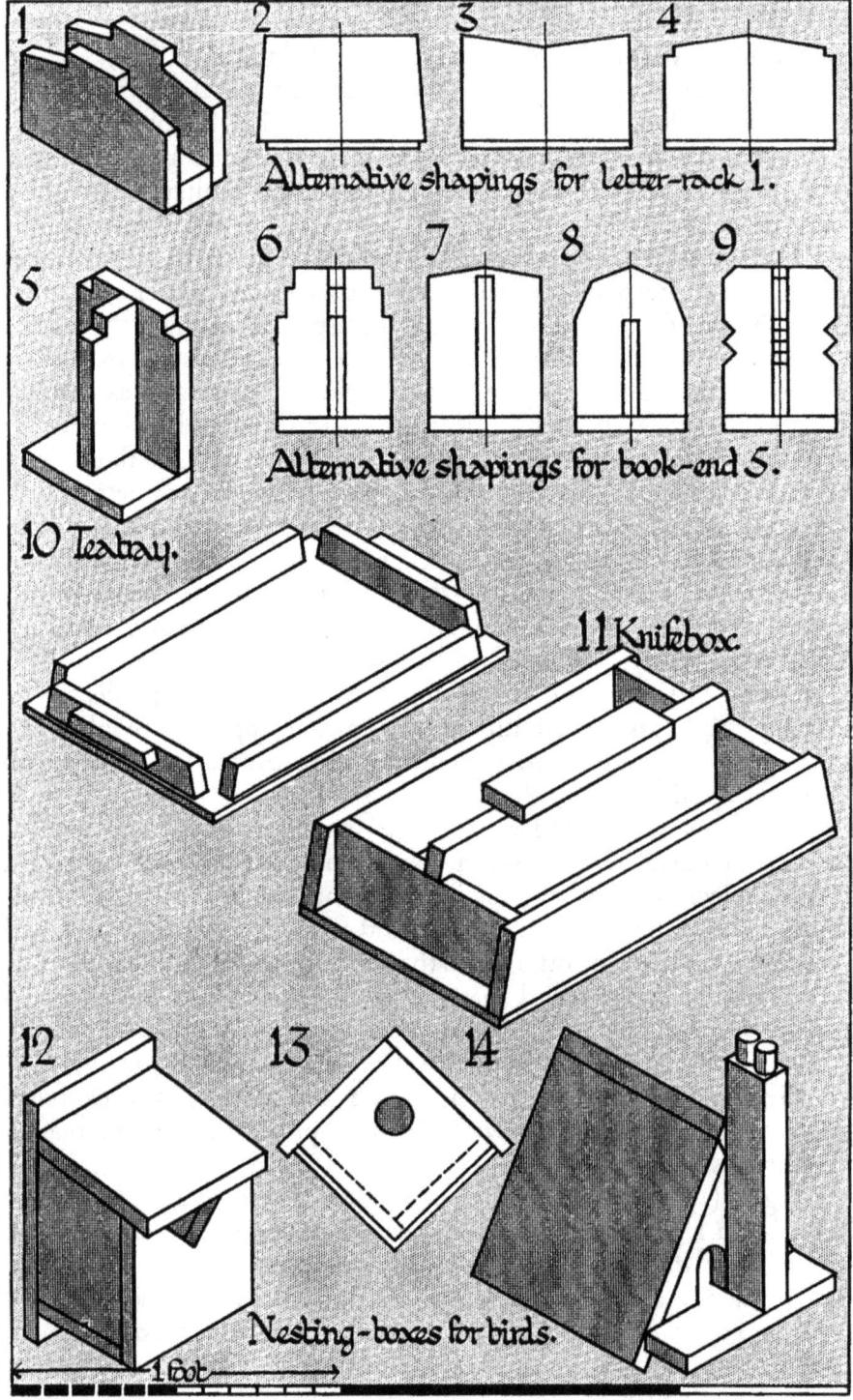

Fig. 2, Group 1. Letter-Racks, Book-Ends, Teatray, Knife-Box, Nesting-Boxes

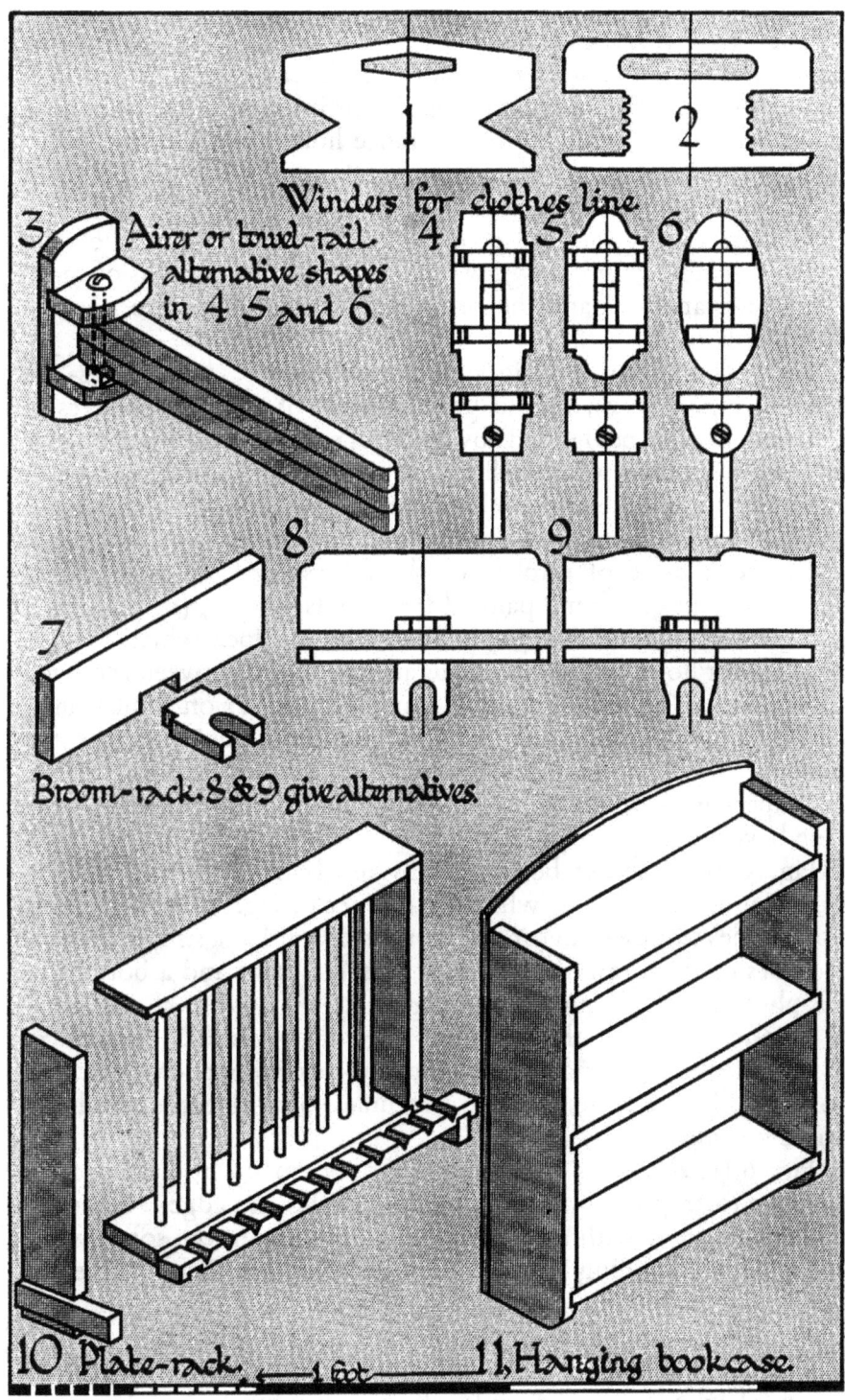

Fig. 3, Group 2. Line Winders, Towel-Rails, Broom-Racks, Plate-Rack, Hanging Bookcase

The letter-rack and book-ends in Fig. 2 (1-9) give some suggestions for shaping by means of straight sawcuts. The nesting-boxes shown in Fig. 2 (12-14) would be interesting to make at a country school; the size of the entrance hole should be adapted to the bird that it is desired to encourage; thus a 1" diameter hole will admit wrens but not the common sparrow.

Group 2.—The second group, Figs. 3, 4, and 5, introduces the use of the plane, chisel, bowsaw, etc. The shaping permits of more interesting variations and the principles of carcase construction are introduced.

Fig. 3 (1-11) shows various shaping exercises; the clothes-line winders, Fig. 3 (1, 2), should preferably be of ply, the grooves in the latter example being made by boring a row of holes and chopping the open part away with a chisel. The plate-rack and bookcase in Fig. 3 (10, 11) show simple rebated carcases.

The book-end, Fig. 4 (1), is made with a shaped block to which is screwed a piece of tinplate or sheet brass covered with baize; Fig. 4 (2-7) suggest some painted treatments. Fig. 4 (8) is a pencil box, the body of which is made of a 2" by 1" block which has had $1\frac{1}{2}$" diameter holes bored at the ends and the wood between removed with a chisel. Fig. 4 (10) shows a stamp or pin box on similar lines, and Fig. 4 (9) an inkstand with one of these boxes at either side, the block for the inkpot being screwed to the lid and turning with it. The paperknives in Fig. 4 (13-16) are made in hard wood with the blade bevelled on one side.

Fig. 5 (1-13) shows book-troughs and book-racks with shelves housed into shaped ends, while the cabinet in Fig. 5 (10) represents a further development in carcase work in that it has a simple drawer. The sides of this drawer are housed into the front and a bottom of thin ply fixed by gluing and pinning.

Group 3.—The third group, Figs. 6, 7, and 8, introduces through-dovetailing and the mortise-and-tenon joint. Most school workshops have a lathe, and Fig. 8 includes some objects embodying simple turning.

Fig. 6 (1, 2) shows bread-boards to be made in hard wood; a groove to trap the crumbs is worked round the edge. Fig. 6 (6) is a cigarette-box with a rounded lid worked from the solid, while Fig. 6 (9) has a sliding lid. Alternative detail for these is given in the elevations and sections in Fig. 6 (7, 8). Fig. 6 (11) shows a rather more advanced type of book-rack with shaped feet.

The construction of a simple rebated mirror frame is given in Fig. 7 (1), detail for the ends of the uprights being shown in

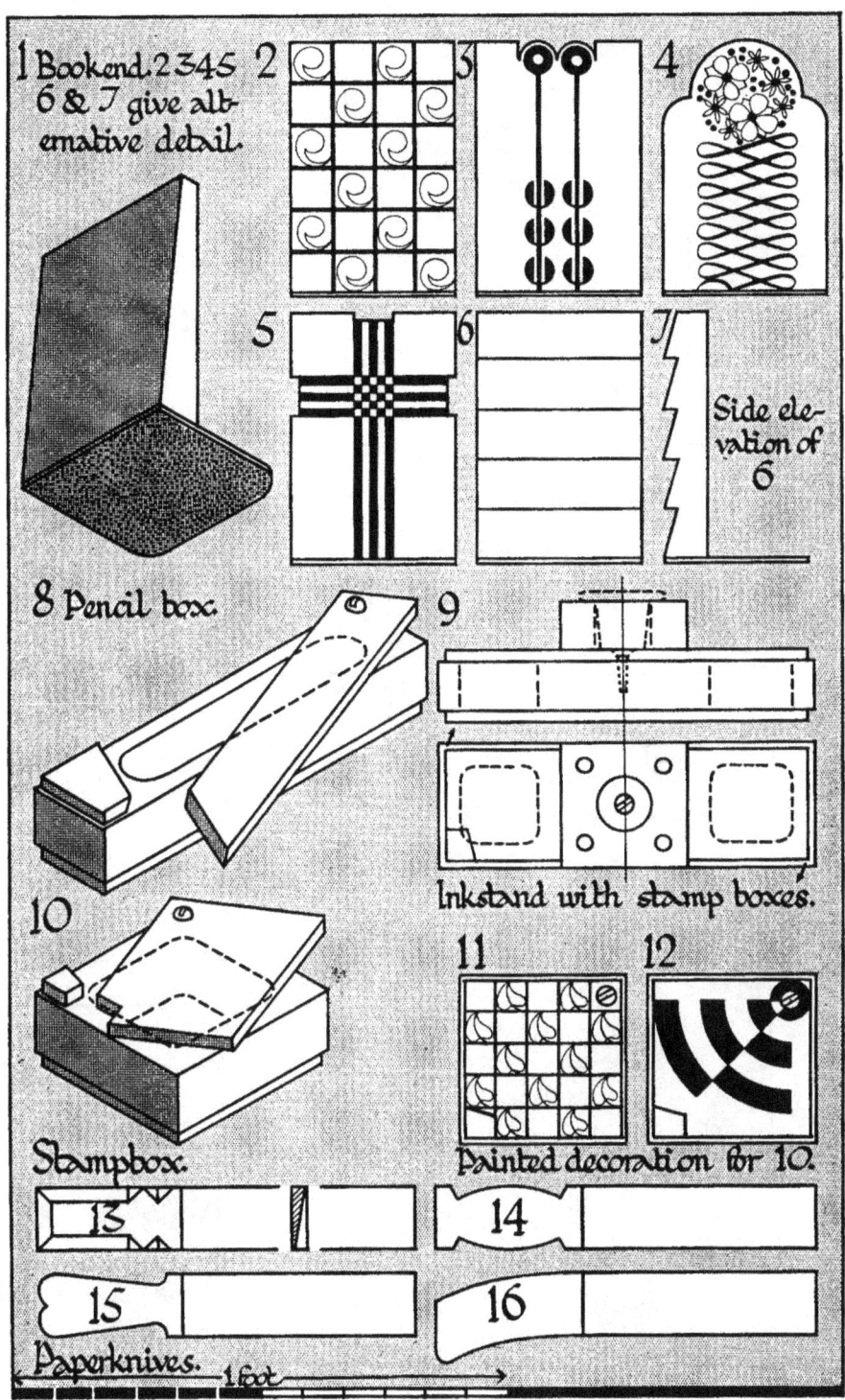

Fig. 4, Group 2. Book-Ends, Boxes with turning lid, Paperknives

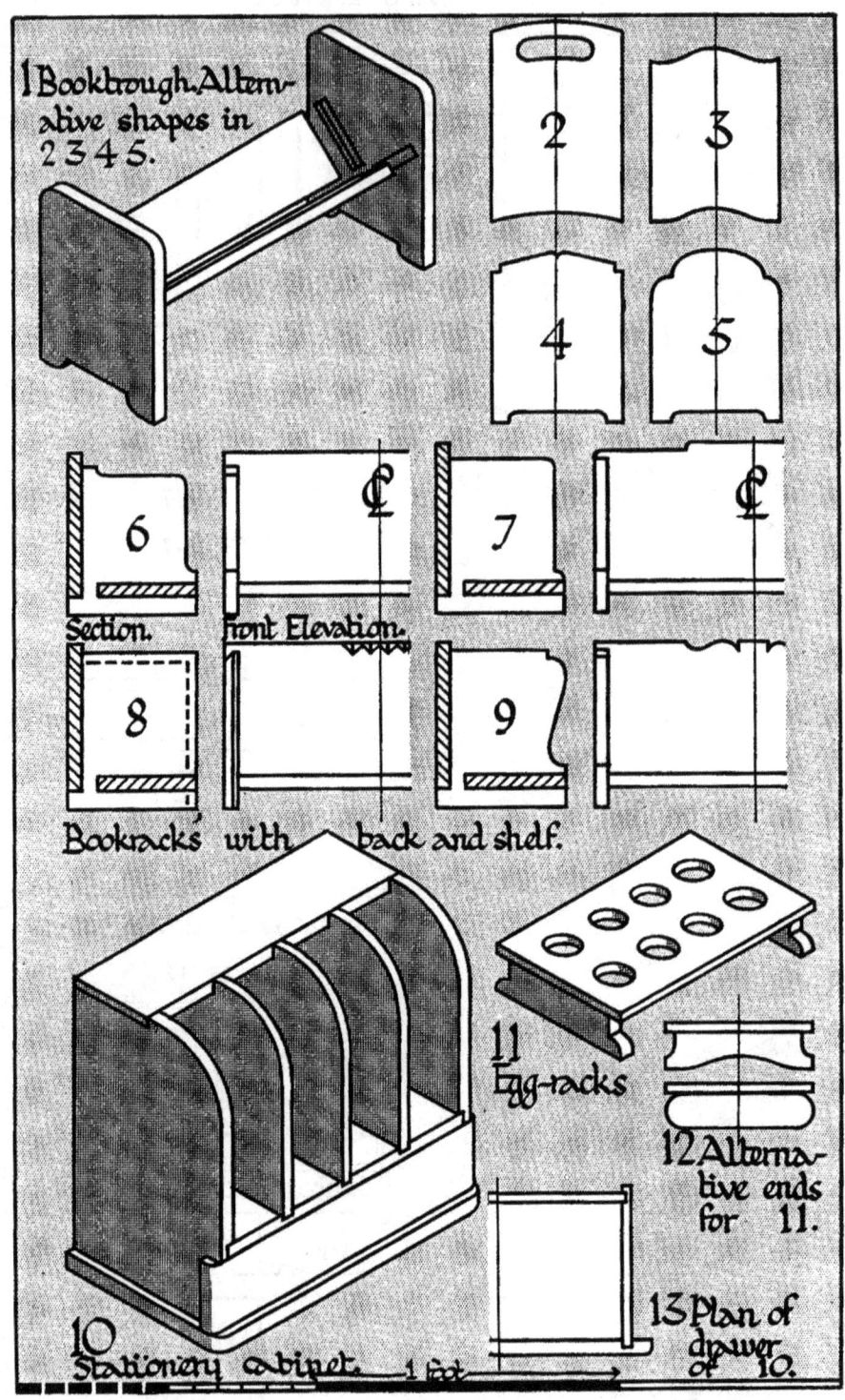

Fig. 5, Group 2. Book-Troughs, Book-Racks, Egg-Racks, Stationery Cabinet

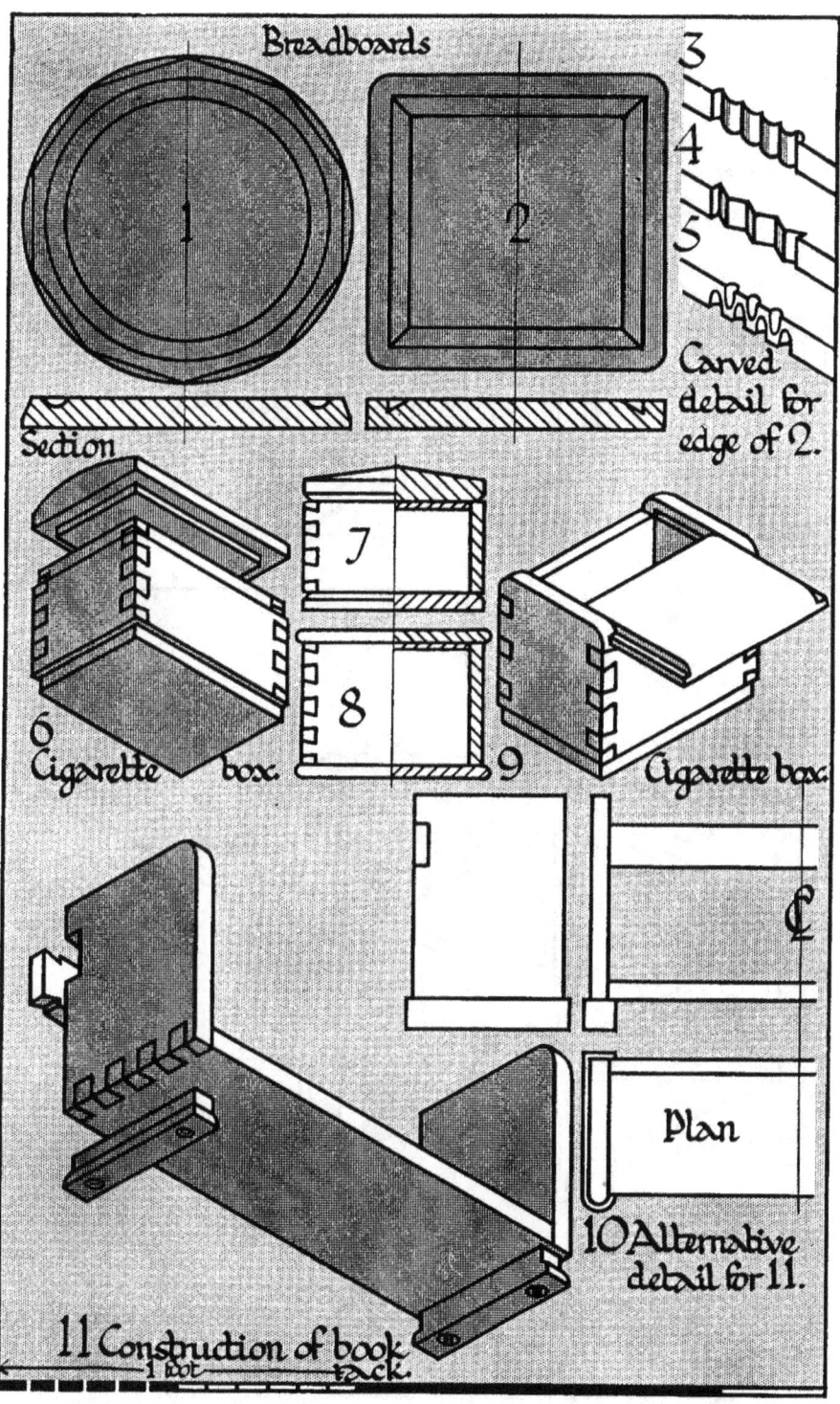

Fig. 6, Group 3. Bread-Boards, Cigarette-Boxes, Book-Racks

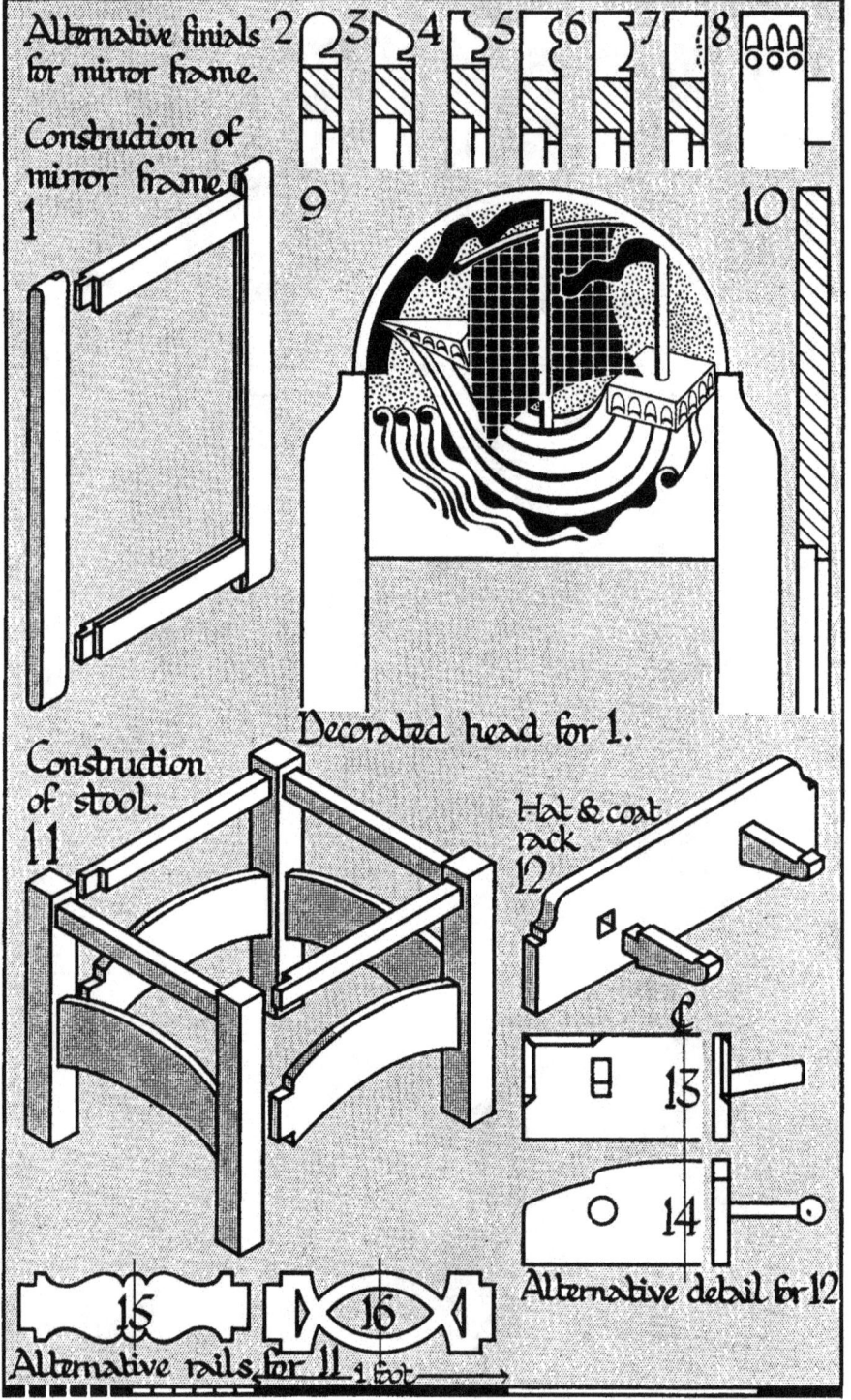

Fig. 7, Group 3. Mirror Frame, Stool, Hat and Coat Racks

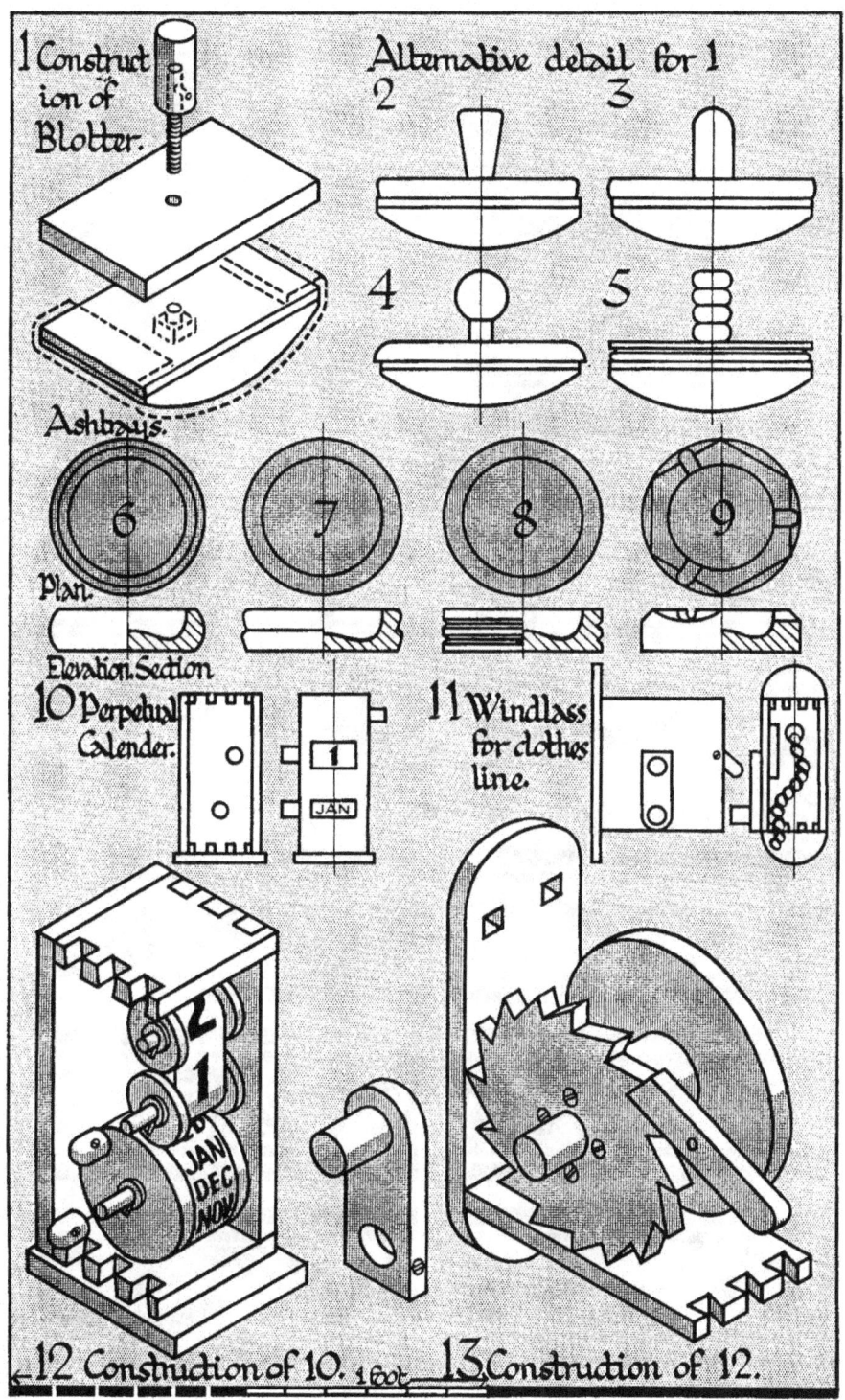

Fig. 8, Group 3. Exercises embodying simple turning—Blotters, Ashtrays, Perpetual Calendar, Windlass for clothes-line

Fig. 9. Suggestions for Painted Decoration; Border Patterns

Fig. 10. Suggestions for Painted Decoration; All-over Patterns

Fig. 7 (2-8). Alternatively, the frame could be made with a head, as in Fig. 7 (9), and decorated with a painted roundel. The ship motif is intended for painting in bright heraldic colours such as vermilion, ultramarine, and gold; pupils might be encouraged to find illustrations of historic ships and to formalize them into decorative patterns. Fig. 7 (11) illustrates a stool made with bare-faced tenons. It could have a woven seat of leather or "sea-grass."

The blotters in Fig. 8 (1-5) have a turned knob bored to take a $\frac{1}{4}''$ bolt which screws into a nut cut in the base and thus holds the blotting paper in position. Fig. 8 (6-9) are ash trays shown in plan and half-elevation and section. They are intended for turning in a hard wood such as walnut or Australian myrtle, the wood being roughly cut to the circular shape and glued to a block which is screwed to the face-plate of the lathe. Fig. 8 (10) shows the elevations of a perpetual calendar, and Fig. 8 (12) details the mechanism. The figures for the days are painted on a strip of linen-backed paper which runs between two bobbins. The axles of these project through the sides of the box and are turned by knobs fixed with grub-screws; spring washers should be fitted to prevent them running too loosely. Below is a larger bobbin for the months, which is turned in the same way. Fig. 8 (13) shows the construction of a windlass for an indoor clothes-line. The drum is $1\frac{1}{2}''$ in diameter with a hard-wood cog screwed to one end. The front of the box has a slot in which a pawl is pivoted so that it can engage with the cog and fix it when sufficient line has been unwound. The casing is tenoned into a backboard which is screwed to the wall.

INDEX

The page numbers in ordinary type indicate references in the text; numbers in black type refer to illustrations or to references accompanied by an illustration on the same page.

Airers, **147**

Bandings, 5
Basket, trug, **144**
Bed-fitments, 97, **100**, **101**
Bedsteads, castors for, 102, **103**
    ,, , fittings for, 100, **103**
    ,, , headboards for, 97, **98**, **99**
    ,, , panelled or slatted, 102, **105**
    ,, , sizes of, 102
    ,, , stump foot, 102, **104**
Bleaching oak, 125
Blotters, **153**, 156
Bolts, coach, 34
    ,, , French, 100, **103**
    ,, , wooden, **120**, 121
Bookcases, bow-fronted, **11**, 12
    ,, , break-fronted, 11, 12, **14**, **15**
    ,, with cupboards, 10, 12, **13**, **14**, **15**
    ,, , enclosed, 10, **13**, **14**, **15**
    ,, , hanging, **147**
    ,, , open, 10, **11**
    ,, , sideboard, **66**, **67**
    ,, , unit, 12, **13**
Book-ends, **146**, **148**, **149**
Book-racks, **148**, **150**, **151**
Book-tables, 15, **16**
Book-troughs, **148**, **150**
Box, cigarette, 17, **18**, **19**, **20**, **144**, **145**, **148**, **151**
  ,, , construction of, 17, **18**
  ,, , glove or handkerchief, 17, **18**
  ,, , housemaid's, **144**
  ,, , knife, **146**
  ,, , nesting, **146**, **148**
  ,, , pencil, **148**, **149**
  ,, , pin or stamp, **148**, **149**
  ,, , window, **144**, 145
Brickwork fashion, **73**, 74

Bureau, 94, 96
Buttons, 69, 71

Cabinets, built-in, 21, **23**
    ,, , cocktail or music, **26**, 27
    ,, , display, 20, **21**, **22**, **23**, **24**, **25**
    ,, , enclosed, **26**, 27
    ,, , hanging corner, 20, **22**
    ,, , radio, 57, **58**, **59**
    ,, , radio-gramophone, 57, **59**, **60**, **61**
    ,, , stationery, **148**, **150**
Calendar, perpetual, **153**, 156
Carcase, dovetailed, 14, **15**, 39, 41, 57, 59, 66, 67, 91, 92, **115**, **116**, **117**, **118**
    ,, , framed, **24**, **25**, 65, **108**, **109**, **120**
Carved decoration, **22**, **87**, **88**, **89**, **108**, **120**, **151**
Carving, application of, 3, 4, 145
Caskets, **19**, 20
Caul, 17, **18**, **19**, 20, 84, 95
Cellaret drawer, 64, 66, 67
Chairs, arm, 28, **30**, **31**
    ,, , bedroom, 28, **29**
    ,, , construction of, 27, **32**
    ,, , dining, 27, 28, **29**, **30**, **31**, **33**
    ,, , garden, 127, **129**, **130**, **131**, **132**
    ,, , single, 28, **29**, **32**
Chests of drawers, dovetailed, 106, **107**
    ,,   ,, , framed, **108**, **109**
    ,,   ,, , unit, 106, **107**
Chimney-pieces for built-in fires, 34, **36**
    ,,   ,, tiled surround, **33**, **35**
Clamps for table top, **75**, **76**
    ,, wagon top, **83**, **84**
Clocks, inlaid figures for, 48, **49**
    ,, , long-case, 38, **39**, 41, **42**
    ,, , mantel, 44, **45**, **46**, **47**, **49**

INDEX

Clocks, wall, 48, 49
Colour, 7, 8, 9
Concrete bird-baths, 136, 138, 139
    ,, garden seats, 136, 137
    ,, , mixture for, 136
    ,, plant-tubs, 140, 141
    ,, posts, 140, 141
    ,, reinforcement, 138, 141, 142
Construction, 2
Curved work, 17, 18, 19, 20, 22, 24, 25, 44, 45, 46, 47, 48, 49, 62, 63, 70, 71, 73, 74, 76, 77, 100, 101, 116, 118

Decoration, 3, 4, 5
Decorative scheme, 6–9
Doors, flush, 12, 13, 14, 26, 65, 66, 67, 121, 122
  ,, , glazed, 12, 13, 14, 15, 21, 22, 23, 24, 25
  ,, , panelled, 39, 42, 63, 120
  ,, , plate-glass, 24, 25
Dovetails, double lapped, 117
  ,, , lapped, 117
  ,, , secret-mitred, 107
  ,, , slip, 79, 81, 117, 118
Drawers, bow-fronted, 100, 101, 115
  ,, , construction of, 106, 107
  ,, , fitted, for sideboard, 64, 66, 67
  ,, with overlapping ends, 66, 68, 115
  ,, , slips for, 106, 107
Dressing chests, 116, 118
Dressing tables, cheval, 115, 118
  ,, ,, , enclosed, 112, 113, 114
  ,, ,, , kidney-shaped, 112, 113
  ,, ,, , knee-hole, 112, 113
  ,, ,, , pedestal, 112, 113, 114, 115, 118
  ,, ,, , unit, 114

Electric fire, 34, 36
Electric lighting, concealed, 20, 21, 22, 24, 25, 100, 112, 113
  ,, ,, , fittings for, 51–57

Feet for cabinets, etc., 11, 13, 14, 19, 62, 63, 64, 91, 93, 95, 151
Finials for bedstead posts, 104
  ,, concrete posts, 140, 142
  ,, mirror frames, 110, 152
Fixing built-in cabinets, 21, 23
  ,, chimney-pieces, 34, 35
  ,, corner cabinets, 21
  ,, electric fire, 34, 36

Fixing feet, 62, 64
  ,, glass for mirror, 87, 89, 109, 111
  ,, handles, 51, 64, 67
  ,, headboards, 97, 99
  ,, tops, 72, 75, 84, 86
Fluted book-table, 16
  ,, casket, 19, 20
  ,, clock-case, 44, 45, 46
  ,, doors, 121, 122
  ,, drawer front, 93, 95
  ,, feet, 13
  ,, lamp standard, 52, 53
  ,, pedestal for table, 76, 77
  ,, pilasters for chimney-piece, 34, 35
  ,, plinth, 36, 37, 93, 95
Framed back, 114, 115, 116, 118
  ,, carcase, 24, 25, 65, 67, 91, 92, 108, 109, 120, 121
  ,, stand, 14, 15, 24, 25, 26, 27, 65, 67, 94, 95
  ,, top for garden table, 131, 133

Gallery for sideboard, 65, 67
Garden chairs, 127, 128, 129, 130, 131, 132
  ,, items in concrete, 135–142
  ,, seats, 126, 127, 135, 136, 137
  ,, tables, 131, 133
Glass doors, 24, 25
  ,, shelves, 20, 24, 25

Handholes, 49, 50
  ,, for trays, 81, 82
Handles, block, 49, 50
  ,, , shaped, 49, 50, 64, 67, 108
  ,, , strip, 49, 50, 90
  ,, for trays, 81, 82, 84, 146
Hanger for trousers, 123, 124
Hanging, wardrobe for, 119, 120, 121, 122, 123
Headboards for divans, 97, 98, 99
Hinge, box, 17, 18
  ,, , centre-pin, 42, 44
  ,, for Pembroke table, 78, 80
  ,, , piano, 61
  ,, , rule-joint, 78, 80

Inkstand, 148, 149
Inlaid decoration, 19, 20, 60, 61, 73, 74, 75, 87, 88, 89, 90, 111
  ,, dials for clocks, 39, 44, 45, 47, 48, 49
  ,, figures for clocks, 48, 49

INDEX

Inlaying, 5
" circles, 41, 44

Kerbs, mouldings for, 34, 35
Keying, 17, 18, 19, 47
Knobs, 19, 20, 50, 51
Knuckle-joint, 78, 80

Lamps, candle, fittings for, 54, 55, 56
" , ceiling pendant, 55, 56
" , non-tipping, 54, 56
" , standard, 51, 52, 53
" , table, 52, 54
Lapped joint, 12, 13
Legs, bevelled, 65, 78, 79, 85, 91, 94
" , moulded, 16
" , shaped, 112, 113
" , tapered, 28
Lid, sliding, 148, 151
Lining box, 17, 18
" with leather, 94, 96
Loudspeakers, grilles for, 57–61

Mahogany, 2, 8
Matching in marking out, 83, 84
" veneers, 5
Mirrors, carved, 87, 88, 89, 90
" , cheval, 109, 110
" , circular, 86, 88, 89, 111, 114, 117
" , clips for frameless, 109, 111
" , convex, 88, 89
" , dressing, 109–111
" for dressing tables, 112–118
" , fitting glass for, 87, 89
" , overmantel, 88, 89
" , stay for cheval, 115
" , swing, 109, 110
" , toilet, 110, 111
" , triple or triptych, 109, 110, 112, 118
" , wall, 86–90, 148, 152
Mortise-and-tenon, barefaced, 152, 156
" " , stub, 84, 117
" " , through, 128
Moulding application of, 4
Moulding sections for bedstead ends, 105
" " bolection jambs, 34, 35
" " cornices, 11, 14, 22, 35, 39, 120
" " doors, 120, 121, 122

Moulding sections for door frames, 23
" " drawer fronts, 108, 109
" " feet, 11, 14, 19, 62, 64
" " handles, 49, 50
" " kerbs, 35
" " legs, 16
" " mirror frames, 87, 88, 89, 110
" " panels, 103, 105
" " plinths, 11, 14, 39, 120
" " table tops, 75, 77
" " wall clocks, 48, 49

Nested tables, 79, 81
" trays, 81, 82
Nesting-boxes, 146, 148

Oak, 2

Paint for joints, 127
Painted decoration, 26, 88, 89, 90, 111, 145, 149, 152, 154, 155
" treatments, 5, 8, 24, 27, 127
Panelled backs, 114, 115
" bed-fitments, 97, 101
" bedstead ends, 102, 105
" doors, 39, 42, 44, 63, 120
Panelling, 2, 7
Paper-knives, 148, 149
Patterns for painting, 154, 155
Pelleting, 127, 128
Pendants, ceiling, 55, 56
Pivots for bookcase door, 12, 13
" gate-leg table, 76
Plinths, 11, 12, 13, 14, 15, 24, 25, 39, 41, 57, 58, 59, 60, 61, 66, 67, 93, 94, 95, 106, 107, 114, 115, 116, 117, 118, 121, 122
Plywood, 2
Proportion of room, correcting, 7

Rack, book, 148, 150, 151
" , broom, 147
" , egg, 150
" , hat and coat, 152
" , letter, 146, 148
" , plate, 147, 148
" , wine glass, 66, 68
Rounded corners for bedstead ends, 102, 104

INDEX

Rounded corners for carcases, 45, 60, 61, 79, 80, 93, 95, 108, 109, 112, 117, 121, 122
„ „ chair arm, 132
„ „ trays, 81, 82

School woodwork, 143–156
Scratch-stock, 41, 44
Screwing, pocket, 84
„ , slot, 34, 35, 97, 99
Seats, garden, 126, 127, 136, 137
„ , loose, 69, 71
„ , over-stuffed, 32, 33, 71
Secretaires, 94, 95
Shelves, adjustable, 14, 15
„ , folding, for chair, 130, 131
„ , plate-glass, 20, 24, 25
„ , sizes for book, 10
Shrinkage in wood, 2, 34, 80
Shutting joints, 14, 25, 27, 120
Sideboards, bookcase, 66, 67
„ , buffet, 65, 67
„ , dresser, 62, 63
„ , fitted, 64, 66, 67
Stay for bureau falls, 94, 96
„ cheval mirror, 115
„ wardrobe door, 120
Stilts, 144, 145
Stools, four-legged, 68, 69, 152, 156
„ , dressing, 68, 70
„ , music, 68, 70
Stuffing, 32, 71

Tables, book, 15, 16
„ , card, 78, 80
„ , circular, 76, 77, 79, 80
„ , dining, 71, 72, 73, 74, 75, 76, 77
„ , elliptical, 76, 77, 78, 80
„ , gate-leg, 78, 80
„ , nested, 79, 81
„ , occasional, 79, 80
„ , pedestal, 76, 77
„ , Pembroke, 78, 80
„ , refectory, 74, 75, 76, 77
„ , side, 72, 73
„ , tea, 79, 80
Table plates, 72, 75
Texture in materials, 9

Tone in materials, 9
Tonks' patent strip, 14, 15
Towel rails, 147
Trays, ash, 153, 156
„ , cutlery, 64
„ , nested, 81, 82
„ , tea, 81, 82, 146
„ , wagon with, 85, 86
„ , wardrobe, 121, 123
Turned ceiling pendant, 55, 56
„ chair detail, 30, 31, 33
„ feet, 11, 91
„ detail for garden seat, 126, 127
„ handle, 49, 50
„ knobs, 19, 20, 50, 51
„ lamp standards, 52, 53, 54
„ legs, 68, 69, 78, 91, 92
„ mirror frame, 88, 89
„ ring for loudspeaker grille, 57, 58, 60
„ terminal for post, 104
„ wall clock, 48, 49
Turning, simple exercises in, 153, 156

Unit bookcase, 12, 13
„ chest of drawers, 106, 107
„ dressing table, 114
„ sideboard, 61

Veneered treatments, 10, 18, 19, 20, 26, 27, 45, 52, 53, 57, 58, 65, 67, 76, 77, 88, 89, 91, 93, 94, 95, 97, 101, 102, 104, 105, 108, 111, 112, 113, 115, 116, 118, 119, 121, 122
Veneering, application of, 2, 4
„ patterns, method of, 95

Wagons, 83–86
Walnut, 3
Wardrobes, fitted, 121, 123
„ for hanging, 119, 120, 121, 122, 123
Webbing, 69, 70, 71
Winders for clothes-line, 147, 148
Windlass for clothes-line, 153, 156
Windows in decorative scheme, 6, 7
Wood, nature of, 1
Writing tables, knee-hole, 91, 92
„ „ , pedestal, 92, 93

www.ingramcontent.com/pod-product-compliance
Lightning Source LLC
Chambersburg PA
CBHW080245170426
43192CB00014BA/2577